# The 30-Second Storyteller: The Art and Business of Directing Commercials

## Thomas Richter

THOMSON

COURSE TECHNOLOGY

Professional ■ Technical ■ Reference

# Acknowledgments

As a director, one quickly learns that it is impossible to create a commercial alone. I've learned that it's much the same in writing books, and I have a number of people to thank for their immense help in authoring *The 30-Second Storyteller: The Art and Business of Directing Commercials*. Kevin Harreld at Course Technology PTR was quickly interested in the original idea and made sure it came to fruition. Author and renegade filmmaker Graham Robertson made the initial contact to Kevin. My good friend Brian Carpenter looked at the early manuscripts with the eye of a Harvard graduate. Marta Justak edited my loosely connected thoughts into a comprehensive text that readers can actually follow. Executive producer John Clark and head of production John Quinn, both at Boxer Films, Los Angeles, provided insight, wisdom, knowledge, and support. Casting director Renita Whited let me in on some casting secrets in return for a boyfriend.

For letting me pester them with questions, I want to thank the interviewees: Joe Murray, who means it when he calls you "brother"; Tor Myhren, a creative genius whom I'm grateful to call a friend; Matt Tolmach, who has been a great domestique and lead-out man in life, career, and on the road, besides being an indispensable friend; Kelly Trudell, for his wise words and the permission to use the Ford project as a case study; Jim van Osdol, for providing valuable insights and letting me use materials from the *Birth* project; and Jim Zoolalian, a great director, whose pitching skills have paid for some of my spec spots.

Sadly no longer with us, two executive producers, Joanna Bongiovanni and Gary Weiss, who believed in me when I first began my career, deserve a special mention.

My parents and grandparents, who instilled in me a love for art, film, and writing. My brother, who hails from some excavation site in the Middle East, where he tells his own stories using a much longer timeframe than I do.

Finally, Stephanie K. Smith, who came into my life at just the right time and whose presence, support, and love has made all the difference.

# About the Author

**Thomas Richter** is a commercial director who works all over the world for clients from all kinds of industries. He began to assemble filmstrips and create movies at the early age of six: he grew up next to a Steenbeck editing table where his mother, an editor, was working. The family trade of filmmaking was a natural choice for Thomas, as his uncle is a director of photography, and his grandfather owned a 16mm camera and was shooting experimental color film of Berlin in 1931. In 1993, Thomas moved to Los Angeles to attend the prestigious Art Center College of Design. He graduated in 1996 with a Bachelor of Fine Arts with Honors in Film. Thomas has won dozens of awards for both commercials and short films, including the John Sayles Award for Best Narrative Short, the Silver Hugo Award for Best Campaign, and the ITVA Platinum Award for Media Excellence.

# TABLE OF CONTENTS

**Chapter 7    Preproduction Meeting . . . . . . . . . . .165**

**Chapter 8    Getting the Shot . . . . . . . . . . . . . . . . .183**

# INTRODUCTION

Imagine a job where you have to work only 10 days a year to make $100,000. A job that allows you to be a respected artist, a savvy craftsman, and a hip partygoer who hangs out with celebrities, superstars, and top models. No need to wear a tie and suit. You can show up in jeans and a baseball cap. No corporate office hours, and no supervising department heads checking your time card. You are *it*, the top dog, the alpha male, the tip of the echelon.

You work all over the world, always fly business class, stay in fancy hotels, and eat at chic restaurants (and you don't even have to pay the bill). At your command, buildings are blown up, cars crash, helicopters fly, and you are expected to spend a million dollars in a week or two. This job exists. It's called a *commercial director*, the creative mind behind the production of a TV spot.

I have been a commercial director for a good number of years now, and I've done all of the above. Believe me when I say that I have often contemplated how great it is that someone pays me for doing this job. I think it's fair to admit that being a commercial director is one of the coolest jobs in town. It is also fair, however, to say that it is one of the toughest jobs to get.

When I say that I've done all of the above, I don't mean to say that it is *always* like that. Not by a long shot. The vast majority of time is spent trying to get there. And once you're there, you have to spend a great amount of time trying to *stay* there. It's quite frustrating to tell you the truth. During production, you feel like the king. Assistants bring you coffee, you sleep in president's suites, and any of your wishes are someone else's command.

But try running around town to get signed with a production company. Showing your reel to over-worked, stressed-out producers, who couldn't care less about the 50th fresh-out-of-film-school-genius-this-week, is not much fun. And even once you're signed, you've only taken the first step towards a successful career. But I'm getting ahead of myself.

This book is for everyone who is interested in the career of a commercial director. It won't teach you how to direct. It will let you in on all those things a commercial director does that go beyond basic directing.

## It's All About the Reel

First, I will describe the environment in which a commercial director works. Obviously, it's different from TV or features. Much different. Then I will go into the process of breaking into the industry in the first place. How do you get your start? You will see that it is all about the reel, which is your portfolio.

You may be a DP, or an agency creative, or even an editor. You may be a TV director, or a feature director, or a film student. But you will need a reel. If your work so far has nothing to do with commercials, you will have to shoot spec commercials. How do you choose which commercials to shoot? You will see that directors are categorized by specialties, and you should choose your niche wisely.

I will go into the process of getting signed with a production company and bidding for projects. You'll spend a lot of time bidding. During the bidding phase, there will be conference calls and treatments, all of which I cover in this book.

## Politics, Production, and Post

Along the way, I hope to shed some light on your relationship with the advertising agency and their client. There are a lot of politics going on behind the scenes, most of which you are not privy to, but all of which have a profound impact on your work. The psychology behind this most uneasy alliance between commerce and art can be befuddling.

Then I will cover the production of a commercial from preproduction through the shoot, all the way to finishing in post production. There are several steps unique to the commercial industry. Again, I will focus on commercial directing and not on directing in general.

*The 30-Second Storyteller* will *not* teach scene blocking, working with actors, camera techniques, editing, or any of the other basic skills involved in the craft of directing, although occasionally I will allude to them.

Rather, I will turn the spotlight on the specialty of bidding, winning, and creating a 30-second spot, the techniques involved, the technologies of choice, and the obstacles that come between you and a successful career.

In the final chapter, there is also a section on international representation and an interview with a major studio executive, providing some great insights into Hollywood's take on commercial directors. *Spots* are considered one of the best stepping stones, and many a commercial helmer (*helmer* is industry jargon for director) has successfully made the transition to features.

Finally, you will find some good resources and a brief glossary to explain some of the more obscure terms used in commercial production.

Throughout the book, I will feature examples from a real-world commercial that I shot in 2006, as an ongoing case study. Look for the case studies in the special sidebars.

I hope this book will help you embark on that difficult but rewarding career path of a commercial director. Who knows, maybe someday, we will be bidding for the same project.

# CHAPTER 1

# THE COMMERCIAL DIRECTOR'S WORLD

I decided to become a commercial director in 1994 when I was a student at the Art Center College of Design in Pasadena, California. The Art Center, with one of the finest film departments in the U.S. and quite possibly the world, was then in the midst of what we students called the Tarsem/Bay era. Michael Bay and Tarsem were Art Center alumni, and in 1994 they were making it big.

During an honorary ninth trimester, Tarsem had made his career by directing the music video for "Everybody Hurts" by REM. He became a hugely successful music video and commercial director by creating a look that would be the trend for several years. He then forayed into features with the Jennifer Lopez vehicle *The Cell*.

Michael Bay was just completing his first feature film, *Bad Boys*. It was a mediocre script, but he turned it into a testosterone-infused action spectacle with Ferraris that broke every law of physics known to man. Prior to directing *Bad Boys*, Bay had made a huge career in music videos and commercials, and was successful enough to buy a few Ferraris for himself.

To us lowly film students, these two men were superstars. And suddenly, we all wanted to direct commercials, because the 30-second ads offered a path to feature directing, which was the ultimate goal.

For example, commercial directing opened the way to features for Ridley Scott. In 1984, Scott directed the famous Apple Macintosh launch commercial, inspired by Orwell's novel *1984*, in which a hammer-wielding wonder woman smashes a giant television screen used by a mind-controlling tyrant to manipulate the masses. I've always thought that this commercial was one of the all-time greatest feats of irony in advertising, because it was a manipulative mass media spot that glorified the destruction of manipulative mass media.

Scott, of course, continues to be a highly accomplished feature film director, creating masterpieces of cinema like *Blade Runner, Alien, Black Hawk Down,* and *Gladiator.* He started out in commercials and pioneered a commercial visual style in the movies, a look defined by a hyper-realistic sense of image.

After Scott and a handful of others had made the transition in the 1970s, however, Hollywood closed the door for a while. The reason was probably fear, the governing sentiment in major motion picture studios. The risk of using a commercial director on a feature film was just too great. After all, their reasoning went, those guys don't know how to direct actors or how to make anything longer than a minute, and aren't really artists or filmmakers in the first place.

But with the Tarsem/Bay era came a renewed interest in ad helmers ("helmer" is industry jargon for "director"). This may be because there has been a trend to distill features down to more commercial fare, essentially treating each movie and each star as a product, and simultaneously a trend in commercials to go for storytelling and entertainment, rather than mere hardcore selling. And don't discount the advent of MTV, which revolutionized the way we watch television. All of a sudden, music video and commercial directors were the cool folks, the avant-garde of filmmaking, and the herald of new technologies.

In other words, commercial directors became viable candidates for studio pictures, because they knew how to communicate, sell, and impress. They knew how to tell a story, and they could shoot beautiful images.

In any case, whether your ultimate goal is to make feature films or commercials, the road is long and hard. Directing is a highly sought-after profession with many pitfalls and setbacks. You stand to make insane amounts of money—some guys earn $50,000 per shooting day. Directors are respected, sometimes even admired and adored, but they are also the ones who carry the burden when everything goes wrong.

The first word of advice: If you have a hard time dealing with rejection, try another career. You will face obstacles every step of the way. As Matthew Tolmach, president of production at Columbia Pictures, told me: "TR, you're trying to break into the most competitive business on the planet." In this book, I will describe many of those obstacles in the hopes of preparing you better for the journey.

## What Does a Commercial Director Do?

A commercial director is a hybrid professional. He is an artist. He is a salesman. He is a communicator. He is a technical wizard. He travels along the edge of two worlds, with a foot in each: the advertising industry and the entertainment business. Commercials are made to sell a product or a service. They are tools by which companies increase their sales. Yet somehow television spots have found their way into the Museum of Modern Art. They're celebrated pop culture. They're entertainment.

Let's start with a brief overview of how a commercial comes to be made. Along the way, I will explain some terms that are common in our industry.

## How Is a Commercial Made?

First, there is a client. The client is the one who provides the money. The client—or rather his company—has a product or a service to sell. To increase sales, there is a marketing department that oversees marketing, advertising, and sometimes public relations. Some companies have one person in charge of all of those areas. Others have several people in charge of just a single product or brand.

A company like Procter & Gamble or General Motors has many different brands and products. Thus, there is a different team responsible for each product within the company.

## The Ad Agency's Role

The client hires an advertising agency to come up with the advertising strategy and to create actual advertising, such as print ads or television commercials. The relationship between client and agency is very important for a director to understand because, contrary to what you might expect, decisions are not always made in the best interest of the product or the commercial. A company may have several advertising agencies, particularly if there are several brands. Sometimes the agency is even part of the creation of the product or the brand. In fact, most product or service launches today are accompanied by an advertising and branding agency, because such a partnership is the only way a company can successfully introduce a new product or service. The airline Song is a good example. It was not just a small, growing airline with an emerging image, but rather a brand where everything—including colors, logo, story, and message —was created before the company ever bought an airplane.

So, a company has hired an ad agency to increase their sales, and the agency comes up with advertising that is intended to do just that. One of the venues the agency can use is a television commercial. The client may ask for a commercial, or may be hesitant about employing such an expensive method. In any case, the agency creates a number of concepts for the commercial and pitches them to their client. Usually, the commercial is tied into the marketing strategy from the start. More often than not, the commercial is actually the centerpiece of the campaign. There may even be an entire series of commercials, called a *television campaign*.

After the agency has created many, many concepts, they pitch a few to their client. The client will sign off on a commercial and charge the ad agency with production. This is where the commercial director comes in. Most of what happens before this point is usually beyond the director's knowledge or influence, although it often has a bearing on his work.

## Wassup?

Who will ever forget the Budweiser "Wassup?" campaign, which became part of American pop culture in the blink of an eye. The creatives saw the idea in a short film and hired that director to make it into a commercial for beer. Not only was it followed by several sequels, but it also spawned a huge wave of spoofs, which became hits on the Internet.

I remember being at the Cannes Lions Advertising Festival the year when this campaign won the Grand Prix. Everywhere you went in that quaint French beach resort, people were yelling "Wassup?" at each other. I particularly remember a Spanish birthday party in the hotel room next to mine, in which I saw guests arrive all through the night only to be greeted by a high-decibel "Wassup?"

Well, I was up. All night.

## The Agency Staff

There are several different positions at an ad agency, and the names of those positions vary quite a bit. To give you a very rough overview: Besides the management, there are the creatives, the production, and the contact people. The term *creatives* refers to the people who come up with the idea. These teams, which usually consist of two or three people, are made up of creative directors, copywriters, and art directors. The creative director is in charge of the team. The copywriter is in charge of the written word, slogans, stories, voiceovers, and the like. The art director is in charge of everything visual and makes sure that the colors are correct and are compatible with brand schemes, logos, and so on.

On the contact side are the people who are the connection between the client and the agency. They coordinate schedules, meetings, and often play babysitter. Mostly, they are neither creatives nor creative, but nevertheless have great influence because the client trusts them.

Finally, there is the agency producer, the person in charge of producing commercials for that agency. The term is something of a misnomer, because the agency producer rarely produces the commercial in a production sense, but instead oversees quality and cost, as well as post production. Agency producers are also on a constant lookout for directors.

The desk of an agency producer is piled high with reels, both solicited and unsolicited. While creatives should be the ones who make the choice about which directors to ask for a bid, the agency producer is very powerful because he can filter out a lot of reels, which the creatives will therefore never get to see. However, many creatives also keep an eye open for what's hot and new.

Often, the agency producer will send the approved concept to sales reps. By the way, that concept is now called the *storyboard*, or *board*. That is because often it will include drawings that were made to sell the concept to the client. But it could also be just a page of text description, simply called the *script*.

The sales rep is the person who tries to sell directors to agencies. The reason he is not called an agent is because he usually has a relationship with a production company rather than an individual director. This means that one sales rep represents all directors in a given production company. In fact, most sales reps represent more than one company. They may be trying to get work for dozens of directors.

The sales rep may recommend certain directors and send reels to the agency producer. At the agency, dozens—sometimes hundreds —of reels are screened and filtered. At the end of the process, a small number are selected, commonly between three to five. These directors will now bid for the job.

The director and the production company receive the boards from the ad agency and go to work. They sit down and figure out how to make the spot and plan a budget. The director comes up with his take on the concept, new ideas, improvements, and suggestions. This is compiled in a *treatment*.

It is likely that there is a conference call between the creative team plus agency producer and the director plus the producer. After a few days, the agency receives treatments and budgets from all the bidding directors. Now the agency looks at them and makes its choice. Then there is a client-agency meeting, in which the agency recommends its choice and the client signs off on the director (or not). Strong agencies will insist that they choose the director, rather than having the client choose that person.

## Production and Post Production

Once there is a green light, the commercial goes into preproduction. The director, together with the production company, preps the shoot down to the minute details. Locations are searched, actors are cast, and equipment is booked. Then there is a preproduction meeting, in which the director presents all of this information to the client and the agency. All the important elements—props, casting, locations, and the style of shooting—are approved by the client.

Then, finally, production comes around. In a few days—sometimes one, sometimes 10—the commercial is shot. Again, the agency and very often the client are on the set and oversee the production. Things may change as new ideas and suggestions come up.

Once the commercial is wrapped, the post production starts. Sometimes the director is very much involved, sometimes he only does a director's cut, and often he has no part in the editing and finishing whatsoever.

As you can see, the commercial director is part of a long process. He is neither the end nor the beginning. To some, like the client, he is but one of many service providers, and not particularly important. To others, particularly himself, he is the king, the master of the art of television commercials.

To all, however, he is a specialist. And not only are commercial directors specialists in the process, they are specialists within their craft. Perhaps the single most important topic for aspiring commercial directors to understand is that you will be pigeonholed and categorized. You will become a "car guy"—AKA a director who shoots cars—or a "people shooter," or someone who "does" snow or birds or hands or whatever else can be done. The reason for these specializations is safety. The agency and the client prefer to see their commercial already on your reel. They want to know that you can do their spot in the way they've imagined it.

## The Specializations

Commercials come in a variety of genres. There are comedy spots, running footage car spots, beauty spots, food spots, and many others. You must specialize to be successful. The single most important asset for a commercial director to showcase both his craft and his specialty is his reel, which must compete with those of many other accomplished directors. More in depth about the reel shortly, but keep in mind for now that the reel is a collection of your best work. It is your calling card, and thus the main tool with which your sales rep will get you work.

If you are up against an established director with a reel full of great car spots, you need to have a reel with better car spots. A food spot or a kids' commercial won't help you in this instance. Therefore, you had better specialize and do it right.

Here are some common categories used in the industry (in alphabetical order).

### *Aerial*

Aerial shooting includes air-to-ground and air-to-air photography, and is often handled by directors who are also directors of photography or even pilots. Because of the obvious obstacles in staging complicated aerial shots, special expertise is required to keep expensive flight time to a minimum. If a commercial includes only a single aerial shot, then a special aerial director is usually not needed. Instead, a quality pilot with an experienced DP and your own imagination will be able to get the shot. However, if the project is—say—for an airline, and the object is a giant jetliner in mid-flight from a variety of angles, then most certainly a specialist will be called upon.

## *Animals*

Working with animals is always a challenge, and it requires experience and patience. I highly recommend shooting with animals that can be trained and are used to film production. While domesticated animals like cats and dogs are easily handled, wild animals like crocodiles, snakes, or even elephants are much more difficult and unpredictable. In those cases, I prefer computer-generated animals. I also insist that animals should be treated kindly and not abused or hurt in any way.

---

### Animal Rights

I once shot in Jamaica, where animal protection laws are loose and the general attitude towards animals is quite different than in the States. For one of the shots, a cow was supposed to carry the company logo "branded" on its side. The logo was supposed to be painted on the animal and made to look like a branding. However, the cow didn't cooperate, and just as the handlers were about to treat the animal with a lot more force than I was comfortable with, we decided not to attempt the shot at all.

---

## *Animation*

The field of animation is wide, from claymation to 3D. Nevertheless, there are commercial directors who have specialized in it. Often, there is no shooting of film at all, because the entire spot is created in the computer. Very often, the animator is also the director.

I've only done one animation project so far, and I was only involved because I wrote the concepts and oversaw the production. The technique we used was traditional line-drawing animation. The animator prepared key poses—about every tenth frame—in order to get client approval. Then the elements were created, scanned into the computer, and animated with the help of an "egg-sheet," essentially a timing sheet on which the animator has marked which cell to use at which point in time.

Animation is highly specialized, and there are production companies who do nothing but that one task. If you are interested in this field, you should get in touch with these companies and try to get an internship to see the inner workings of this genre.

## Baby

Any commercial with an infant or baby in it has very tight parameters attached to it for legal reasons. Babies can only be exposed to film lighting for a short time, which is why you often see twins or triplets getting a lot of film work. (They can work in shifts, so as to make better use of the film crew's time.) The director is required to have a certain "touch" or "feel" to work with very young infants and should be adept at tricks to get babies to do certain simple actions. Patience is a virtue in this field, as often the babies don't follow instructions very well. Most likely, the parents are present and almost always they're the ones actually working with the baby to get certain performances, simply because they know their child better than anyone else. You should also be aware of the decency laws in the country that you are shooting the commercial for. Once a spot had to be pulled from U.S. television because the bare behind of a baby could be seen!

## Beauty

A beauty spot usually has to do with women's cosmetics, very often skin lotions and creams. The emphasis here is on making skin look young and fresh. Perfect makeup and a soft look, with lots of whites or primary colors in limbo, are trademarks of this genre. (In theater and film, "in limbo" is used to describe a nondescript, featureless background, such as all black or all red.)Other products that might be useful here could include lip-gloss, teeth whiteners, nail polish, eye makeup, or even shaving accessories.

It's actually not that easy to make skin look as perfect as it appears in commercials. Lately, more and more of these hurdles are being solved in digital post production. Yet, if the film is shot right, it certainly makes things easier. A basic but important skill in this genre is the art of making models feel comfortable, particularly when you're dealing with bare skin, shower scenes, or "problem zones."

The director will try to create a quiet, private, and intimate atmosphere on the set when the shooting starts. It is common courtesy for everyone who is not essential at the moment of shooting to leave the set. This often leaves but a handful of people in attendance when the model has to undress, and that obviously will provide a much greater comfort zone.

## Car—Action

Action car spots require expertise in mounting cameras on vehicles, vehicle-to-vehicle filming, and helicopter shots. Obviously, the main goal here is to make the car look fast or tough or rugged or robust. Dirt and dust are okay here. It's all about testosterone and the projection of strength or towing capability. Trucks, quite obviously, usually fall into this category, and so do many spots for SUVs.

A director in this genre needs to be able to break down an action sequence into single shots that tell a dynamic, entertaining, and interesting story when they're all put together. Having done a number of action-driven car spots, I can say that you can never have enough footage at your disposal once you go into the editing process.

One very simple rule to remember here is that things always look faster if either the camera or the object moves. Driving next to a fast car will make the car look slower. Having the car blast by while the camera pans, however, will create the energetic and dynamic image you might be looking for.

Very often, you will find variable frame rates in this genre. This means that the film is not being shot at 24 frames per second. In many car spots, you may have wondered why the vehicle doesn't look like it's leaning "out of the curve" when taking a turn at high speeds. The reason is that the car was actually driven much slower —slow enough that the gravitational forces didn't push the chassis enough for it to be visible. The film was running at a slower rate, say 16 frames per second, and when it is played back at 24 frames per second, the car appears to be going fast. The effect is that the viewer believes the car to be more stable and thus safer in turns.

Then again, in a lot of truck and SUV spots, you want that aggressive sports look where the car is thrown about while traversing rocky terrain. You may even want dirt and dust to fly every which way. A common technique here is to use a smaller shutter on the camera, which results in a sharper image. (It cuts down on exposure time, which means there is less motion blur.) The result is an almost strobelike effect, particularly when small particles fly through the air. The beach landing sequence in *Saving Private Ryan* was shot this way.

### Dig That Mud!

These famous mud-spraying commercials are also carefully crafted. An effects crew actually digs a trench, which is then filled with a specifically created mix that gives you the perfect viscosity and texture. You can dial in the color of the mud to perfection.

## Car—Beauty

In these types of spots, cars do drive (as opposed to studio beauty shots), but the emphasis is on the look, the beautiful curves, and the awesome landscape (as opposed to the performance aspects). Lighting the car in an exterior environment is very difficult, and that's why clients will look for this very specifically. As opposed to action car spots, here it's not about strength and horsepower. Rather, the commercial tries to evoke a certain emotion, like the joy of driving or the car's serenity in crazy traffic.

Making a car beautiful is a long process because of the many details involved. Special "car prep" companies work on every inch of the vehicle and make it film-ready. This process may include tinting the windows (blocking any light that shines through the grill or other seams in the car), changing the entire electrical system so that each light can be switched and dimmed individually, cleaning or greeking (a term used to describe the eliminating or blocking of any unwanted stickers, tags, letters, or logos), and obviously cleaning and polishing the sheet metal to its finest shine.

Additionally, specific cars may have specific angles from which they look the best. The client may actually have a "brand guide" in which the approved lenses and angles are listed. The style changes every few years: profile shots are hip, frontal shots are hip, three-quarter shots are hip...you get the idea. One important term to know is the *aggressive stance*. Sports cars and SUVs look fairly good in this stance. It's a three-quarter angle with wheels turned so that the rims are facing the camera.

Otherwise, it's really up to your own preference and sometimes the light. Lighting cars in an exterior environment can be difficult and time consuming. Often, it's simply a matter of being in the right place when the sun goes down. The classic car shot shows the reflection of a sunset horizon on the car's body as a perfect line. Because lighting a car is all about defining its form, soft, even light is usually the way to go. And because of the reflective nature of the metal, you need large surfaces to be reflected. That's why the sky is such a perfect light source for cars.

### Car—Studio

Studio shoots with cars are all about lighting and set design. Often, you will see lighting effects, like a streak of light traveling across featured parts of the car—for example, the hood in a close-up. Since the shape of the car can only be brought out by the correct light, the emphasis is clearly on a perfectly lighted car.

Large light boxes are put overhead and white bounce boards all around the sides. What you perceive in the car as light is actually a reflection of one of those tools. In the case of the traveling streaks of light that you see in so many spots, the thing that's actually moving is the car. It's sitting on a huge rotating platform. Lately, we've seen a lot more energy-infused light traveling along cars. This is done in digital post production rather than in the camera.

### Celebrity

There seems to be a notion that working with celebrities is difficult or demands certain talents. While I have not found that to be the case, clients will often ask to see a director's reels with celebrity work on them. However, some celebrities will insist on seeing the director's reels and approving the choice in advance.

My experience is that celebrities have a lot to lose, and that is why they are protective of their image and reputation. They may ask for a certain light or angle, because they know what makes them look good. I've yet to have problems with a celebrity other than their usual idiosyncrasies, which are summed up in the term "amenities." For example, they usually want a special trailer, a special car, a special makeup artist, and special food. All that is simply a matter of providing a certain level of comfort.

---

### Celebrity Notes

It gets more complicated if you have time constraints. I was on a shoot once with Lance Armstrong, and he was supposed to show up at 11 a.m. and had to leave by 1 p.m. He arrived at 12:30, and everyone else just had to deal with it. When I worked with Barry Bonds, he shook my hand without even looking at me. I had barely finished my sentence when he said, "You're rambling, let's shoot."

Then again, I've worked with celebrities who couldn't have been nicer or more accommodating. The cast members of ABC's *Extreme Makeover: Home Edition* were a blast to work with, as were the National Cricket Team of the West Indies. As long as they're professional and respectful of the people working hard to make them look good, they deserve the same treatment.

---

### Comedy

Comedy spots are huge, because more and more emphasis is being put on entertaining the audience. There are many types of humor in this genre. From slapstick to smart jokes to odd Scandinavian humor, this specialty is very large and very competitive.

However, it is a tough genre for another reason. Comedy is not easy. Ask any stand-up comedian trying to make a crowd laugh. The humor could be in the situation, in the character, in the action, or in all of the above. In most cases, it's really the timing that makes it work.

Additionally, comedy works with a number of other genres. Traditional jokes have a setup and a punch line, and this works well in commercials. However, more and more spots have complete story-lines, consisting of three acts with all the bells and whistles. And all that in 30 seconds.

As a director in this genre, you most likely need to be comfortable working with actors. Most of these spots involve human beings and the situations they get themselves into.

## Dialogue

Somewhat similar to storytelling, dialogue commercials are those in which people talk mostly with each other and not into the camera. Sometimes there is an actual story; sometimes it is just moments or beats. What clients look for in these snapshots of life is often a sense of realism and intimacy.

Directors need to be able to work with actors and have a talent for timing and staging, as well as creating the right environment to allow actors to perform with open emotions.

## Documentary

Here, the commercial attempts to impersonate a documentary or has a documentary feel to it. To create a certain kind of realism, it is often shot in black-and-white or grainy stock. The camera is also less "staged," but rather accidental in its movement—like it would be in a documentary. Therefore, this genre is essentially a full style with its own motifs and techniques.

Actors have to be believable as regular folks (and sometimes regular folks are used as actors). The director not only has to direct the talent in a way that makes them credible, but must also create that sense of reality and randomness inherent in documentaries.

## Emotional

This category is often teamed up with storytelling or people or vignettes. Pharmaceutical products and health insurance providers fall into this vein. There are not many words spoken, but the images are very touching and moving. A technique often used is to shoot in invisible slow motion, which means a slightly higher frame rate. This slows down the action by a tiny bit and adds a layer of softness and dramatic impact.

For a director, the pitfalls are kitsch and cheesiness, both of which should be avoided. Instead, these spots work well if there is a credible substance to the imagery.

### Food

This is another highly specialized category, with a lot of crossovers into the liquids genre. Food has to look great, and a lot of chemicals are used to make it so. This also makes those normally delicious foods inedible in the process. Swirling raspberries, crunchy-looking cereal, juicy steaks—you get the idea. Often, there are temperature issues to be dealt with, or effects like fake smoke. Similar to the liquids category, food directors often are also directors of photography.

### Graphics

This category actually has very little to do with normal directing techniques, because neither a camera nor a single roll of film is ever used. Mostly, these spots are made by graphic designers and art directors on computers. Occasionally, there will be live action involved and two separate directors will work on a spot.

### Hair

Hair products are advertised by showing impeccable hair, which is a combination of actual hairdressing and lighting, as well as slow-motion work, particularly for moving hair (the famous head-throw). Clients will want to see well-done, fabulous hair on your reels, because that's what makes their product sell.

### Kids

Strictly speaking, there are two categories here: commercials for kids and commercials with kids. The ones for kids are sometimes called Saturday morning spots; they advertise toys, Barbie dolls, and model cars. Commercials with kids could be almost any other category, but kids have to deliver a performance. This is considered to be a tough assignment for a director. Usually, the greatest challenge is to get a natural-looking performance from kids, but this is something you should deal with in casting. The second greatest challenge here is the parents, who frequently make the most trouble.

When working with kids, you can avoid a lot of trouble if the casting is done right. I'm amazed at how many kids come to casting against their will. It's fairly easy to spot natural performers and the ones trained to artificial perfection. Some kids can actually be called professionals, and as long as they come off naturally, that's great.

Most kids, however, are intimidated, as if they're visiting the dentist. One great trick is to sit on the floor during the casting. By putting yourself on their level, the kids don't have to look up at you and automatically feel more comfortable.

I also have found it helpful to do magic tricks on the set, which earns you eternal attention and begging for more. Once the kids understand that there is "play time" and "work time," everything runs smoothly.

---

### A Gifted Kid

Nothing, however, beats working with a natural talent. I will never forget one Tom Watson from just outside London, who was eight when I first worked with him.

He had the aura of a 40-year-old, the wisdom of a 60-year-old, the talent of Sir Anthony Hopkins, and the face of an alien (really!). He was incredibly talented, intelligent, and polite, and he became the "face" of a yogurt product for a few years.

---

## Lifestyle

Lifestyle is a category that can be applied to many genres. It's somewhat murky, because it describes everything from *Sex in the City* shopping expeditions to friends enjoying dinner to rich people on yachts. It's best described as anything that shows a certain style in life.

### Liquids

One of the more obscure specialties, liquids can be very rewarding work. Whenever you see the flow or freefall of liquids—milk or cream or beer or oil or brake fluid—you're seeing the work of a specialist. He must have knowledge of special cameras for high-speed photography, the behavior of different liquids, and the lighting required for them. Obviously, this is very technical and camera-driven work, and it is common that directors in this field also do the photography.

### Music Video Style

Also referred to as "urban," this category is mainly a "look." It is ironic that even though music video style is what clients ask for, what they really want is a slick, high-quality commercial that borrows a few motifs from music videos. The look is mostly defined by camera movements, colors, and editing.

### People/Real People

Being able to film people and make them feel comfortable and safe in front of the camera is essential in this category. It has many crossovers with other genres. "People" is usually centered around natural and genuine photography of people, while "real people" is a more documentary version. Being good with people should be a trait of any director, yet some are considered better people-shooters than others because they bring out that special something. It is actually incredibly rewarding to find true emotion on a set and be able to capture it on film.

### Slice of Life

More down to earth than the lifestyle category, this genre is the average man's daily experience in commercial interpretation. Like a window into a person's world, this category applies to everyday products.

The director has to be able to catch the essence of certain moments, as mundane as they may be. As the word "slice" indicates, each moment is a mere snapshot, and often there are more than one per spot. This results in the necessity of communicating something very effectively in one shot.

### Special Effects

The advent of computer graphics has created this category, in which highly complicated and technical visual effects call for expertise in expensive techniques like green screen, motion capturing, and rotoscoping. The possibilities of digital post production are truly endless, yet a lot of time and money can be saved if the live-action part is shot correctly. Seamless integration of CG (computer graphics) work starts in preproduction.

If you are not a specialist in this area (like me), you will still face digital post production issues on virtually every project. While you grow with every challenge, I recommend working closely with a post production supervisor and the appropriate digital artists to achieve your vision. Project by project, your experience will grow, and you will feel more comfortable in the high-tech environment that creates dinosaurs and great—really great—apes.

### Sports and Athletes

Sports-related photography falls into its own category, because the director may need to accommodate extreme situations and plan his shooting accordingly. It is not uncommon for directors to be DPs in this genre. These guys actually climb, surf, and trek with the real athletes in order to get their shots. Yet it's not only the physical demands that make this a specialty. Images of sports are sometimes hard to master. When it comes to creating a coherent sequence of a very fast sprint, for example, it helps to have experience with editing these events.

### Storytelling

Here the concepts tell an actual story. These spots involve working with actors and a knowledge of drama. These commercials have a beginning, a middle, and an end, all in 30 seconds—in other words, a true story structure. This is a very large category, covering products in all ranges.

A director should be trained in the dramatic field and understand act structures of both newer and older styles. The reason it is so hard for many seasoned feature directors to create a functioning commercial is that in order to get the story to work in 30 seconds, one needs to strip it down to the bare essential key beats.

### Tabletop

*Tabletop* refers to the technique of shooting a still or moving portrait of a product on a fixed or rotating table. This is essentially a studio shoot, and it often focuses on packaging, like rolling lipsticks, perfume bottles, or fountain pens. Somewhat related to still product photography, the specialists have come up with incredible ways to move the product and the camera.

### Testimonials

Whenever there is an on-camera customer talking about his or her experiences with a product or a service, it is called a *testimonial*. Often, these people are actors, and the goal is to make the commercial look like it was shot in a neighborhood mall with real consumers. These spots are considered hardcore selling, and you will find that they are often shot on video to add realism by degrading the image. They can be very effective, and sometimes spots from other categories include a testimonial part.

### Time Lapse

Time lapse is a technique in which the camera exposes far fewer frames per second or minute than usual. When played back at regular speed, events unfold compressed in time, such as clouds moving very fast or stadiums filling very quickly. Combined with camera moves on motion-control rigs, this can be technically demanding.

### Tourism

For some reason, tourism has developed into its own category. Some trademark techniques include swooping helicopter shots across mountain ranges and along beaches, the happy couple at the fabulous dinner, and an overall feeling of being happy in paradise.

The photography is very landscape-driven, although romantic Jacuzzi scenes may appear as well.

### Underwater

For obvious reasons, this is a narrow specialty. Mostly, the director of photography will direct, in addition to being a diver. Knowledge of exposure, focus, and other underwater-related issues is a must.

### Vignettes

Vignettes are motifs, quite often centered around locations. A spot about New York, for example, may contain such vignettes as the Statute of Liberty, Central Park, the Museum of Modern Art, 5th Avenue, and so on. Often, the challenge here is to assemble various vignettes into a spot with an uninterrupted flow.

## Survival of the Specialized

These specializations are very important. I cannot repeat this enough. You will be astounded at how much the agency and the client will want to see the spot they're planning to make already on your reel. The reason for this, undoubtedly, is fear and an overwhelming desire for safety. The company will spend maybe $500,000 on the production of the spot and upward of $5 million on buying media time on television. Their investment needs to be safe. Their jobs need to be safe. If the commercial is screwed up, they may lose their jobs. They have kids in private schools and mortgages to pay. Fear reigns supreme.

Yet specializations often make a lot of sense. I wouldn't want to bid for a stop-motion animated commercial or a food spot. I simply don't have the expertise. Likewise, a director who knows everything there is to know about shooting liquids may know nothing about working with actors.

Finally, specializations are useful as a means of getting the attention of an agency producer. When an agency producer views a reel and gets a clear impression of a director's specialization, he is more likely to remember that director and his particular expertise.

For years, I had had the problem of being too diverse. I had emotional black-and-white spots, funny kids spots, beautiful images, and music video-style work all on the same reel. "Yeah okay, but what does he do?", agencies would ask. Apparently, it is inconceivable to them that a director could do more than just one genre (although most directors can).

Or, if a director has six beauty car spots on his reel, agencies think it must mean that he does them really well. Their logic is not readily apparent to me; maybe it is to you. However, that is the way it works, because it gives agencies and clients a feeling of safety and comfort.

What does this mean for you, the aspiring commercial director? Well, your first obstacle is getting signed by a production company. The way to do this is to create a spec reel, which is a reel full of fake commercials. You will have to create this reel largely on your own. It will cost quite a bit of money, because you will want the commercials to look and feel just like real commercials.

However, this may be the only time in your commercial career when you have full control—over the ideas and the spots, of course, but mostly over the course of your career. The spec reel is where you will determine your specialization.

In the next chapter, I will go into detail on how to create a spec reel and get signed by a production company. First, however, let's look briefly at the most important relationship you will ever have— besides the one with your mother.

## The Director's Relationship with a Production Company

The most important relationship in your professional career is the one with your production company. The reason is that the production company basically acts as your agent. In the interest of simplicity, I speak here of the "company" in singular terms. However, if you are represented in several countries, you may have several production companies. I will get into international representation later.

The business of the production company is to produce commercials. The company receives a production fee or markup of the budget in return for its services. But to book commercials, the company must have something to offer to agencies. Their products are their directors.

A production company may have one director, several dozen directors, or any number in-between. It may have two employees or 30; it may have one local office or six offices all over the world. Production companies come in many shapes and sizes. Yet when they vie for a spot, they do it in tandem with a director. And the reason they were asked to bid is very often the director's reel.

As I mentioned before, the production company may employ a number of sales reps on a retainer or a percentage basis. Mostly, these sales reps have their own offices and represent several production companies. Commonly, they only serve one specific market. The U.S. television ad market is divided into four major regional markets: West Coast (California, Seattle), East Coast (New York, Boston), Midwest (Chicago, Detroit, Minneapolis), and South (Texas and Florida).

Sales reps will visit these agencies and stay in constant touch with them to sell directors.

An aspiring director breaks into the industry through the production company. Once a production company signs you, it will send out your reel and try to acquire work for you. That's why your relationship with your production company is so important.

The next chapter of this book deals with how to jump that first hurdle: signing with a production company by creating a spec reel that they can use to sell you.

# Chapter 2

# Breaking into Commercials

## Creating a Spec Reel

Your single most important sales tool in the commercial industry is your reel. It is your portfolio, your body of work, your calling card. Reels will be scrutinized by agency producers, agencies, clients, and even those crew members who have enough clout to decide if they want to work with you in the first place.

On any given project, an agency might look at hundreds of reels. In fact, DVDs and tapes float around production offices and agency hallways like blood cells, in never-ending circulation. They're sent out on demand, as cold submissions, on recommendation—you name it. They're everywhere. There is hardly a desk in the commercial industry without a stack of reels on it.

John van Osdol, executive vice president and director of broadcast at Leo Burnett Detroit (this means he is the agency's top producer), says he receives up to 40 reels a month. Kelly Trudell, who is senior producer at J. Walter Thompson, also in Detroit, explained that he has virtually no time to screen any of the dozens of reels he is sent, except when there is a project pending that could be a fit.

Directors will be judged, pigeonholed, selected, and hired based on their reels. You *are* your reel. But how do you get a reel if you've never shot a commercial? This is where the spec reel comes in. Spec commercials are fake commercials. (These are not to be confused with spoof commercials, which poke fun at a product or a spot that already exists).

A good spec commercial looks and feels like a real commercial. It is done for a real product, preferably a well-known brand like Nike, Coke, Levi's, BMW, and so on. There should be nothing about it that identifies it as a fake commercial. The quality of the images and the sound, the voice of the narrator, the performance of the actors, and the conceptual idea should all be indistinguishable from a real commercial. And it must stand out from the crowd. It must be great, intriguing, entertaining, and persuasive, so that producers have an interest in signing you. If it's not, you'll end up wasting a lot of money.

---

### Get Reel

Tor Myhren is executive creative director at Leo Burnett Detroit:

*The reel is the second most important weapon a director has in his/her arsenal. The first is reputation. Directors have their best work on their reel. So it is very easy to see what they have done, what they are capable of, and what spots they like enough to represent them. Sometimes you might see something in a spot on someone's reel, literally one small scene, that convinces you he or she can do your entire spot. A good reel will get you good jobs. Period.*

---

## It's All About the Idea

Good spots start with good creative ideas. Some directors can write good commercial scripts. But most aspiring directors should try to find rejected scripts—real agency work that was turned down by the client. Just because it was canned doesn't mean it was a bad spot. The client may not have liked that particular strategy behind the concept, or perhaps it was simply no longer necessary to advertise a certain model of a car because it was already selling well. Or maybe the creatives had a great idea for a product they didn't even advertise! In either case, find a full-fledged, professional, real-world script, because it's most likely a hundred times better than anything you can write yourself.

---

### Who's Got an Idea?

Jim Zoolalian, a busy commercial director, had this to say about his spec reel:

*I had worked at a few ad agencies and had become friends with art directors and copywriters. These friends were more than willing to provide unproduced commercial concepts in order to get another spot in their portfolio. From the start, I knew that you had to always have a great idea—an idea that other creatives (the people who ultimately give you jobs) would be impressed with. I went for the ideas that really made me laugh or think. Yes, I also made sure they had elements that I could bring my directing eye to, but most importantly they had to be really good ideas. The kind of ideas you would see in the award books. Another good thing to do is to study the award books, and learn to think like the best people in our business.*

---

Try to get your hands on these so-called dead boards, and you have a good shot at finding something that's cutting-edge creative. Where do you get dead boards? You'd be surprised how many agency creatives are interested in having their ideas shot to use on their own reels. There are newsgroups and advertising communities that can help. You can try to get in touch with agencies directly. Hang out at screenings and AICP parties. Make connections.

This book is not about how to be a copywriter or create the perfect advertising script (in fact, there are plenty of publications about that already). There is no silver bullet for a great commercial, so don't believe anyone who tells you there is. Commercials are made to sell products or services. Consequently, they have to fulfill certain requirements, such as communicate product features, building an image, or evoking emotional associations. They should be appealing on many levels. They should be entertaining, beautiful, edgy, impacting, moving, emotional—and much more.

At the same time, you have a very specific goal: You need commercials that the producer or the sales rep can use to sell you as a director. Tastes and trends change fast in the commercial industry. Study the spots you enjoy, and research what has been winning all the awards. Chances are that this is the stuff everyone considers top creative right now.

## Brand Yourself

As I said earlier, you *are* your reel. I mean that. Your reel will define you. It will give everyone an idea of who you are and what you do. Commercial directors specialize in such categories as storytelling, cars, kids, food, tabletop, comedy, beauty, and so on (for a more in-depth exploration of specialties, see Chapter 1). Your reel is where your specialization is manifested.

Therefore, when you are planning your spec reel, you are also planning your career, your niche. In fact, in recent years it has come to the point where directors think of themselves as a brand. Think of Michael Bay, Tarsem, or David Fincher. (If you don't know these names, go on the Internet and research them.) These guys have a look, a style, a signature that people in the industry will refer to. "We want this to have a Fincher feel," or "It should look very Tarsem," is what they say. In Michael Bay's case, he has even transported his style into movies, where he is now a brand name. Mention a Michael Bay film, and everybody has the same associations in their heads.

---

### Find Your Genre

Joe Murray, a commercial director with a 20-year career, about branding yourself:

*I did a lot of fashion and female products early on, as well as music video-style stuff. I did high-speed planes. I'm really into the whole "You have to be able to shoot anything" philosophy. Right now, I'm in-between genres. As an artist, you don't want to be branded, you want to be free in a certain way, but you have to have a strong genre these days. The downside is that people have shorter careers.*

The good news is that you have the power to brand yourself before you enter the fray. You must specialize. You have no choice about that. But you can choose your niche—and once you choose it, you had better make it your own.

Most likely, you will have a preference. You like car commercials. You prefer working with actors. Maybe you are a storyteller. Or you see yourself as a visual graphic artist. Whatever it is, find your niche and do research on it. Watch the commercials that fit your category, study them, and learn about your competition.

## Shoot the Same Commercial—Again and Again

Let's say you are a photographer experienced in tabletop still photography. You know all the tricks, from softboxes to penlights, from upside-down cameras to temperature control. You would like to move into commercials. Sounds like a good idea, because tabletop directors are rare, sought-after, and make a lot of money.

Look at every tabletop commercial you can get your hands on. This includes spots with liquids (where the fluid is the hero: beer, lotion, cleaners), packaging (where the package is the hero: perfumes, bottles, lipstick), or rotation tricks (where choreography is the star). Research the technology involved, with emphasis on gadgets like high-speed photosonic cameras, motion-control rigs, and snorkel lenses. And then specialize.

### My First Genre

When I began working on my spec reel, I thought that storytelling and kids would be good genres for me to try out. I've always been great with kids, and storytelling was certainly my strength. Additionally, "kids" is a strong niche, and if you are good in it, you'll have fast success.

I began writing concepts based on those two genres, pitching them to instructors, classmates, and people in the industry I knew. I wanted a specific smartness and cleverness in the kids. I found that often kids were much more grown-up than commercials made them out to be. Yet, I didn't want to do commercials *for* kids, but rather commercial *with* kids as actors.

Let's say you've decided you want to be a tabletop director specializing in beautiful package-driven commercials. These are spots where lipsticks rotate, perfume bottles slide in, and fountain pens roll around with incredible choreography. Find existing storyboards, or pick a number of products and come up with ideas. Many ideas. Run them by friends or—better yet—people in the industry. You may want to draw storyboards or conceptual presentations to hone your ideas further. Agency creatives, after all, go through a hundred ideas before they find one that they like, and why should you do any less than the professionals?

---

### I Kid You Not

I wrote at least 20 different concepts before I decided on three that I wanted to shoot while at Art Center. One was a McDonald's ad that took place in a Russian barbershop: The only way the kid was going to get his hair cut was if he was promised McD's afterwards. The next one showed a role-reversal situation: Three kids in the bleachers of an amateur league baseball game watch their parents play ball and talk about them as if they are the parents. At the end, one kid says that his dad wants him to buy the new BMW. Finally, I came up with a futuristic Lego spot, in which three judges atop a high tower sentence toys to destruction if they require imagination, like Legos do. When the executor tries to destroy a Lego block, the block is stronger than the iron of the sledgehammer—because imagination cannot be destroyed.

---

Remember, you want to create a reel that defines you as a tabletop director specializing in beautiful packaging spots. Essentially, you must shoot the same commercial four or five times over, each time with a different product, different colors, and different music. But you must have an overarching feel and theme. The more your spots are alike, the easier it is for producers, agencies, and clients to file you in their internal database as the beautiful-packaging-tabletop guy. If they have a project involving beautiful packaging, they will automatically think of you.

## Thinking of You

Tor Myhren, agency creative, has a director in mind when he writes a script:

*Often, by the time I have a concept, I have a director in mind. Any creative person can visualize what they want the spot to feel like. So once an idea is down on paper, you begin to think about which director can capture the feeling of your script. Is it beautiful and slick? Is it gritty and real? Is it funny? Though there are many talented directors in the commercial world, there are only a handful of great directors. These are the very few who can cross genres and capture moments that are funny or sad or cinematic, depending on the concept. Usually, you'll start with these guys. If they're booked, you focus in on directors who specialize in whatever it is you're trying to create. Most directors are known for one or two things. This guy is a small-moment comedy guy. This guy shoots beautiful vignettes. This one does big-budget special effects.*

## Stay Away from Variety

The same applies for all categories. If you want to do running footage action cars, you had better have a bunch of running footage action car commercials. If you prefer beauty studio cars, you had better have beauty studio cars. Don't put a comedy spot on a car reel. Don't put a kids' spot on a comedy reel. Don't put a food spot on a graphic design reel.

Naturally, there are crossovers. You might have a car spot that is also funny. Or a storytelling spot with kids. But you must make sure that the spot fits your primary category. Variety is not a good thing when it comes to your niche, except when it's within it. For example, you could have action car spots in snow, in the desert, in the forest, and in the city. But leave that Nike spot off, because it's not a car ad.

Agencies and clients need a certain level of comfort, and they get it by hiring a specialist. If you have a plumbing problem, would you prefer hiring a handyman who "kinda" does everything, or a professional plumber? You get the drift.

## Budget Concerns

Shooting a spec reel is expensive. Without any support from a school, university, or production company, you could easily spend $20,000 per spot. That is especially the case if you are interested in expensive categories such as cars or effects-driven spots. To be able to compete against all the other reels out there, you must use the same gadgets they use, like helicopters, Russian arms, and car trailers. Be realistic about your budget and write your concepts with that in mind.

On the other hand, for a filmmaker, it has become easier and cheaper than ever to create. What used to be an almost unattainable art form for the regular artist is now quicker than painting in oil. The digital age has brought us DV cameras, cheap yet powerful editing platforms, and even viable online and effects solutions on affordable home computers. It is entirely possible to create a great spec commercial on an $800 budget. If the concepts are smart and you are resourceful, you can complete your reel for under $10,000. How? This is where your talent comes in.

### Spec on the Cheap

A year after I had left Art Center, I wasn't so sure anymore about wanting to be locked in as a kids' director. I decided to do another spec spot, this time involving snowboarding, comedy, and storytelling. I had just lost a job because I didn't have any snow on my reel, so I guess it was a reaction to that. Five actor friends, two DPs, and a producer drove up to the mountains around Los Angeles with me at 3 a.m. By sunrise, I had them running in snowshoes on mountain ridges and back-country valleys. They were an expedition on a search for that elusive creature: the snowboarder. Suddenly, the snowboarders showed up (portrayed by the producer, one of the DPs, and myself), and the expedition shot one of them with a tranquilizer dart in order to put a tracking tag on his ear. We shot the entire spot on video, because we wanted it to look like a National Geographic documentary. In editing, I added gaming scenes from *Coolboarders 2001* for the Playstation, plus some jumps we shot while boarding in Mountain High, a ski resort not too far from L.A. The whole thing cost me $800. It has been the single most successful spec commercial I've ever done.

It would be far beyond the scope of this book to explain how to produce a commercial within a certain budget. There are too many factors involved, and it depends on the resources available to you or your producer. However, there are some helpful tips.

The specialty you pick has a huge bearing on the amount of money you will need to spend. Traditionally, car commercials, beauty commercials, and elaborate art direction cost a lot of money. Comedy and storytelling can be cheap. Graphic design can be cheap, provided you know how to do it yourself (and if you don't, you probably shouldn't be specializing in it).

Once you have decided on your niche and you start thinking about products, it's much the same. Nike spots may look cheap, but they can involve expensive special effects. Mercedes Benz commercials demand that you have a certain production value. Advertising for high-performance cars usually involves rigs, Shotmaker camera cars, and remote-control cranes. Remember that your spec spot should look just like a real spot for that brand. So you have to adhere to the look and class of that product.

Let's say you have concepts for three or four spots you want to shoot. There are a few production tricks that can save you money without cutting corners. Think about shooting the spots back-to-back, rather than doing three separate shoots. Many equipment rental houses will give you a much better deal for a full week, rather than for three separate two-day rentals.

### Shooting from the Hip

Once you are working with a production company—or even if your friends are—it's a good idea to have a few simple spec ideas on standby. Last year we had a 35mm camera for a weekend and decided to take it out on an impromptu shoot. With only five people involved, we shot a beautiful black-and-white car spot in and around Las Vegas. Also, production companies often keep "short cans," film left over from shooting. If you can score a few short cans here and there, you can save up a nice stack of stock.

Then there is the obvious question of what format to shoot in. Film or video? Again, car and beauty spots will have to be shot in 35mm, simply because that's the industry standard. Running footage, cars in particular, looks horrible in video, and it's not useable for car advertising. Comedy, on the other hand, lends itself well to high-definition video or even DV, depending on the idea behind it. Sometimes, you actually want it to look like video.

### The Digital Route

> With newer, progressive DV cameras and the Final Cut Pro line of editing equipment, you can do some quite amazing stuff. The software tools available might sound expensive, but compared to a film shoot, they are a pittance. Also, you will end up using Final Cut Pro to compile your reel over and over again. This also works with Adobe Premiere on both Mac and Windows.

A large cast will cost you more money, even if you don't pay the actors. Usually, one of the biggest budget items in a spec shoot is food. If you don't pay crew or cast, at least you should feed them well.

Also, reserve money for post production. A great deal of a commercial's look is determined in telecine and online. A single hour on an Inferno or a Henry can cost you $1,000.

It certainly helps to be aligned with a school or a production company that supports you. Schools may provide free equipment, insurance, and student discounts at many rental houses and post production facilities. Production companies have the wherewithal to produce things cheaply as well. They can use existing relationships with vendors, they have production insurance in place, and obviously they have a whole lot of experience you can tap into.

## A Few No-Brainers

Finally, a few nuts and bolts things about your spec reel. You should have a minimum of three spots. All of them should be good. If you have four spots and one is mediocre, take it off. If you have five good spots, put them all on.

Think about the order of spots on your reel. You want a good opener and a good closer. The opener should grab the viewer's attention and make him watch the entire reel. The closer should stay with the viewer and etch an image or a look or a feel into his brain, by which he will remember you.

Before your spots play, there should be a plate with your name on it: John Doe, Director. Keep it simple. Keep it unpretentious. Put the same plate on the end of the reel. Don't put music to it. If you need music with your name to sell yourself, you've already conceded that your reel is weak.

If you use a DVD (which you should), and you have a Web site (which you should), you should have a link to your site at the end of the reel.

The design of all your materials should be branded. This means the cover of your reel, your business cards, your Web site, and everything else you might hand over to someone. All of these features should have the same graphic design that communicates who you are with colors, fonts, and maybe even pictures. This will help you to stand out, and people will have an easier time remembering you.

Your contact information should be on the DVD and—more importantly—on the cover. If the disc is in the DVD player, you want people to be able to read your name off the cover and follow the disc menu on the inset.

Naturally, it is a good thing to look at reels of other directors. They are your competition. Check out their graphic design, their order of spots, and their nameplates.

Spend a lot of time developing and planning your spec reel, with emphasis on researching the state of the art. In the appendix of this book are some good resources to help you find out what's hot and what's in demand. It's worth spending the money for a subscription to gain access to a library of thousands of spots.

Remember that you are competing with real-world budgets, extremely creative people, and high stakes. Once you step into a production office in New York, Hollywood, or Santa Monica, you are one of 2,000 aspiring directors, not to mention the other 4,000 working directors against whom you will bid. The doors are usually locked. Your reel is the key.

## Contacting Production Companies

After you have completed your spec reel, it's time to hit the production companies. This can be a daunting task. It is generally agreed that there is an oversupply of directors. Therefore, a lot of production companies will simply ask you to send in your reel. And then you will never hear from them again.

First things first, though. Where do you find production companies? There are a several publications that list names and numbers (see these sources in the appendix). That doesn't mean it is prudent to use the shotgun approach and mail out 400 reels.

Most production companies have Web sites. Go check them out and see what kind of work they do. Some companies are very specialized in the kinds of commercials they produce. You want to find a company that fits you. You also want to feel that the company has a good vibe. Often, you can already tell by the design of their Web site if they might be a match for you.

Reading the trade papers will give you a good idea who the big players are. The Internet offers great resources for tracking down specific spots and the people who were involved in the production, which ultimately leads to the production company.

While you are compiling a list of production companies you want to contact, I recommend that you set it up as a database that allows for many, many entries. For example, you might want to use these categories: first time contacted, names of important people, names of the receptionist or assistants, date of reel sent, date of follow-up, remarks or comments someone made, and so on. The data will accumulate quickly, and soon you won't be able to stay on top of it without notes. Trust me.

## The Matrix

When I began compiling addresses and names, I started an Excel sheet and kept updating it. I used different colors to mark things like "first contact," "reel sent," "turned down," etc. Incidentally, I ended up handing the file to many other Art Center students who graduated with me. It's good to share information, because even though you are all in competition, the benefits of sharing are much greater than the danger of someone taking your place at a production company.

Naturally, it is better to get signed by a well-known production company. The prestige of a powerhouse, plus their connections, can be decisive. Agencies tend to want to work with famous names because it increases their own prestige. And the assumption is that powerhouse companies are successful because they're good and they know what they're doing.

However, it doesn't help you to be signed with a world-renowned production house that keeps you on the shelf. More important than the prestige of the company is how the staff will sell you and whether they believe in you. You want the production company to push you, which includes the following: The company's sales reps will aggressively work to get you in front of agency producers' and creatives' eyes. The company will announce in the trade papers that you are signed. And the company will commit to sending you to meet agencies, invest money in your treatments, shoot more spec spots, and generally support you in any other way possible.

So more often than not, new directors tend to sign with smaller companies who have more time to invest in building a director, and who have more at stake in making that director successful. If your fate is intertwined with the production company's fate, clearly they will work harder. If you're one of 20 directors (all of whom are working), you might become a "floater," somebody who is tossed into the big pool and then watched to see whether he comes up for air. But don't expect help.

## Tales of Horror

Rumors are that sometimes production companies sign young and promising directors to keep them off the market. They offer a guarantee, which makes the director sign, but then they don't send his reel out because they prefer to get the jobs with one of their other directors. The $60K retainer that they have to pay to the young director is nothing compared to the loss they would suffer if someone else marketed him successfully. Whether this is actually true or not is open for debate. It could just be a tale told by young directors who aren't working.

You also don't want to sign with a company that already has directors in your niche. Unless those directors are very, very successful (in which case, you may profit from boards that they reject in a trickle-down effect), why would you go into a situation where there is in-house competition?

So, while you are looking for production companies, keep in mind that you want a company that jibes with your work, is willing to push and support you, and is set up for and committed to accommodating and helping a new director.

## Catch the Crumbs

Some directors have benefited greatly from being mentored by a superstar commercial director. If an A-list helmer throws his weight behind a spot and promises the agency a successful project, they will accept almost any director. Trickle-down effects—a bigger director turns down a board, and it goes to another director from the same company—are rare, but they do happen.

When you contact companies, the first problem is usually getting access to someone of decision-making importance. Getting past the receptionist is tough for some people, while others seem to strike up friendships within minutes. Some of the people who answer phones seem to have a standing order to block as many calls as possible. Don't be deterred.

The person you want to talk to is the executive producer or the head of production. You want to get that person on the phone and make an impression. If the receptionist tells you to send in your reel and hangs up, you've lost.

So what do you say to the receptionist? Well, you're a director. Period. If you say that with enough confidence, most receptionists will concede. That's how simple it can be. Directors are important. They make lots of money. Sound like it, and you're halfway there.

Once, I tried the you-have-no-idea-who-you're-talking-to approach with the receptionist. It worked, but I didn't like the feeling it gave me. Some guys I know are great at it. On another occasion, I pretended to return a call. Sounded like this:

*Is Frank in?*

*May I ask who's calling?*

*It's Tom.*

*And this is regarding…?*

*I'm returning his call.*

*Let me see if I can get him.*

It has worked, but it can backfire. I don't recommend it, particularly if the producer is on top of things and knows that he hasn't called you.

In general, anything goes in your attempts to get through. What do you have to lose? It takes determination and perseverance to succeed. Be polite, or adamant, or annoying, or truthful…whatever you need to do.

Once you have the producer or the head of production on the line, you've won the first skirmish, but the war has only just begun. Keep in mind that no one is waiting for you. Chances are you're interrupting someone's busy day, so be brief and to the point.

The goal is to make the producer look at your reel. And you need to impress him enough to get him interested in you as a person. Ideally, you want to walk into his office and sit down to show your reel. Most of the time that won't happen. But how do you approach the first telephone conversation?

You're a director, you love the work the company has been doing, and you would like to show your reel to them.

*Sure, why not.*

*How about I swing by next week? What time would be good for you?*

*Look, I'm really busy. Just send it in, we'll look at it and get back to you.*

*Great, I'll send it in and follow up to make sure you got it. Thanks for your time.*

This is how the majority of conversations will go. Note that you don't rely on them calling you back. No way that's going to happen. Do the follow-ups yourself. Once you have the hook in the producer's flesh, don't release him. It is important that you take charge, because that is what a director does. A director is in charge.

It helps to believe you are talented and good, but don't be full of yourself. You are the artist. You deserve respect. If they don't see that, it's their loss. But it's also possibly the end of your own career, which may never really get off the ground.

Maybe you have a family friend in a production company somewhere or—even better—in an agency.

*My good friend Paul over at the Great Creative Agency recommended that I talk to you guys. I love your work, and I think we could be a great fit.*

*Really? Can you send in your reel?*

*I'd prefer to meet in person to get a feel for your company.*

Bang. Who's your daddy now? Suddenly, it's you who chooses the company, and they're asking you to send in your reel. Ideally, that's the way it should be. Meeting someone is obviously a hundred times better than sending in a DVD. If you just send it in, you'll never know where the reel ended up or who watched it (maybe that narrow-minded receptionist). If you meet them face-to-face, there is a different connection. This is what may happen:

*I like your reel, and I think you have potential, but I'm not really looking to sign anyone right now.*

*Do you have any recommendations about who else I could talk to?*

*Yeah, why don't you call Jim over at the Incredible Film Production? He's a good friend of mine, tell him I sent you.*

Very often, you will follow lines of established networks from production company to sales rep to producer to production company. People know each other. In fact, a common question you'll get is, "Who else are you talking to?" I'll say more about that one in a moment.

If you're a creative and you're trying to move into directing, it can be to your advantage to come from a good film school or a good agency. In my case, the fact that I went to Art Center opened a lot of doors because of the prestige of the school.

Your goal—however you accomplish it—is to get your reel in front of the executive producer or whoever makes the decisions. Do not accept anyone lower in the hierarchy, unless they have the power to send it up the chain. Depending on the time of year, the state of the industry, and about a billion other things outside your control, the answer will be one of three: "Let's talk," "Not for us," or "Keep in touch."

Obviously, "Let's talk" is the most desirable one, because it means that the producer likes what he saw on the reel and wants to spend some time to get to know you. More about that in the next section.

"Not for us" can mean a lot of things. It can be genuine, or it can be a polite lie—there's no way of knowing. Rarely will people tell you that they didn't like your reel or that it was bad. They know that in a few years you may be a huge director, so why burn bridges? In any case, it means you can strike that production company from your list for now.

If you get rejected (and you will), take it in stride. Don't get mad at people, don't scream at them, and don't be nasty. It doesn't serve your best interests. Just say "Thanks for your time" and concentrate your efforts on someone else. It's their loss.

"Keep in touch" may sound ambiguous, but it's very common. It usually means that they see something they like, but they either can't sign anyone right now or don't want to invest the time to build your career. Maybe they're under financial stress, or the company is being renamed, or someone will be leaving soon. You never know. But you do know that you can keep in touch. That means you can call every two to three months and try to build a relationship with the executive producer.

### Today in the News

Send out an email newsletter as often as you can, to get people to come to your Web site. Obviously, it's better if you actually have news to report. These things may not pay off immediately. It may take you 10 years to reap the benefits, but you are in it for the long run.

Even if you sign with another company, you want to stay in touch with as many people as possible. Your career may develop in unforeseen directions. Companies fold, and people change jobs. Once, I had someone tell me to call back in three weeks. I thought the person was not really interested, but I called back anyway. It turned out that the person had left their old company for a new one and didn't want me to show up at the old office. The bright producers know that personal relationships are as much in their interest as in the directors'.

It's a good idea to have a Web site and set up a little email list to send out updates of new work. Anyone who says "keep in touch" should be on that list.

## Into the Lion's Den

Meeting an influential person at a production company—such as the executive producer—is the first step toward creating a vital professional relationship. I've found that there is no set way a meeting will happen. In London or Paris or Berlin, meetings are much easier to get than in the U.S., and they are usually more serious and in-depth. In the U.S., and particularly in Los Angeles, there is a lot of small talk and schmooze. One time I had to play pool for an hour.

(To this day, I'm not sure if I should have let the producer win.) At one meeting we played computer games, and at another we fixed a videotape machine.

## Be Yourself

I've had people ask me, "What should I wear for a meeting?" and "Should I bring a resume?" Remember that this is not a job interview. You are a valuable commodity for the production company. They should be after you, not the other way around. Today, some of my friends and I laugh about our first few attempts at meeting with companies. Some of us wore suits, others brought chocolates, and yet others talked about their high school grades. It's normal to be nervous and insecure about the process. It's very, very hard to "sell" yourself to someone you've just met. The most important tip is to be yourself. That's why someone will want to hire you—because of your own specific sets of talents and skills, because of your viewpoint, and because of your creativity. If you normally wear jeans and a t-shirt, go in with that. If you prefer to be dressed up in designer clothes, feel free. Both the commercial industry and the advertising industry are very "cool." People think of themselves as being at the very forefront of creativity, pop culture's avant-garde. Thus, they're very open-minded, and no one will take offense if you're not wearing a tie.

The content of meetings can vary greatly. Some producers want to know a lot about your history, while others care only for the reel. One producer showed me a dozen directors' reels and raved about how great they all were. (Thanks a lot, but what about *my* reel?) At another production company, I met every single person who worked there. I also once had a meeting at a café, because the producer, for some unknown reason, did not want me to go to the production office.

The truth is that you can't know what to expect, and it doesn't really matter. What matters is what *you* want. It's not a job interview. It's not an application. You are checking out the production company. You are the artist. Is this a place where you will feel comfortable? Are there people you can trust? What's your vibe, your feeling? Your gut instinct?

You should ask the following questions:

*How many directors do you represent?*

*How many jobs have you done this year?*

*Have you worked with new directors before?*

*What is your experience in building a director's career?*

*How do you plan to build my career?*

*Where do you see chances and opportunities for my reel?*

*What specifically do you like about my reel?*

*How would you market me?*

Make sure that you watch the company's reel and ask questions about the work on it. How recent is it? How many different directors are on the reel? Have directors recently left the company? (Certain resources will give you directors' histories, including where they have been repped and for how long. So if you find out that directors have left a company, ask them why.)

You want to gain a full picture of the company and its philosophy. You want to know who its sales reps are and who else it represents. You want to talk to the reps before signing. Is the company repped all over the States? Only in the States? Are there relationships with production companies in Canada, Latin America, and Europe?

Good answers are the following:

*We are passionate about your reel.*

*We will announce your signing and launch you with press in the trade papers.*

*You should think about some more spec work that we could do together to keep your reel fresh.*

*We have very specific agencies in mind that would like your work.*

*You will fill a genre that our roster has been lacking so far.*

*We have deals with production companies in Toronto and London, and you would automatically have representation there as well.*

Of course, the producer will ask a lot, too:

*Where do you see your career going?*

*What do you expect from us?*

*Are you willing to shoot low-budget commercials?*

And the routine question: *Who else are you talking to?*

That question comes from a place of deep uncertainty. No one really knows who will be the next big director. No one knows the next trend. If you're talking to a lot of people, it may mean that a lot of people like you. You could be a hot property. It may also mean no one wants to sign you. It's one of those questions that solicits information beyond the actual answer.

The best response I've heard is the one recommended by Bob Peterson, Film Department Chair at Art Center and veteran commercial director: *I'm talking to everyone.*

Both you and the producer will want to walk away with a good feeling and a lot of good answers. If the meeting went well, the two of you will want to think about it and set up another meeting soon. If he hasn't done so already, the producer will show the reel to his sales reps, because they are the ones who have to go and actually sell you. It is important that they are supportive and believe in your work. If things progress positively, you have to talk to sales reps yourself and "read" them.

The most important rule to remember: *Never entrust your career to anyone else.* No one will ever care as much about it as you do. It is okay to question—even doubt—the sales reps and the executive producer. If they seem uncertain about you, how can they possibly sell you with confidence?

Ideally, you will be meeting with a number of people. Hopefully, a few of them will be interested in signing you. Then you'll have to talk details.

## Signing, and What to Look For

Signing with a production company means committing to exclusive representation for a set amount of time. No other production company can offer you to agencies, and usually you cannot work for any other production company. The executive producer commits to getting you work. That's the keyword: *work*. He can be nice and wonderful, supportive and helpful. If he doesn't get you work, he's not doing his job.

In the United States, exclusivity is common. Canada and the United Kingdom are pretty much the same. The rest of Europe and Latin America are much looser, and you can be represented by more than one company (more about that in the chapter on international representation).

A lot of producers will ask you to sign a contract. That's okay. The producer is investing money and resources in you, and he deserves some security. Sometimes, there is a guarantee or retainer involved. A guarantee is basically a salary that the producer believes you will earn back over the course of the contract. Look at it like an advance.

Let's say the producer pays you a $60,000 guarantee for one year. You have the security of earning that money. Great. Once you do your first couple of jobs with the company, you won't get your director's fee until you go past $60,000. If you stay under the guarantee, the producer hasn't done his job right, and you've made a basic salary to live on. There are many variations on the retainer, including one guaranteeing a salary that is accounted for monthly.

There are also signing bonuses, although most likely not for a new director. Rumors have it that some guys on the A-list have gotten up to a million dollars to change companies. If they bring in $15 million in jobs, that is totally agreeable.

Also, in some instances, directors are offered a profit share in lieu of a higher director's fee. Depending on the budget, there is a sliding percentage scale of markup share per project.

In either case, don't just go for the best financial deal. The sweetest promises of money are worth nothing if the work doesn't come in.

The regular contract or handshake agreement is good for a year. Don't commit to more than that the first time around, because you simply never know how things will work out. The sales rep who really liked you may leave for another company, and the new one may hang you out to dry.

Usually, both the company and the director will realize that things aren't working out, and both sides will agree that the relationship should be resolved. Rarely does a production company try to force a director to stay. It's not in the company's interest to retain an unhappy director.

There are a number of details that deserve special attention and that you can discuss with the producer, particularly if those details are part of a signed contract.

Is the contract only for commercials, or does it include music videos and industrial promos? Some companies are active in more than one field or have a divisional arm that works in, for example, music videos. However, if a company has no involvement in the music industry, don't bind yourself to them for music videos.

Your day rate is usually set in the contract, although it is commonly assumed to be flexible. Make sure the day rate is agreeable to you, particularly if other terms of the contract (like a retainer) are dependent on it.

Travel expenses and level of travel may or may not be talked about in the contract. Terms of payment may be set, such as when the director's fees are to be paid and who is responsible for tax withholding.

The right to a director's cut may be included (a director's cut incurs additional cost for the production company), and there should be a clause that you are to get a high-quality copy of each project at no cost, for your personal collection.

Breach of contract, confidentiality, non-compete clauses, and all the usual contract terms are included as a matter of course. (You can find a sample contract in the appendix.)

You may have to join the Director's Guild of America (DGA). It's a costly endeavor, and the production company should pay for it. If you are not a U.S. citizen or resident, you may have to deal with immigration or work permit issues. The costs for that should also be covered by the company.

The extent of financial support is an important issue. You definitely want to know whether a company can finance a spec spot or two, to keep your reel fresh and interesting. Will a company produce low- or no-budget spots to get them on your reel? Sometimes agencies have no money for certain projects (like a PSA), but a smart producer knows that the $10,000 required is a good investment. The project will get the director working with a real agency, it will help create a relationship between the creatives and the director, and it will give him some exposure.

The production company is also in charge of making copies of your reel, at their expense. When handing over your master tapes to be copied, make sure that you know where they will be and that they will be returned. Ideally, ask the production company to make copies of the masters. I almost lost a very expensive master tape when a production company with which I had worked moved to a new location. I found my digital tapes sitting in a plastic bag in a corner of the empty office. So make sure there is a clause that defines how your materials are cared for, and by whom.

## I'm Signed—Now What Do I Do?

Pat yourself on the back, if only this once. You've taken the first major hurdle, and now you can concentrate on the real problem:

getting jobs. The bidding process is described in detail in the next chapter, but you must keep in mind that this is no place to rest.

While you are waiting to receive boards, you should be actively working on your career. Remember that no one else cares as much about your success as you do. If you are lucky, the boards will start pouring in, and you'll be busier than you've ever been in your entire life. It is more likely, however, that you will find boards are hard to come by.

---

### You Are Your Career's Engine

While I was working in Europe in 1999, I watched CNN constantly, following the Kosovo conflict, which was raging at full force. Here we were, fighting over little frames in the editing while people were being killed, raped, and driven from their homes a mere 1,000 miles away from us. I told my producer, "We should go down there and shoot something." He agreed and got the production company to give us $10,000 as a budget. From a local rental house, we got a free 16mm package, and off we went to Albania.

We flew into Tirana, the capital, and started to make contacts, eventually finding a police captain who offered to escort us to the border of Kosovo. After an eight-hour ride over back-country roads in a completely undeveloped country, we arrived in Kukes, the border town where 300,000 refugees were piled into camps. With two concepts loosely in our heads, my producer and I began shooting—in the camps, at the food distribution places, at the border stations, and in farmhouses. After 10 days, we returned and edited four spots for the UNHCR (United Nations High Commissioner for Refugees).

The spots screened in 60 countries, were translated into 13 languages, and were even adopted for a print campaign in Canada. The campaign won many awards, including the Silver Hugo for best campaign, right behind the Budweiser "Wassup" campaign—a multimillion-dollar account.

My point is that your own drive and motivation as an artist will further your career. Don't wait for anyone else.

---

Stay in constant touch with your producer and the sales reps. You will hear the feedback they are getting from agencies. More importantly, you'll keep the pressure on them turned up. What's going on? Where are the boards? What did the Great Creative Agency say? When are you meeting that other Great Agency?

*If you slack, they slack.*

If you have contacts with agencies yourself, keep them going. Stay on top of developments in the industry—technologies, trends, new ideas, new agencies, new directors, awards, and so on. Go to industry events and parties. Network.

And do maybe the most important thing: create. Hone your craft further. Write concepts, screenplays, short stories—whatever makes you happy. Shoot something, even if it is on video. Cut it. Experiment and play around. Expand your knowledge of directing and filmmaking. Take photos. Paint a picture. Write a song. Stay sharp. Stay sane.

# Chapter 3

# Getting the Job

## The Boards Come In—Now What?

The boards—those elusive pages of creativity, stardom, and wealth that everyone is waiting for. You may hear that you are "up" for a project, that you are in the running, or in the pile, maybe even on top of the pile.

*There are some boards floating around for you.*

*You're going to get some boards.*

*We should get the boards next week.*

*They want to bid you.*

The tension rises, the anxiety increases. And finally they show up. You never quite know what to expect, because they differ so much (see Figures 3.1-3.2), for example:

- A single paragraph, describing a vague idea.
- Two pages formatted like a movie script.
- An agency template of two columns (visuals in the left, audio in the right, see Figures 3.1 and 3.2).
- Storyboards of eight black-and-white frames, roughly sketching out a spot.
- Two beautiful full-color pages of detailed illustrations.
- An animatic completely finished with sound, voiceover, and music.

| Creative | Creative Dir. | Proof | Legal | Prod. Accuracy | Claims | Exec. Prod. | Account | Client/GM |
|----------|---------------|-------|-------|----------------|--------|-------------|---------|-----------|
|          |               |       |       |                |        |             |         |           |

**Leo Burnett Detroit**

TELEVISION – JOB #

[CLIENT] Leo Burnett Detroit

[PRODUCT LINE] House Ad

[Creative Team] Cusac/Cymbal

[PROJECT TITLE] "Birth"

Origination Date: 10/23/05
**Revision Date: 11/16/05        Revision #: 4
Scripts/**

[LENGTH] :60 ALTERNATE ENDING

ISCI #:

| VIDEO | AUDIO |
|-------|-------|
| Open on two creatives (Steve and Tom) sitting in an office cubicle working. Thinking. Occasionally SOMEONE passes by. | |
| Closer on Tom. His expression changes as if he's feeling something deep inside. An overcoming (Think ALIEN). Steve makes notice. | Steve (OC):    What? |
| Tom doubles over in pain, holding his stomach. | Tom (OC):    Oh… Oh God. I think it's happening. |
| Steve shakes his head. | Steve (OC):    What? Dude, do you have indigestion again? You need to see a doctor about... |
| Tom is in major pain now. He breathing begins to quicken. | Tom (OC):    No. This is it. It's coming. |
| Steve now realizes that the situation is more serious. | Steve (OC):    Really? |
| A grunt and the commotion causes another creative to stick his head into the scene to see what's happening. | Tom (OC):    Do I look LIKE I'M JOKING?! |
| Steve sweeps his desk empty with a careless wipe of his arm, sending notebooks and junk flying. | Steve (OC):    Alright people. Let's make it happen. We're gonna need some paper towels and some chewing gum, this is gonna happen RIGHT HERE. RIGHT NOW! |
| Another woman sticks her head in. | Julia(OC):    The CD is on his way. And I told Deano to boil some water. |
| People are running off and gathering at the same time. Steve grabs Tom's chair and puts it into full recline and pulls his jeans off. One of the women cringes. | Steve (OC):    Good. Alright. Breathe buddy, breathe. Stay calm. |
| The Creative Director bursts into the scene, dressed from head to toe in black. He is pulling on a pair of rubber gloves. | Brian (OC):    What've we got?? |
| Steve looks at him. He smiles as he speaks. | Steve (OC):    Looks like a big one man. |

Birth rev4                                                                                    02/15/06  10:53 AM

**Figure 3.1**
This is a script from Leo Burnett Detroit for a 60-second spot.
It's divided into a video and an audio column.

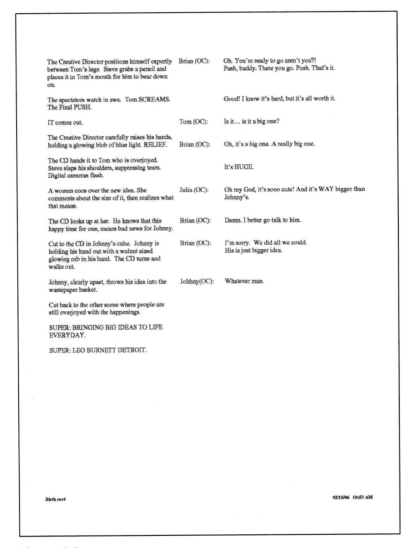

**Figure 3.2**
The script continued.

All of those are legitimate boards. Yet they differ greatly in presentation. Usually, what you can derive from the state of the board is the degree to which the client is involved in the process. The more color and fireworks, the more layers of corporate blessings the board had to survive.

No agency will do full-color boards for fun, or for you, the director. The only reason those are made is because the client has to sign off on them, and the client is tough—or the client wants to get them tested in market research focus groups—which is synonymous with being tough.

In other words, there is a lot at stake for the agency, and colorful storyboards simply leave less to the imagination. Yet if the agency is strong and powerful and the client trusts his advertisers, then the conceptual idea may be written down on a napkin. There simply is no standard.

The next thing you can determine by the state of the board is how much flexibility there is. Concepts that are in the third stage of approval and the fourth stage of testing are less flexible for obvious reasons.

### This Is Only a Test

Testing, by the way, is a dubious method of judging how a commercial will play with the audience. A select focus group gets to watch an animatic and then fill out questionnaires about how they liked it. In some way, it's a safety net for marketing managers when they justify their decisions to superiors. ("But it tested well!") But how can you possibly "test" a commercial before it's shot? That's like gauging the driving abilities of a car based on a colorful drawing.

In either case, you are presented with a concept. Most of the time, the concept is just that—an idea, a story, a core message. Sometimes, it may not be thought out very far, but your job is to make the concept shootable or "round." And the agency will usually be looking for your input.

Warning: We're entering a gray area. The circus act you will have to attempt is a difficult one. On one hand, the agency wants your input; on the other, they don't want you to change their idea completely, because they're attached to it. They want you to improve it, even though it's already next to perfect.

From the beginning, you should realize that you are dealing with two distinct layers. First, there is the layer of the actual commercial. How good is it going to be? How entertaining? How effective?

Second, there is the layer of politics and ego. You must never forget that there is a complex relationship between the agency and the client that you will never be privy to.

This can lead to complicated situations. What's in the best interest of the commercial may not be in the best interest of the agency. Sometimes, it may not even be in the best interest of the client! But don't fret. That's what your producer is for. His experience, his cajoling, and his cunning interrogation of the agency producer should gain you vital information about what's really important.

## CASE STUDY

### The Boards Come In

Throughout the book, I will use a Ford project from early 2006 as a case study. From the first moment I received the board all the way to the airing, I will take it through the steps of bidding, prepping, preproduction, production, and post production.

In mid-December 2005, I'm traveling in Europe for meetings and holiday celebrations when I get an email from my executive producer, John Clark, back in Los Angeles. His company is called Boxer Films, and I've been signed with them for two years.

In the email, John—in his sparse style—lets me know that there is a Ford board coming in for me. I should call him. So I get on the phone, and I hear that this board is coming in, and that it's got a short turnaround, which means that it has to be on-air very soon. How soon, he will have to find out, but just in case—can I come back before the Christmas holidays?

Of course I can, although my grandma will be bummed. In any case, he will send me the board as soon as he receives it. This, by the way, means that the agency has already seen my reel, and that I'm one of three to five directors being bid for this job.

The next day I wake up to an email attachment containing said Ford board from the J. Walter Thompson agency in Detroit, and a note from John to call him. When I call him, he tells me that the conference call is supposed to happen the next day, 9 a.m. Los Angeles time, 6 p.m. European Central time. Is that fine? Absolutely.

CASE STUDY *continued*

Word is, they have okayed money for two days (which means it could be more but it's doable), and the schedule is breakneck. Air date is January 7. Here, I do the math. Usually, it's a week post production—and that is without knowing the concept yet. Some concepts take a month in post. But let's say it's a week. Puts the shoot right at New Year's. So, shooting two days before the year ends means December 28 and 29. Really bad timing. People are on vacation or don't want to work. However, not primarily my problem at this point.

My problem is the conference call. I have two days to look at the board and make up my mind about a number of things. Come up with good ideas. Come up with good questions.

## Your First Look at the Board

I approach a project like this: First, I look at the board and think of ways to improve the idea, to make it more interesting, entertaining, and effective. This involves a lot of my personal taste and style— and my taste and style are part of the reason the agency asked me to bid *in the first place*.

Then I look at the board from the agency's point of view. Their main emotion is one of concern and fear. What could go wrong? What is not clear? What could be misunderstood? Is this going to work?

The governing principle is safety. If the agency people feel they are sticking out their necks for you, you may as well not bid. Their jobs are on the line. Your job, besides making the concept a better spot, is to make the agency feel safe and comfortable. They must be able to trust you, because by extension they are trusting you with their kids' college funds.

### Let the Board Speak to You

Here's director Joe Murray's approach to a storyboard:

*I'm very intuitive about it. A certain take or beat might interest me. Every board is a process and discovery. Everything is different. There are no two boards that are the same. What resonates with me, what do I like about it? What does it lead to? What's the dynamic? Quick pace, slow-paced? I tap into my visual lexicon to tell the story. I look for inspiration in books, magazines, sometimes a certain lens will pop in my head. It's about finding the personal inspiration, your point of view. You hit a certain style and talk a certain language, and that becomes your style. But it has to come from the inside.*

Luckily, you have ample time and opportunity to gauge where the agency stands. Usually, the first step after you receive the boards is a conference call with the agency. Therefore, your first goal at this stage is to come up with ideas and questions that you can pose in the call.

The ideas and questions must be good. Do not scare the agency with mediocre suggestions. Make them feel that whatever you do will make *them* look good.

I commonly try to find a core theme for the spot. For me, the core theme usually has to do with story line (because of the genre I work in). So the theme could be "odd-funny." In a tabletop spot for perfume, it could be "classic-elegant." In a car spot, it could be "action-filled yet beautiful."

Then I try to come up with one major idea that I want to add to the concept. I may have a million ideas, but I want to identify the one that has the biggest impact and will resonate in the agency's mind. It could be an image, an action, even a piece of music or another character. It's that one thing which enhances their idea and takes it to the next level.

## Go to the Core

Director Jim Zoolalian approaches a new project like this:

*I always start with the idea. I peel away all of the stuff that often sur-rounds the pure thought. If you can get to the core idea, it's much eas-ier to pitch your new ideas and unique thoughts if they're based on that original idea. I then start thinking of all the interesting visual imagery that might spring from illustrating that main idea. And then sometimes I look at the location stills that I've taken of the proposed location. For me, visual ideas can materialize from looking at pictures of the actual location. And then finally, I might go back to reference films to get shot ideas. All of this is done simultaneously, because sometimes an idea in one area can spark an idea elsewhere.*

This idea should show the agency a few things. For starters, it shows that you understand the concept and that you are on the same wavelength. The agency should feel that their concept is improved. It should also reinforce their decision to bid you in the first place.

The theme and your main idea will be your "sell." However, you should be prepared to answer any question the agency might throw at you.

*How do you see the look?*

*What do you think about the casting?*

*Do you think there should be music?*

*How are you going to solve the special effects?*

*What acting style do you see here?*

Once you have the board, sit down and think hard about it. The conference call is coming up, and you will have a chance to down-load a lot of information from the creatives. Come up with the right questions. Think of good answers. And have some good ideas and your own interpretation ready to impress them.

## CASE STUDY

### First Look

I look at the boards and am exhilarated (see Figures 3.3-3.5). They look like fun. There are two climbers hanging from the face of a mountain, and I'm a sucker for climbing and high-altitude mountaineering. Immediately I notice the weird arrangements of bivouac platforms. Those are the hanging platforms on which the climbers sleep overnight in a vertical environment. The process of overnighting is called bivouacking, and the site is the bivouac.

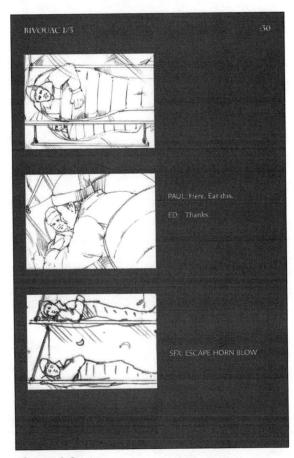

**Figure 3.3**
In this agency board, there are three images per page—there is no norm.

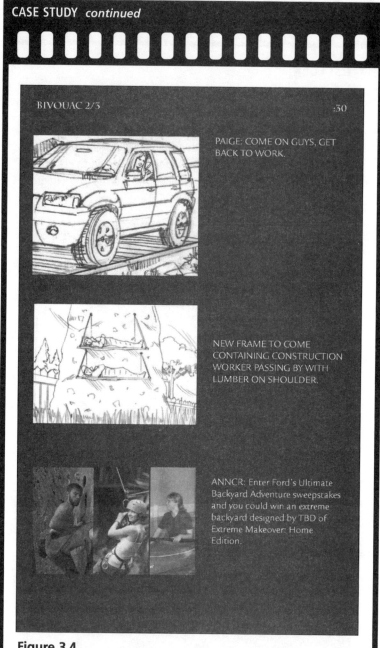

**Figure 3.4**
Occasionally, you see a mix of drawings and photographs.

**Figure 3.5**
The logos and the car shot are placeholders, and you are
expected to make suggestions for these frames.

I read on. A car appears, driven by a woman named Paige, and she is yelling at the guys on the side of the mountain. Then there is a reveal. It's not a real mountain, but rather an artificial climbing wall. This is the major turning point in the story. The rest of the board is almost entirely art card stuff, which means it's nothing that will be filmed. In the top-right corner, it says that it is a 30-second spot, but I'm not holding my breath on that. Those things change quickly. Thirty would be nice.

A closer look at the art cards reveals that this is a sweepstakes in cooperation with ABC's *Extreme Makeover: Home Edition*. I've never watched the show. Oops. Thank God for the Internet. A quick look tells me that the entire cast of the commercial is from the TV show: Paige Hemmis, Paul DiMeo, and Ed Sanders. This has a few implications, since they are celebrities. But right now, I'm not concerned with that.

In the sweepstakes, you can win an extreme adventure backyard makeover. So the cast will show up and put an adventure park behind your house. A climbing wall and…what else? Will we have to shoot any of the other extreme sports stuff, like kayaking or snowboarding? This brings up a ton of production questions. But again, right now I'm not concerned with that. My main focus is the conference call.

In the conference call I will be talking to the creative team, Chris Sadlier and Matt Dimmer, as well as the agency senior producer, Kelly Trudell (whom I've also interviewed for this book). Also on the phone will be my executive producer, John Clark, and our head of production at Boxer Films, John Quinn.

The goal of the conference call is to download a lot of information from the agency. For example, how final is the story? When celebrities are involved, concepts are often preapproved by "their people," and changes are always a big issue. Since it is a Ford commercial, and in the storyboard Paige is driving up in a car, I'm wondering whether it is mandatory that the car moves. I want to talk to them about the arrangement of the platforms on the wall because my feeling is that the staging and framing of shots could be problematic in this setup.

**CASE STUDY** *continued*

On another story-related issue, I need to make up my mind about the wall: Should it be clearly recognizable as an artificial climbing wall, or should it look like fake rock? Obviously, fake rock will "sell" the idea that they're at a high altitude much better. On the other hand, it may not be completely credible if it looks like real rock, simply because artificial climbing walls don't look like that.

So, I'm intrigued by the idea and the story; I love the setup with the climbers on the wall. There are a few issues I'm concerned with. My next step is to break down the story into beats for myself. So far it's a very simple dramatic structure with these beats:

◆ Two climbers are hanging precariously on a vertical wall, waking up.
◆ They rise, and we're led to believe that it's a cold and tough environment.
◆ A car drives up from out of nowhere with a woman calling out to the climbers.
◆ It is revealed that the climbers are but a few feet off the ground on an artificial climbing wall.

It's pretty much a one-liner joke. Setup with a punchline. To me, the meat is in the fact that we're led to believe that these guys are tough, high-altitude mountaineers, when really what they are is boys playing at camping in the backyard. That's the funny stuff. How can I make it even funnier, or is it already at its funniest?

In this case, the two opposites—mountaineers versus boys—are what create the tension and the humor. I can increase the dramatic tension by pushing each of the two opposites farther while loading them up with more punch. In other words, I should look for ways to make them tougher on one hand and more boyish and nerdy on the other.

How about if I add a blizzard? If I create a really freezing cold feeling up on the "mountain," it's going to raise their external conflict. Each story should have an external and an internal conflict for the main characters. The external conflict deals with outside forces that are acting against the protagonist or making his life a living hell. The internal conflict consists of all those psychological obstacles a character has to overcome in order to continue his quest and succeed.

CASE STUDY *continued*

So by adding a blizzard I would certainly increase the external conflict of the two climbers because it creates a more adverse environment and puts them into a more exposed situation. My concern with a blizzard is that it won't be credible if we start in an environment that is filled with ice and snow, and then end in a sunny backyard somewhere in America. I think that would be a stretch.

Also, the blizzard isn't funny. And it's already cold anyway. So the blizzard was a bad idea. Next. In the boards, Paul hands Ed something to drink or eat. I really like the fact that there is so little talking going on. It feels like the guys are conserving every ounce of energy. So, what if Paul hands Ed a Thermos bottle? Presumably with something warm in it. And Ed is freezing, and he is wearing mittens. When he tries to open the bottle, he drops it, and it falls down the mountain.

Now that's working. It ties into the cold and freezing feeling—in fact, it offers relief by being some sort of warm beverage. So when Ed loses the bottle, it is double-bad. It ups the stakes, because not only are they stuck on the side of a mountain, but they've also lost their hot fluids. And I can see the attempt to open the bottle performed in a very funny fashion. In fact, I can direct them to act like the boyish nerds that they turn out to be by the end of the spot—like amateur climbers. There is potential for some physical comedy when the bottle slips. Both guys could be trying to grab it desperately.

So I think this is going somewhere. My next major question is how to shoot the reveal. It's not really funny when Paige drives up in the car. It seems like this may be a typical concession to a client in order to show the car in motion. However, Paige needs to be that grown-up person who simply shakes her head about the guys playing backyard adventure. That's funny. But will it work when she is in the car?

An idea arises: how about having the bottle hit green grass pretty much immediately? So there is no 1,000 foot fall, which the audience expects. The bottle drops only five or six feet, and we see it smack onto a neatly cut lawn. And then we see Paige walk up to the guys and have a bit more of a spatial relationship between them. If she is in the car, they are very separated, and it's going to be difficult to stage. If she is on foot, I can create a sense of space between the characters. If she can walk right in front of them, why are the guys making such a big deal about "being on the wall?" It makes them look even nerdier.

Great, now I have two major ideas for the story which I think improve the comedy and take it to the next level. I know how I would shoot the spot in terms of colors and camera movement. Pretty simple and without any attention-grabbing camera movements. It's about the story. It's cold. Nothing moves much. So the camera won't move much either. Slightly bluish in tone, and then a nice change to a warmer overall hue when we reveal that they are, in fact, in a backyard.

Time to think about the product. It's a Ford spot, so the Ford Escape is the product, even though it's not really a Ford Escape commercial. Nevertheless, the car is shown and that's my client's main concern. I favor products that are integrated into the story and the environment. Pack shots in limbo (on white or plain background) are not my favorites. I would like to shoot the car in the backyard while construction of the adventure park is in progress (which is the setting of the commercial). I'm not sure yet if that will be possible, because staging a full backyard under construction may be too expensive. We may only have a small part of a backyard that we can afford to dress. Lots of open questions.

The location choice is a very important issue to deal with early on. We need a backyard that is large enough to accommodate an artificial climbing wall, a car, some sort of construction site, and, last but not least, a film crew. This brings me to the question of how big the wall should be. Without doubt, this will be one of the first questions John Quinn, who runs the production, will ask me.

I quickly realize that we need a location with a free view of the sky as well. For the shots of the guys on the wall, there cannot be any buildings or trees in the background. And the wall has to be big enough to create the illusion that these guys are on a mountain. The shots must be completely filled with the rock behind them, and any edges need to be in front of clear sky.

In fact, I'm increasingly aware now that the wall presents quite a challenge in terms of designing the shots. It will be very difficult to plan the shots and angles with these limitations in mind. Maybe this would be a good project to do some previsualization on. Brain fodder for later. My focus is on getting the job, and the conference call is an important step in that process.

I break the story down into beats again:

- ◆ Two climbers are hanging on a vertical wall, waking up.
- ◆ They're very cold, so one hands the other a Thermos with warm fluids.
- ◆ When he tries to open the bottle, it slips from his hands and falls down the mountain.
- ◆ The bottle immediately lands in green grass.
- ◆ A woman appears from out of nowhere and speaks to the climber.
- ◆ We reveal that it's an artificial climbing wall in a sunny backyard.

So now that there is more stuff going on, in this case, it's a mislead. My intention is to mislead the audience into buying into the conflict of the lost bottle. I want the viewer to feel the cold and isolation and then react "Oh no!" when the Thermos falls. In the audience's minds, the question now will be, "What are they going to do? They're out of water!"

Rather than letting the audience dangle on the weak conflict of two climbers on a vertical wall in a cold environment, I choose to show something that is happening in the moment: two climbers on a vertical wall in a cold environment lose their warm fluids when they fumble the Thermos bottle and it falls into the abyss. At the moment of highest tension (the bottle is lost, what will happen now?), the reveal comes in: The bottle isn't lost, because they aren't on a mountain. They're grown men playing like little boys.

I feel confident that this is a good idea, and I'm ready for the conference call. Most of it will be asking questions and listening.

You are also dealing with the beginnings of the production, even though you haven't been awarded the job yet. The person in charge of compiling a budget—either the producer or the line producer in charge—will ask you many questions, such as the following:

*Where do you want to shoot?*

*How many days do you need?*

*How many actors will you need?*

*Is there any special equipment?*

*Are there digital effects?*

All these questions are very preemptive because at this point everything is a bit vague. However, a budget must be made somehow, based on something. Also, your style may have an impact on the budget. Additionally, the budget constraints may have an impact on your ability to shoot the commercial the way you want to. If there is only $50,000 for post production, you can't create ideas and shots that cost $200,000.

Together with the production people and sometimes a location scout, you will begin to investigate possibilities for the right location, looking for the perfect street, house, or beach. You may have to talk to specialists about certain aspects of the production, taking into account that the agency might ask you about them.

The agency realizes that at this stage you won't have all the answers. But as you go into the conference call, it is good to know that you've done your homework.

## Nuts-and-Bolts Stuff

As I said before, storyboards can come in many different forms. Here are some detailed descriptions of terms and formats you might run into.

## Pages Formatted Like a Movie Script

A movie script format centers dialogue on the page, while action runs across the entire width of the page (see Figures 3.6-3.8). The format is based on a long-standing norm that is used in feature production to estimate the length of scenes and shooting schedules. Usually, one page is estimated to run one minute (a movie script has around 120 pages).

```
                        "Birth" - Page 1


      "Birth"


      INT. ADVERTISING AGENCY OFFICE - CUBICLE

      Two CREATIVES (TOM AND STEVE) are sitting across from each
      other, at their desks. They're... creating. Thinking.

      CLOSER on TOM. His expression changes. As if he is feeling
      something very deep inside. An overcoming (Think ALIEN).

                           STEVE
                        (notices)
                  What?

                           TOM
                  Aw god.

      TOM doubles over in pain, holding his stomach.

                           STEVE
                  What's going on?

                           TOM
                  I think... it's happening.

                           STEVE
                  Really?

      A GRUNT, which causes STEPHANIE to stick her head around a
      cubicle wall. TOM SCREAMS in a sudden attack of pain,
      causing others to notice, including JOHNNY.

                           STEPHANIE
                  What's going on?

                           TOM
                  This is it! It's coming!

                           STEVE
                  Alright people. Let's make it
                  happen. Let's move everyone! Get
                  Brian!

      JOHNNY runs off.

      STEVE sweeps his desk empty with a careless wipe, sending
      his notebook and everything else flying.

      STEVE grabs TOM and pushes him into the birthing position on
      his empty desk.
```

**Figure 3.6**
Remember the agency script in Figures 3.1 and 3.2?
This is my version of the same commercial.

"Birth" - Page 2

                    STEVE
          Good. Alright. Breathe buddy,
          breathe. Stay calm. Brian's going
          to be here any second.

TOM's pain increases.

BRIAN arrives with JOHNNY.

                    BRIAN
          What've we got??

                    STEVE
          Looks like a big one, man.

BRIAN expertly positions himself between TOM's legs. STEVE
grabs a pencil and places it in TOM's mouth for him to bear down
on.

                    BRIAN
          Oh. Push, buddy, push. There you
          go. That's it. Come on.

The SPECTATORS watch in awe. TOM SCREAMS. The FINAL PUSH.

                    BRIAN
          Good job! Good job! Right on.

IT comes out.

                    TOM
          Is it... is it big?

BRIAN carefully raises his hands, holding a glowing blob of
blue light. RELIEF.

                    BRIAN
          Oh, it's a big one. A really big
          one...

BRIAN hands IT to TOM who is overjoyed. STEVE slaps his
shoulders, suppressing tears. Flashes of digital cameras.

BRIAN turns to the SPECTATORS.

                    BRIAN
          People. Now this is a big idea.  A
          really big idea. Congratulations
          Tom.

                    STEPHANIE
          Oh my God, it's soooo huge!
          (Oh my God, it's so cute!)

**Figure 3.7**
The script continued.

```
                        "Birth" - Page 3


        APPLAUSE.

        ABRUPTLY sad, tragic MUSIC is heard.

        JOHNNY is looking at a tiny green light blob in his hand. He
        is totally bummed and walks off. BRIAN notices.

        BRIAN follows.

        BRIAN gives JOHNNY a pep talk. He drops the tiny green idea
        into a wastepaper basket.

        BRIAN returns to the celebrating group.

        TOM, STEVE, and BRIAN pose with the big idea for a
        photograph.

        SUPER: LEO BURNETT DETROIT

        SUPER: BRINGING BIG IDEAS TO LIFE EVERYDAY.


        A shot of the tiny green idea in the corner, dying off.
```

**Figure 3.8**
The script continued.


## An Agency Template with Two Columns

Agencies have their proprietary formats for scripts. They'll include the agency logo and information, like the names of the creative team, the name of the producer, the name of the client, the dates of origin, the date of revision, the type of advertising, the length, the project title, the brand title, the campaign title, and on and on.

Below the header, you will find two columns, divided into video on the left and audio on the right. The video column lists everything that is seen. The audio column lists everything that is heard, including voiceover, dialogue, music, and sound effects.

## Storyboards with Frames

This page is usually divided into three columns. Video description is on the left, audio description is on the right, and the center column is made up of storyboard images. The images might be very concise and detailed, or simply just a rough sketch.

## Animatic

An animatic is an animated storyboard. Drawings are scanned into the computer or taped on video and then edited along with music and voiceover or sound effects. This is often done for testing purposes when the concept is presented to a selected audience for research. Also, it gives a good indication of the timing of the spot.

## What Is Copy?

The term *copy* is used for any words that can be seen or heard, written by the agency. Very precisely, it stems from print advertising, where the copy is the actual text or slogan in the ad. In TV advertising, the *copy* means voiceover, dialogue, claims, slogans, explainers, etc.

## Pack Shot

Sometimes, you see the term *pack shot* at the end of a concept. It refers to a shot of the product and is derived from packaging photography. However, *pack shot* is also used for car or service ads where there is no more packaging (no box to speak of).

## Super

The term *super* comes from superimposing. Supers refer to all text or graphics that are laid on top of images in post production.

## Treatment

The *treatment* on a spot (not to be confused with the director's treatment) usually refers to the design and layout of the final logo plate or product shot. Placement, size, and many other variables must be taken into account, including how the treatment will be integrated into the spot.

## The Conference Call

The conference call is usually your first direct contact with the agency. It's a very important call, and you need to be focused, not only on presenting your view and take on the creative, but also on what you can "mine" from the agency. As I said earlier in this chapter, your initial storyboard prep should be about two things: your interpretation of the project and the questions you can ask in the call.

You will probably not book a job based on a conference call. The best you can do is woo the agency— for example, give them a confident, safe, and comfortable feeling about your work, and improve their idea in a way they like and which makes them look good. You can put that idea, image, or action in their heads, and hope that it will be so compelling that they won't be able to stop thinking about it. However, you can lose a job based on the conference call. You may simply not be on the same page as the agency, and the call can go badly. Don't worry. Learn from the experience.

There could be a large number of people involved in the call: the creative director, the copywriter, the art director, the agency producer, the contact manager, your producer, your post producer, your sales rep., and so on. No matter how many people there are, however, it is important that you take charge at a certain point. It is your call. The agency doesn't come to you to tell you what to do. They want you to tell them.

Most agencies, particularly the good ones, are looking for someone to step up and make their spot something special. John van Osdol, executive vice president at Leo Burnett Detroit, puts it this way: "We look for a definitive point of view. A confident skipper in a sea of potential mediocrity." For Kelly Trudell from JWT, "The call is huge. I look for someone who is relaxed, friendly, and gives us a sense of confidence: someone who brings original ideas to the concept. The rapport that develops during that first call can be the difference between the director being considered or not."

## Listen

Commercial director Joe Murray has had years of experience with conference calls:

*I choose three points I want to get across. But more important is downloading. Get information from them. Really, it's getting a sense of who they are and what they're looking for. Listen. Hear what they are saying. You have to walk the line between having a point of view and not being too specific. The difficulty is that you say one thing that is almost meaningless to you, and they hate it. It's so easy to misstep.*

*Serendipity is a good word. You know, conference calls only started within the few last years. And I'm a horrible salesperson. A lot of people get jobs because of conference calls. It's kind of like combat. You never know what you're going to do. You can train and be prepared, but it's not the real thing until you do it. Go jogging.*

*It's very hard to discuss visual things over the phone. Green is not green. And agency people are not visual. You have to be highly developed visually to understand the world, to see the world from a visual viewpoint. Toughest thing is that you cannot do it alone, so you need support. Always make sure to hire people who are better than you. Get the input.*

## Listen More

Director Jim Zoolalian on teleconferencing:

*The biggest piece of advice I can give is LISTEN, LISTEN, LISTEN. This is something that I have to constantly remind myself. It really is helpful for me to hear the background and framework for why a spot is being produced. So I usually start the call by having the agency take me through the boards in their own words. You really can learn a lot about the thought process behind the concept, and if you're fast enough, you can use this information to help pitch your own ideas.*

Usually, your producer will take care of polite introductions. Then one of the creatives will quickly run through the idea and often give additional information as to what is important to the client. This information is extremely important because you will learn the underlying strategy of the commercial.

For example, the creatives might say that the car has to be red, or that the couple has to be Latino, or that a certain key visual has to be repeated several times. Some of these issues will be very mundane and often make no sense from a storytelling or artistic viewpoint, but they are the inevitable problems you face as a commercial director.

Other issues are very important because they are related to the ego of the creative or the person in power at the agency. For example, a creative may say:

*I'm all for authenticity.*

*I just hate three-quarter angles on cars.*

*Really, I prefer the odd kind of acting.*

*I don't know, but monochrome is so out.*

These utterances are worth their weight in gold. They show you the direction in which the creative would like to take the project, and it would be foolish to go against his wishes.

The agency will adhere to certain parameters and give you their basic interpretation of the concept. Then it is your turn to take charge. Remember, you must impress the agency with your ideas and make them feel safe. Also remember that the agency may have up to four other conference calls lined up with other directors.

I usually open with how much I like the concept and why. A certain element—perhaps the humor or the feel or the storyline—appeals to me, and that is why I want to shoot this commercial. This approach makes it clear that I chose to bid for the project as much as the agency chose to bid for me. My attitude validates the agency's work. Hey, if this guy agreed to do it, the agency thinks, it must be pretty good. While this may sound a little simplistic, I truly believe that you must like the concept in order to make it become a reality. There are spots that are hard to like, but with luck, you will not run into too many of those.

After my initial validation of the agency's work, I will ask questions:

*How old do you see the boy?*

*Did you see this as being very Spielberg-esque, or shot in a more modern, reduced style?*

*Why do you have the hero go back and wave one more time?*

*What was your reasoning for the wide shot of the house?*

All these questions are intended to give me an understanding of the agency's positions on important issues. It also shows them that I have thought about the concept, and I have very specific questions about it. Finally, it forces the agency to respond. If they are weak or uncertain about certain issues (which they almost always are), I have a chance to present them with a solution. And that makes me look good.

Obviously, I want to see if my initial ideas are on the mark. If I feel the agency will like my ideas, I present them.

However, if I feel I'm off the mark, I keep asking more and more specific questions, which may include details like locations, casting, or sound. These questions are designed to bring up certain points of information, which I write down during the call. Then I go into a phase where I agree with everything they say and underscore how much we are on the same wavelength. One by one, I reiterate some of their points and reinforce their vision, which of course I now present as our common vision.

This strategy works remarkably well because all creative people like to hear that their work is good. And it's not a bad thing to do. It doesn't mean that you are tricking the agency. It's just that your initial ideas were off, and they have to be rethought. This is what the call is for.

However, if you are right on the mark with your interpretation and your ideas are strong, it's time to impress them. I tend to present ideas as rough thoughts, intuitions, or flashes of insight that automatically appeared to me when I read the concept—even though I actually put in a few days of hard thinking. Also, I present them in a very non-committal way:

*I wondered if it wouldn't be good to…*

*It occurred to me that it could be great to…*

*I think it would just be so funny to…*

*Did you consider having him…?*

*I think a great way to shoot this would be to…*

*What do you think about…?*

I don't want to roll over the agency and make them feel like their concept is incomplete, not funny, or weak. I want to improve, push, heighten, support, and foster. To such an approach, the perfect answer from the agency is this:

*I like that a lot… if he takes the bottle in his hand, he could even just walk away right there, so we save a couple of seconds…*

The creative likes it. But even more, he's made it his own and expands on it and acknowledges how it would improve the spot (in this case, by simplifying things and saving a bit of time). If you hear this, you've done a great job. From now on, keep hammering away on that same idea. Why bring up something that the agency might not like? You've found something they've responded positively to, so keep talking about it. How will you shoot it? What will it do to the story? Hammer it home because this is the association you want them to walk away with from the call.

This conference call, as you will remember, is not about actually deciding how the commercial will be shot or who gets the job. You will not book the spot based on the conference call. So, after getting a lot of good information about the agency's viewpoint, you must leave them feeling safe and comfortable and empowered. You want them to walk away and say, "That was a great call."

Look at it like a hook. Try to hook the agency. Don't give them too much. You need to save more for later. If this were a movie, it would be the teaser. If it were sex, it would be foreplay.

Obviously, you want to appear professional and not make a fool out of yourself. There are a large number of answers you simply can't give at this point:

*Will you use a crane or a dolly?*

*How will this or that digital effect work?*

*What director of photography are you using?*

*How will you create all that snow?*

---

## Connect the Chemistry

Creative director Tor Myrhen, who regularly is on conference calls with the industry's leading directors, notes this:

*Conference calls are funny. And yes, they are also very important. Funny because they are your first taste of the director as a person, rather than as a reel of commercials—and rarely do they live up to the image you have in your head. And important because on a good job, there are probably several talented directors competing for the work. So as an agency guy, you've got three great directors wanting to do your job. Which one should you choose? At this point, it really comes down to chemistry. I would say calls have less to do with nailing exactly how to shoot the thing, and more to do with making a connection with the creatives. When we hang up on the agency side, we ask ourselves one thing: Can we trust this guy to make it great? If the answer is yes, chances are he's gonna get the job—even if his visual references and his treatment weren't exactly what we had in mind.*

With growing experience, you will be able to "wing" these kinds of questions, but, doubtlessly, it is better to do the research and have some answers ready—even if they're not final. Often, they're options:

*We could use either a crane or a dolly, or even a steadicam. Once I see the location, I'll make the final decision, and we will use whatever is necessary to get the shot we want.*

*We've talked to the effects guys at the post production house, and they had some great ideas as to how to accomplish that effect. They're true artists, and once we get rolling, we'll sit down with them and go through it shot by shot.*

*There are a few guys I really like working with, and we're getting their latest reels. For this spot, I would really like to use someone who has some experience in shooting with elephants.*

*We looked at some tests from a real effects company, and their snow looks just fantastic. At the end of the day, we'll have to tie down a tight shot list so we can figure out exactly how much snow we need, and where. But I'm not concerned at all, the snow looks very convincing.*

All these answers sound professional and reassuring, while being contingent upon the job actually being awarded. It's a polite way of saying: Give us the job and we'll give you the answers.

In the earlier part of this chapter, I said that you want to present something that resonates with the agency and stays with them. I talked about that one idea, that one image or piece of music by which the creatives will remember the call. It's all about the power of association. You would rather have them leave the call with only one strong idea than several which they can't remember without looking at their notes. This, by the way, goes back to the branding idea that I talked about in Chapter 2. You are selling yourself in this call and staying within your own brand. This is how you should do it.

CASE STUDY

## The Conference Call

**5.59 p.m.**, Frankfurt, Germany. I'm ready for the call. On the other side of the planet, the production team is about to dial in, while somewhere in the middle, in Detroit, the agency takes their seats next to the telephone. This is not uncommon. A lot of this business happens over the phone and the Internet—to the point that people wonder what we ever did without them.

I once had a conference call between Paris, Miami, Los Angeles, and Kingston, Jamaica. I heard later that it cost $800 for the 20 minutes we talked. Sometimes, you have to do a call on your cell phone (I once had to do one while driving!), because scheduling is not always perfect. It gets really funny when you have an additional translator. Only a few weeks ago, I was on the phone with an agency in Moscow. Everything was being translated between Russian and English, and who knows how well. Good enough for me to book the job, but it certainly forced me to communicate even clearer.

**6 p.m.** I call in to the conference call number: "You will now be joined to the conference." A chime announces my arrival, and there is that uncomfortable moment of "Hello? Anyone there?"

Agency and production are already on board, chit-chatting away. Everyone says hi and introductions are made. The atmosphere is friendly and professional—one of the good things about working with a top agency. The creative team quickly runs through the storyboard, pointing out the moments and issues that are important to them. Here and there, they give some secondary information about client preferences and comments.

Chris and Matt sound like the pros they are, and they present their ideas the way I expected: "Here is the idea; where would you take it?" They're open to suggestions, as any good creative should be. This is the moment when it is decided whether the creatives and I will be able to work as a team. Whether we jibe, are on the same page, on the same wavelength.

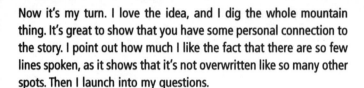

Now it's my turn. I love the idea, and I dig the whole mountain thing. It's great to show that you have some personal connection to the story. I point out how much I like the fact that there are so few lines spoken, as it shows that it's not overwritten like so many other spots. Then I launch into my questions.

First, I ask them whether the car has to drive—if the client demanded that the car be in motion. The answer is no. They say that they thought it was a nice way of introducing the car into the story. I agree for now, but voice my concern that it's hard to stage and get a feel for Paige if she's inside the car. I would prefer to have a spatial relationship between her and the other characters. They agree. Really, what they need is for the car to be present in the backyard.

No problem. I was wondering, I continue, what they thought about pushing the dramatic envelope a little by adding this nuance: Ed could drop the bottle, and have it fall down the mountain. We could even shoot that part in slow motion to overdramatize it a little bit. Then the bottle hits the grass a mere five feet below them. It's a different way to reveal the turning point.

Chris immediately seems to like it, and says that Paige could step into the shot when we see the bottle in the grass. I like that idea a lot. Okay, let me work on it for the treatment. What about the wall? Should it look like real rock? The agency is leaning towards a yes. I agree. I think it could be a nice climbing wall, where the handholds are not yet attached. After all, the place is under construction.

We go into the issue of other items present in the backyard: A snowboarding simulator, a kayaking pool, a BMX trail, a rappel, or a traversing wire. In my opinion we're going to have to choose a few of those, because the final shot will be very wide, and if it's too full, nothing will be recognizable. The agency agrees.

We talk about the pack shot. They don't like pack shots in limbo either, and we agree that a final shot with the car and the wall and the backyard is what we're going for. The agency is apologetic

**CASE STUDY** *continued*

about all the retail information and the logos at the end, but there is no way around it. There will also have to be a disclaimer at the bottom noting any legal issues in regard to the sweepstakes.

This brings me to the length. They say it's going to stay at :30. Great.

John sums up the proceedings and says that I will be preparing a treatment, which will be sent along with the budget. We all say goodbye, and that's it.

# Chapter 4

# The Treatment

After the conference call, you should have a very good idea of what the agency wants and how your interpretation jibes with it. Now you have to put together a treatment—basically, the written presentation of your vision of the spot. This is usually submitted together with the final budget. Based on those two documents, the agency and the client will make their decision.

---

### Make It Better

This is what creative director Tor Myhren looks for in a treatment:

*Any commercial is made three times: Once on paper, once at the shoot, and once at the edit. In other words, what we as agency people bring to the party is only 33% of the finished story. So I look for treatments that take our idea and make it better. I look for that moment where I say, "Hey, that's really cool. I never would have thought of that." It's really this simple: Does the treatment make the spot better, or not?*

---

## The Appearance

Treatments come in many different shapes and sizes. In some countries, they're called "the director's interpretation." In other countries, you don't have to write a treatment in the first place.

However, the norm is that a treatment is required. The most basic treatment is the written word. A single page of ideas and notes is not uncommon at all, although sometimes, to cover all your ideas, you will end up writing three or four pages. But a word of caution: Don't get lost in the details. Imagine that the agency and the client have three or four other treatments to go through, and they don't want to read 20 pages full of 12-point text.

A treatment is not a thesis, it's a presentation. Therefore, you should be entertaining while still being professional. You want to give the reader a quick idea of how your vision would play out—for example, the changes you would make and the improvements you would add.

The trend has been toward very visual treatments. It is not unheard of to prepare a treatment with an attached DVD or CD containing video clips or music. Textures or fabric may be included. On occasion, people have gone out and filmed something on digital video. Today's computer technology has enabled individuals to put together stunning presentations quite easily. I have used programs such as Word, Quark, Corel, Photoshop, Flash, 3D Swift, and Acrobat to create treatments. In such cases, a treatment not only requires you to be a good director, but also a good writer and a good graphic designer!

Even if the written word is not your strength, there are solutions. Directors use treatment writers and layout artists all the time. If you have a supportive production company, it will supply a researcher, a storyboard artist, and anyone else whose skills you might need.

Obviously, you will want your treatment to look nice, communicate your vision, and show your professionalism. Your spelling should be impeccable, and there is really no excuse for mistakes. If you submit your treatment electronically, make sure that the file is not too big and that it opens properly. If you send a printed version, check it carefully. And use a high-quality binding.

I tend to create elaborate treatments with lots of images. I also try to find a graphic design that relates to the feel of the spot. I may use a special format (often horizontal pages) and pick several interesting fonts. I spend a lot of time finding the right images from any number of sources. The Internet is full of free pictures, for example, and you can scan photographs from books or magazines. Or you can even go out and shoot some photos yourself.

---

### Fireworks

Director Jim Zoolalian has this to say on treatments:

*Usually, I only get one or two days to put the treatment together. In order to do this, I have tons of images already on the computer. And if we need to complement that, we hire a visual consultant to pull additional images. The written treatment and visual search all happen at the same time, so that I am adding to the written treatment once some great image sparks an idea, or vice versa.*

---

### Stimulate—Even Objections

And here is what director Joe Murray says about creating treatments:

*There were no treatments when I started. Now I do a visual presentation, writing, something personal, something that resonates with me personally, reminds me of something that happened. Text and images. Literature. Poetry, music, it's a bit like workshopping. Maybe a piece of film or a painting.*

*They may like some pictures, they may hate some. If they object it helps, because you know that's not it. You throw it out there for consideration. A stimulation for ideas and focus.*

## The Content

A treatment should be concise yet complete. You need to cover a lot of ground briefly and answer the most important questions. The stronger your reel is and the more prestige you have, the shorter and more artsy your treatment can be. For a new director, it is probably better to be diligent and detailed. The agency and the client will have to take a greater leap of faith to award you the job. Besides your reel, the treatment is your main tool to win the commercial.

I usually divide up the treatment into sections that deal with artistic elements first, segueing into the more technical questions later.

---

### Treat It Right

Senior agency producer Kelly Trudell on treatments:

*The treatment is very important. Quite often the treatment is the deciding factor in who gets the creative recommendation. Usually, the executive creative directors are not involved in the calls, and reading the treatments helps get them on board with the selection.*

---

### Title Page

Some treatments don't have a title page—perhaps they consist of only one page. They may have a headline. If your submission is elaborate, a title page is a good idea. It should include the client's name, the product or brand, and the name of the spot or campaign. Also, the director and the production company should be mentioned (see Figures 4.1-4.5).

**Figure 4.1**
Title page for a 36-6 drugstore treatment.

**Figure 4.2**
Title page for a Goodwrench treatment.

**Figure 4.3**
Title page for a Nestlé treatment.

**Figure 4.4**
Title page for an Ingosstrakh insurance treatment.

**Figure 4.5**
Title page for a Warsteiner treatment.

## Concept

On the opening page, I like to write a few paragraphs about the overall concept. I want to show that I have a good, strategic understanding of the idea and how it affects the product or brand. I also allude to the "engine" or central theme of the commercial and describe my angle on it. If it's still relevant, I go back to the original idea I pitched in the conference call.

Sometimes I include my specific interest in the spot and describe what appeals to me. The opening paragraphs could be something like this:

*What a cool idea! I'm really into this one. I have a very clear and strong vision of how to shoot this commercial, and I hope I can sufficiently communicate this in the following pages. I'm very excited to be bidding for this project, and I can't wait to share my thoughts and ideas with you. I hope you enjoy this treatment as much as we enjoyed compiling it.*

*At the core of this concept is the great service and maintenance rendered by The Great Car Garage. Because of the outstanding quality of The Great Car Garage, the driver has no trouble at all beating rush hour traffic.*

*The morning commute can feel like a race—we all know that feeling. To communicate this, we're having a little fun with the driver's morning chores: In his fantasy, rush hour is a Formula One race. He is allowed to live out a daydream of sorts, which will play extremely well with the audience, particularly males. Which man has not had the fantasy of being in a race car, let alone on regular streets and in rush hour?*

*The driver lives it for us, and we experience it vicariously. The fun here is that he has to drop off the dry-cleaning, a truly mundane and boring task. Yet, by imagining he is in a race, he makes it work. And he can imagine he is in a race because of the good work of The Great Car Garage.*

*As I mentioned in the conference call, I added a scene in the beginning that sets up the story very nicely. I also came up with a new ending. It reveals clearly that the driver is in a normal car, and it plays very nicely into the daydream idea, as well as the marital setup. The light humor in this typical husband-wife experience adds a nice counterpoint to the Formula One racing scenes.*

*I would like the racing to be very exciting and full of action. While staying within the boundaries of what's legally possible, I'm convinced that we have to meet the audience's expectations for racing. The viewers will not pay attention if we fall short and end up with tame and watered-down footage.*

In this text, I clearly show that I understand the core message of the spot as the agency has created it. Additionally, I express my interest in the project and show that I'm passionate about it. I describe my approach to the story and present the changes and additions—some of which I had mentioned in the conference call.

I also put in a word of caution as to what I think is important to the audience. It's always good to see yourself as the advocate for the audience, because ultimately if the viewers don't get it, the spot has failed.

If you are working on a board that has no story, the concept takes on more significance. Then it will necessarily be longer and more detailed. For a tabletop spot, you could describe the exact setup you would like to work in. For a commercial with visual vignettes, you could go through the different vignettes and explain which emotions you want to evoke each time. In a running footage car spot, you could describe the shots, the backgrounds, the angles on the car, the colors, and your visual inspirations (see Figures 4.6-4.10).

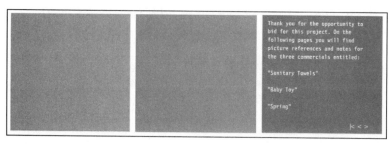

**Figure 4.6**
This page serves more like a table of contents.

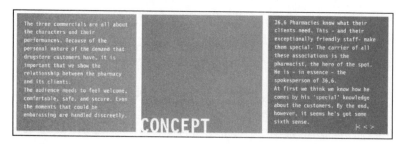

**Figure 4.7**
Describing my take on the concept.

**Figure 4.8**
And a special section about the emotions the spot is supposed to evoke.

**Figure 4.9**
The intro page for the insurance treatment.

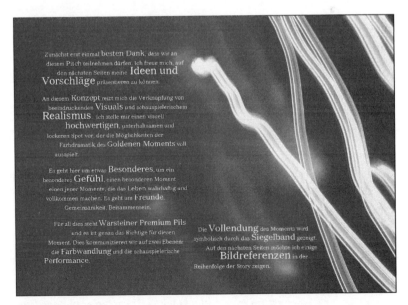

**Figure 4.10**
The opening page of a treatment for a Warsteiner spot, in German.

## Story

In the next section of the treatment, I begin to describe the story the way I see it. This part is very much like a movie script. I tend to use active verbs and short sentences. The story evolves in beats and moments, and that's the rhythm I try to find. Sometimes I will interject a note or a comment. Sometimes I have an extra box on the same page that comments on the action next to it. Here is a sample:

*We open on the familiar steel girders of the Golden Gate Bridge passing overhead, bathed in the golden light of the sunset. We are in a convertible crossing the bridge. The camera pans to the driver, an attractive woman in her 30s who smiles at us. We are in the passenger seat, looking through the passenger's eyes. The entire spot is shot from this perspective, until the final reveal.*

*Still without a cut, we see a couple also in their 30s in the backseat—maybe marveling at the bridge or just enjoying the air streaming by. Here, we're setting the mood and the style: The camera is hand-held, free, and has a nice sense of reality to it. It doesn't seem staged at all. It's emotional, fun, and not overacted. It's very cinema verité, almost documentary style.*

*The first cut: We are now driving on a highway in wine country. Vineyards pass by, maybe we see the setting sun through the trees on the side of the road—all from the POV of the passenger.*

*We cut to the car pulling up in front of the casino. A valet opens the passenger door, and we exit the car.*

*Cut to a dinner scene: wine is being poured, dinner served. The woman who was driving the car toasts to us like she would her partner. This is the first glimpse of the POV person's hand we're getting, but it should be so quick that nothing is given away.*

*Cut to a hand betting chips on a blackjack table. Pan up to show the other three members of the group and the dealer. There could be a series of cuts here, showing a look at the cards, the dealer when he pays out a win, or a celebration over a blackjack. The casino scene needs to convey fun and entertainment, but not in the plastic Las Vegas sense.*

*Rather, I think we should evoke a more upscale and classy, but not conservative, mood here—one that fits with the wine country.*

*After the graphic treatment, we cut to a scene where the woman (driver) is pulling our POV person by the hand to a window overlooking the beautiful Alexander Valley. As soon as our POV person turns to look outside, we see the reflection of the couple in the window and reveal that both are women.*

There is a certain flow to this that you don't want to lose. Try to captivate the reader with the story.

If you are working on a board that is not a storytelling board, the section about the concept will be much longer, and the story section will disappear.

## Notes

In this section, I describe and explain all the changes I've made to the original board. My reasoning for adding or omitting something shows the agency my take on their concept. Here, I will also slide in the occasional detail, like a very specific shot or action (see Figure 4.11).

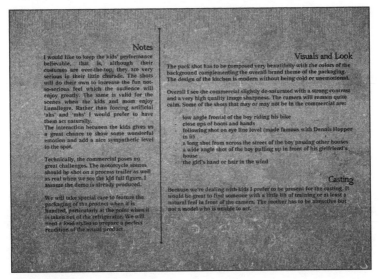

**Figure 4.11**
A good example of a page full of notes, as well as some look and style remarks.

## Look

The Look section describes—sometimes with picture references—the commercial's visual direction. This includes color grading, quality of light, contrast ratios, choice of lenses, camera style, and art direction. Unless the spot is based on the look, this part is usually very short and to the point. Use images with care, because sometimes you limit your flexibility by giving the agency or the client too many visual examples:

*I would like to shoot this commercial in a realistic fashion, utilizing just a bit of stylization to heighten the drama of the metaphor. This is also necessary to bring about the wintry feel. The overall tone should communicate the cold atmosphere by using a soft light look paired with a strong contrast ratio. The shadow areas will have rich blacks, whereas highlights will be sparse but bright. I imagine virtually black trunks of trees between mid-level mist and white snow. Colors will be desaturated to represent a landscape covered by a thin layer of icy frost. The overall hue will be pushed into the blue spectrum.*

*The calm shots of the woman will be in stark contrast to the scenes with the skaters. Her close-ups will be shot from a mount outside the car, using the windshield as a layer of reflection. Her POV from the inside out will be handheld, but not shaky. (I call it the "breathing camera.") Some of the passing-car shots will be from a crane.*

*The shots of the skaters will be dynamic, raw, fast, and action-oriented. We will probably handhold the camera while sitting on a camera car. These shots will be mixed with wider shots of the skaters shooting by.*

## Sound

This section describes everything that will take place in the sound level of the spot, from music to dialogue to effects (see Figure 4.12). Music is a very powerful tool in evoking emotional responses, and thus it deserves a lot of attention.

*I really like the idea of in-race radio chatter. It will add a great texture to the sound layer of the commercial. It brings reality and humor, while advancing the story and serving as a tool to communicate the core ideas of the spot. I've really come to like the idea of a kind of pit-lane conversation between our driver and the Great Garage, which juxtaposes the race action with casual conversation between pros. Nothing is better than keeping calm in a storm.*

*The soundtrack will be composed of radio chatter and the race noises. We may want to add some music or musical sound design, but certainly nothing that stands in the foreground.*

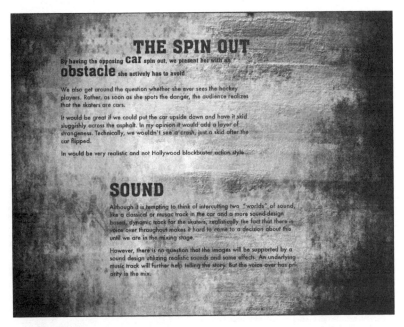

**Figure 4.12**
Here is a brief blurb about sound.

## Casting

Casting is extremely important in any spot that has serious performances. In your treatment, you should describe who and how you will cast. Picture references are helpful here as well, to define types and clichés (see Figures 4.13-4.16).

*We want real people as actors. I see the parents as ordinary people, maybe even innocents, who resort to desperate measures. They must* be able to perform, which means that we have to look for trained actors rather than "real" amateurs. Naturally, Mom and Dad should look like a couple and should fit age-wise.

The son in the first story is the type who likes to sit and watch TV, which inevitably leads to a few extra pounds. However, he is by no means overweight.

The daughter in the second concept is pretty, if not beautiful. She could work at a bank or office, and regularly visits a hair stylist. I could see her on the petite side, and she appears to be quite independent— except for the fact that she still lives at home.

The son in the final story is employed at an insurance or engineering company, and maybe is not completely happy with that. I can imagine him to be a bit skinnier, like someone who didn't make the high school hockey or football team.

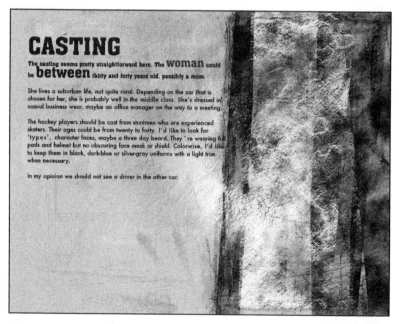

**Figure 4.13**
A casting description as you would see it in a treatment.

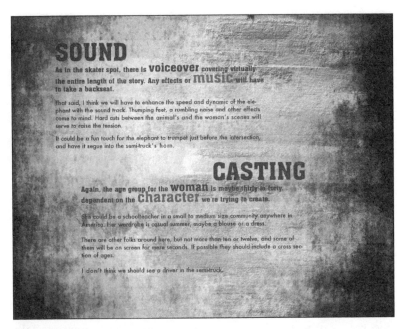

**Figure 4.14**
A page with both casting and sound description.

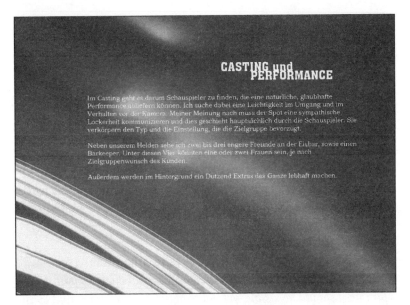

**Figure 4.15**
Sometimes, performance is a good point to talk about. Is it slapstick or serious?

**Figure 4.16**
And for good measure, a page that mixes style and casting.

## Technical Considerations

Depending on the concept, this section can be quite extensive and important. If you're dealing with digital effects, inevitably you will have to deal with a truckload of technical challenges—quite literally. The agency will want to know how you plan to make certain things become a reality. For this section, good research is mandatory. Talk to those who know about this subject—post-production houses and effects supervisors (see Figures 4.17 and 4.18).

*There are several technical challenges in this project, which I'd like to address briefly.*

*We will be shooting a cold winter landscape in the middle of summer. To achieve the desired look, I'd like to use a mix of art-directed, on-set fake snow and digital matte painting techniques. The fake snow will be used on multidimensional objects close to the camera (trees) or on areas that change in perspective. The fake snow will be extremely convincing.*

*The digital snow will be used for areas in the distance or those which are hard to reach. Also, there will be several layers of atmospheric effects, such as fog, snowflakes, and haze.*

*The impression that the road and several other items (sign, leaf) are covered with frost will be created as a digital effect in post. In my opinion, it should be visible, yet not exaggerated. We are bound by the limits of reality, but at the same time we need to communicate clearly what's happening.*

*The building storm in the sky will also have to be created digitally, but it is rather simple.*

*The skaters present a greater challenge. While the obvious choice would be to shoot them on an ice rink, I think another path offers more flexibility. Rather than getting bogged down with motion control equipment, an extra shooting day, and time-consuming compositing in post, I think we can shoot the skaters in the actual location.*

*We will attach rollerblades to the ice skates, enabling us to film the players on the actual road. In post, we will digitally exchange the rollerblades for skates and add ice effects. In many shots, we may not even see the skates in the first place.*

*We gain flexibility in this way, since we can shoot the skaters on the road without having to match shots between their movements and background plates. And since we will create the ice on the road in post anyway, this just makes the most sense.*

*The spinning car would be a live-action stunt with digital enhancements, such as spraying ice. If we shoot the crash, I'd like to shoot it in live action as well. Most likely, this is up to the stunt specialists.*

*There are other, more ordinary effects, like reflections in the windshield and wire removal.*

*Obviously, the main question in the second spot is the elephant. I have reservations about shooting with real animals, unless they're doing something that comes naturally to them. Running is something that elephants don't really like to do. In fact, all the trainers we asked quoted no more than 7MPH as their top speed. That's hardly the kind of impact we need.*

*After a lot of research, I feel that the best option is to use a digital elephant. Not only do we have more freedom during the shoot, but we can also previsualize the elephant's scenes and have him do exactly what we want.*

*To tie the digital animal into the live-action scenes, he will affect the environment by hitting branches and trash cans, and leaving a wake in which dust, leaves, and newspapers are swirling. We will also use his reflections in the storefront and in the water puddle.*

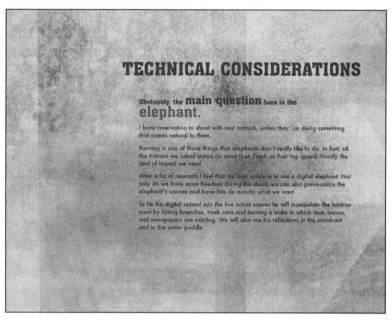

**Figure 4.17**
Here the question was whether to use a real or digital elephant.

**Figure 4.18**
Technical remarks in German.

CASE STUDY

## The Treatment

After the initial conference call, the situation is as follows: Between three and five directors and their production companies are bidding for the job. The agency has had conference calls with all of them and may already have a preference, although not a solid one.

The production company will now prepare the budget and "hit" the numbers. All the directors are preparing their treatments. Each director has to outline his vision for the project, describe how he would shoot it, and explain any new ideas he would like to shoot.

So the challenge for me now is to hammer home the ideas I mentioned in the conference call, particularly the ones the agency liked and expanded on. I should find some visual references to communicate the look I'm going for. My first task is to write a brief for my researcher. The researcher is a person who looks for images and sometimes even does the entire layout of the treatment. They can also look for movie clips, music, fabrics, or whatever else you feel should be included in your treatment.

Here is what I write to my researcher:

*I'm looking for mountaineering pictures with guys in full gear. Cold environment, high altitude, exposed to the elements, that sort of thing. It'd be great if we found bivis rather than climbing pictures. Like morning or evening hunkering-down kinda stuff. I'm thinking Everest, K2, Annapurna, and the like. Gear close-ups are nice, too.*

*I also need pictures of artificial climbing walls, the kind that have variable handholds that are screwed in. Preferably exterior, but the surface texture is what I'm looking for.*

*Then, anything that has to do with adventure sports, snowlikeboarding, kayaking, mountain biking, free-climbing, parachuting, etc. I'm looking for active pictures rather than product depictions.*

*In terms of climbing gear, what's really important is the Thermos bottle. For that, I'm actually looking for catalogue-type images. I guess for the platforms, catalogue-type images would be good, too.*

CASE STUDY *continued*

*Anything that looks related should be cold, freezing, uncomfortable, oppressive in nature.*

*Then, I also need pix of all-American houses, an upper middle-class single-family house with like four to five bedrooms and two stories. It needs to have a large lawn or backyard.*

*That's all I can think of right now. Call me for questions.*

*Cheers*

*-tr*

---

My primary job now is to write. Some directors—particularly very busy ones—have treatment writers. I prefer to write it myself. In fact, I prefer to do the layout myself, and I also do a lot of research—because it puts me more in touch with the project. Often, I find out new things in the process. This is already part of my prep.

In my head, I have a pretty developed idea of the final project. It's not "cut in my head" to perfection, and not nearly all questions are answered, but I have a vision. That's what I have to put on paper. I usually begin with either a runthrough of the story the way I see it or a more strategic description of the concept. In this case, I'm writing the story:

*We open on a wide, low-angle shot of two climbers in a bivouac suspended on a vertical rock wall. We don't see the ground; we don't see much of the rock wall.*

*However, we do get the feeling that these guys are in a precarious place, with 6,000 feet of free fall beneath them.*

*The sun is just coming up. It's a very serene and quaint moment, of the kind you can only experience at high altitude. The climbers are wrapped up tightly in high-altitude gear.*

*The nights up here are cold. Their bivis are either platform- or net-based, but not enclosed.*

CASE STUDY *continued*

The two climbers are Ed and Paul from the Extreme Makeover *show*. They look at each other, and Paul looks for a water bottle buried somewhere in his backpack.

It's cold, and Ed slaps his hands to get the blood flowing.

Paul finds the bottle and hands it down to Ed, with the words: "Here, drink this…"

Ed reaches for the bottle. His hands are cold. His mind is slow. He mishandles it.

With a dull "thonk," the bottle hits a carabiner and twirls off into oblivion.

To heighten the drama, we cut to a slow-motion, low-angle shot looking up at Paul and Ed, who stare down after their lost container.

The bottle falls towards the camera. It's lost forever.

Or so we think.

We cut to a shot of the bottle hitting green grass, almost immediately.

No 6,000 feet here.

A pair of workboots steps into the shot.

It's Paige. She looks at the bottle. Then at the guys who are directly in front of her at the same level.

"You guys ready to go?"

Ed and Paul look at each other, embarrassed.

Then they wriggle out of their bivis as we show… what really is going on.

The camera pulls back and reveals that we are in a backyard in not-so-high-altitude America.

An artificial climbing wall is the centerpiece of an extreme adventure park that is being built in the backyard.

Ed and Paul did a little backyard camping and are now getting ready to continue work.

**CASE STUDY** *continued*

Paige climbs into a Ford Escape, which is parked dominantly in the shot, and drives off in an arc toward the camera.

Other workers are busy on different installations around the scene.

You can see clearly how the story is divided up into beats, almost into shots. The sentences are kept short, and I'm using active verbs a lot: *Paul finds, Ed reaches, Paige looks…*

A story takes place in the now and is driven by action. So you want to use active, present-tense verbs. In the actual treatment, I will illustrate this story with pictures that somehow reflect the moment, the look, the atmosphere, or the location. If their relationship to the story is more obscure, I will explain it.

In the next few pages, I could go into the look, the style, the location, the casting, the sound design, the technical challenges, and so on. On this particular project, I opt to be a bit shorter because of the time pressure. Instead of writing sections, I simply create a single page with observations and notes:

*I really love this story and the reveal—maybe because I have a passion for mountaineering.*

*As I said in the conference call, I like the sparseness, the fact that the guys only speak three words while "on the wall."*

*Their "suffering" and exposure to "extreme conditions" makes the reveal even funnier. I also feel that the addition of the falling bottle heightens the drama and increases the payoff. It's a bit of a misdirect, because the audience thinks that the climbers now have another predicament to overcome.*

*I intend to push that moment with the use of slow motion in almost a B-movie style (think* Cliffhanger *or* Vertical Limit).

*When Paige comes into the picture, I think it's hilarious that she is on the same eye level as the guys in their bivis. It's always great when TV personalities poke fun at themselves.*

*The car obviously will look great. I intend to have it drive in a very dynamic arc through the foreground when we pull back to show the entire situation.*

*Throughout the entire commercial, the camera will stay quite calm. I don't foresee major dolly moves except for the final reveal, in which we will dolly back and move up slightly.*

*We will adjust the image to go along with the story. This means that in the beginning, the sunrise feeling at cold, high altitude should prevail. However, once the bottle lands in the grass, the colors will change accordingly to a more natural, broader palette.*

*The soundtrack should support the visual impression by being calm and quiet in the opening, whereas later, working noise and sounds come in.*

These notes recall some of the things we talked about in the conference call and underline a few major points. I reiterate how passionate I feel about the project and the story, and draw attention to a few moments that I really like. I allude briefly to camera style and colors, and also to the sound design.

Every page of the treatment is in a specific layout with images and background pictures. I sometimes try to convey action by using different fonts and certain spacing. There is not always enough time to be that creative, but it helps because it shows the agency that you are putting in the extra time. And presentation is everything, right?

## Locations

You may also want to talk about locations in your treatment, focusing on which kinds of locations you are looking for, but not necessarily which ones you'll actually use. This is particularly true if the concept is not locked into one location, or if you decide to propose a location change.

## Copyright

You may think that once you present an idea that the agency likes and wants to use, you've got the job. Unfortunately, several times my ideas have been stolen and subsequently used for the commercial by another director. That is a very upsetting situation and one you cannot do much about. Yes, you could make a fuss and probably even sue for copyright infringement. But then you would almost certainly never work with that agency again. And if word got around, no other agencies would work with you, either.

So rather than expending energy on being angry at the thieves, content yourself with knowing that your ideas were stolen because they were so much better than anyone else's.

# Budget

The other major part of the bidding process, besides the creative treatment, is the budget. Sometimes you will find that the numbers are more important than the ideas, because every client looks at the bottom line. However, on more than one occasion we succeeded in getting a higher budget, explaining that with more funds, we could deliver higher quality.

Producers will sit down and make a budget based on their concept of the board and the experience they have collected over years in the industry. Then they will come and ask you the pertinent questions they can't answer themselves.

First, they will want to know how many shooting days you will need to complete the spot. There is no rule of thumb here. You should sit down with the producer and figure out what to shoot, where, and how. How many locations are there? Is there travel between them? Are they nearby?

How many shots do you have per location? Ten or 40? How difficult are the shots? Are they all different setups (shots that require a complete relighting)? What are the possible time multipliers? The common ones are animals, kids, cars, shooting on water or in snow, aerial shots, motion control, major rigs or effects, difficult stunts, or massive scenes that need a lot of coordination.

The more days the budget accommodates, the bigger it will be. However, very often you will get parameters from the agency producer that pretty much lock you into a specific number of shooting days.

Your producer will also ask you what special equipment you need that's not usually on a film set, like certain large cranes, helicopters, steadicams, or other camera rigs. The next big item is talent. If you are shooting a national spot, each actor stands to make a fortune on residuals. Most of the time, the agency will be in charge of paying the actors, so this is not an issue for your budget. But you still have to answer the question.

When it comes to digital effects, you may find yourself caught in very detailed conversations with post production houses about specific shots and how to turn them into a reality. You are often forced to make creative choices before you ever book the job, so that you can assemble a realistic budget. That, unfortunately, is the nature of this business.

## CASE STUDY

### Money Talks

In order for John Quinn, the head of production, to prepare a budget, I need to preemptively answer questions for him. First up is the location. Over the phone, we agree on a location description, which is sent out to a location scout. The brief details involve what we are looking for specifically, including all the limitations of open sky, large backyard, and two-story house.

Then the next-biggest issue: the wall. Since we're obviously going to have to build the wall from scratch, this will be a major art-direction expense. I've decided not to use any preexisting or mobile prefabricated climbing walls because they simply don't look right. We're going to have to build a realistic-looking rock wall.

CASE STUDY *continued*

At this point, I'm guessing a 15' x 40' structure is what we need. I want a granite-type rock surface, rather than, say, yellowish sandstone, because the gray communicates cold. The wall also needs to be supported by a scaffolding, and must be able to hold the talent suspended on a platform on its front side. So this is not a flimsy backdrop set, but a sturdy construction that needs to hold weight.

The production designer is onboard by now, and we talk about the specifics some more. He is going to price the wall out. Although the climbing structure is our centerpiece, there are a ton of other art direction issues to consider— for example, the climbing gear, including the platform, the other extreme sports goods, and the construction equipment and material that is used in the shot as props.

Simultaneously, I'm bringing in the D.P., Aaron Barnes. After looking at the boards and having a few conversations with me, he is able to give John an approximate overview of the equipment he will need. Mainly, this concerns "special" items, such as cranes, steadicam, unusual lenses or lights, and also the amount of film.

For example, in order to get the slow-motion shot for the falling bottle, we will need a camera that is capable of shooting 100 frames per second. Those cameras are noisy and aren't useable for sync sound shooting. Therefore, we will need two cameras on the set to accomplish both tasks. Having two camera bodies is not a bad idea anyway, in case one of them breaks down.

We also decide on a long jimmy job arm, which is a cheap crane, in order to save some money. Given the high-angle shots I envision, we need to get the camera lens at approximately 20 feet of vertical height.

Bit by bit, John puts a budget together, a process that takes a long time to master, because the devil is in the details. Casting is not an issue in our case, because the cast is already decided. Because of budget and time constraints, we also know that we will only have one shooting day available.

While John is in charge of the production budget, our post producer Beth is working on numbers for post production, which the agency has

CASE STUDY *continued*

asked us to supply as well. In a lot of cases, the agency takes care of post production directly, but sometimes they want support in getting the bids. Beth's main focus is on questions about 3D and compositing work, which are expensive and out of the norm.

In this case, we're dealing with only a few, relatively minor post tasks. There may be sky replacement, which—as the name says—is a technique used to replace sky that is not to your liking with a new sky. In many cases the sky—even though it's blue on the day of the shoot—comes out white on film because of exposure issues. In that case, you can easily replace the white with a perfectly wonderful blue sky.

I mention that there might be a wire removal. In case we have to secure the climbing tower with wires because of wind or other security concerns, the wires may run through the shot. Safety is always important, and wire removal is an easy task. The wires will be painted out in post.

Because this commercial is a car shoot, there are always many corrections to be made to the vehicle. The perfection that is expected by clients simply cannot be achieved in an exterior environment. It is impossible to control every reflection of sunlight off the thousands of surfaces surrounding the car. So that is another task that has to be addressed in post.

Otherwise, I don't foresee any digital post production besides the regular telecine and online processes. All of the preceding issues can be handled in the online process, and no extra 3D machines have to be used. This makes it a fairly simple assignment, except for the fact that there is no time to do it all. On an average commercial, post production takes about a week. You shoot, the film gets developed overnight, and the dailies are transferred the next day (or sometimes that same night).

Then the dailies are loaded into the editing system, and the editor or his assistant sorts and syncs them (syncing, of course, means that picture and sound are lined up in sync and then "married" so they can be worked with). This may take a full day, although the editor may get a little time to work on selecting the takes that he likes and the takes that were noted as "selects" during the shooting on the set.

**CASE STUDY** *continued*

So, by now we are at the end of day two of post. Figure two days for editing, which puts the total at four days. Then the agency will come in to take a look at the edits and do changes. Add another day for the agency and the director to agree on a cut, which is then sent off to the client for approval.

Day five. The client approves the edit and everything goes into the online process. There is a telecine session for the selected takes (one day), then the online (one day), and finally the sound mix (one day). So seven to eight days is pretty much the minimum.

On this project, we have three days. The shoot date has been set for Tuesday, January 3 to allow for one day of prepping the set. The spots have to be on-air that Sunday, which means they have to be shipped on Saturday, which means they have to be done on Friday night. So Beth's challenge is not so much controlling cost as squeezing eight days of work into three.

The budgets are compiled into a bid, and together with my treatment it's sent off to the agency for review. Depending on the number of directors who are bidding and the client's involvement in the final decision, the wait can be a week. In our case, we are so short on time that the decision will come down very, very fast.

In fact, we've heard already that we are going in as the "agency recommend." This means that the agency presents us as its first choice, and unless the client has major issues with that decision, they concur.

John checks flights back to the States, while I check my family's Christmas schedule in Europe and spend another few days in limbo. What else is new?

## The Waiting Game

The treatment and the budget are at the agency. Now the waiting game begins. A certain day will be assigned as the "award" day, when the client signs off on the agency's choice of director, along with the production company and budget. If you are lucky, you will hear that you are the "agency recommend," in other words, the agency wants you and will suggest you to their client.

If you lose the job, try to find out why and learn from it. It's important to remember that losing the job says nothing negative about you, your ideas, or your future. The simple fact is that you have persevered against hundreds of other directors to get signed and against dozens to get selected for the pitch, and you have been beaten only by one—the one director who booked the job.

Yes, it's painful and depressing. As I write this, I'm in preproduction for a job but lost another—both decisions were made in the same week. While I'm excited and exhilarated about the awarded job, I'm also blue about the lost one.

It can be a frustrating experience, simply because it may be completely out of your control. Remember what I said about safety. Most decisions at agencies are not made on the basis of the best creative ideas or the most promising talent. They're made to secure jobs and positions, not to expose them.

In the vast majority of cases, the deciding factor is that the director has a similar spot on his reel. The creative sees it and thinks: *That's what I want. That's exactly like the spot I want to do.* He feels safe.

It's unfortunate, but true. There are few creatives who are strong enough to take risks and stake their own careers on believing in someone. Ask yourself whether you would.

Thus, the jobs you will book at the beginning of your career are the ones where there is little at stake for the agency, or where the budget is too low to hire a superstar director. You must slowly work your way up the ladder, booking bigger and bigger jobs, building a reputation and prestige.

John van Osdol, VP/Director of Broadcast at Leo Burnett Detroit, says that in order for him to even consider a director for a pitch, his reputation within the industry is important. Besides the quality of work and the director's personal style, Osdol says the deciding factor is "whether his or her past work has any resemblance to the idea you are currently working on."

Think back to the earlier chapters in which I talked about branding yourself, and you will see once again why I mentioned it.

Then again, it's a great moment when you hear your producer say, "You booked it." It's time once again to pat yourself on the back— and you can pat harder this time. You'll be a working director shooting a commercial, and you'll be making some serious money. What could be better?

# Chapter 5

# Director's Prep

This is the news you've been waiting for. Your producer calls and tells you that you have been awarded the job. It's an exhilarating moment, and you should savor it—because now the real work begins. Everything before was merely dry runs and dress rehearsals.

All the pitching, "concepting," and thinking now will be put to the test. You're about to move into that most exciting of all aspects of filmmaking—production.

More precisely, production is divided into three parts: preproduction, production, and post production. In this chapter, we will be dealing with the director's prep, which is the director's own preproduction. There is also the technical preproduction done by the entire production team, as well as the director. It involves hiring crew, booking locations and talent, organizing the schedule and the shoot, getting permits, and a whole lot of other things.

As the director, you are at the top of the decision-making echelon and thus are involved in technical preproduction. Your decisions will trickle down the pyramid to every department head and to every single person on your set. But how do you make all those decisions? This happens in the director's prep.

The director's prepping phase is the period in which you make up your mind about how to shoot the spot. Which shots do you want to get? What kind of location do you need? What is the cast you are looking for?

Preproduction for a one-day shoot takes at least a week for an easy job. Only a few shooting days are allotted to a commercial, and that means preproduction is intense, detailed, and long. The same is true for feature films. As Alfred Hitchcock once pointed out: "We've made a wonderful film. Now all we have to do is shoot it."

Hitchcock was very picky in his prep, designing shots in detailed drawings. That's not a bad approach at all. The more prepared you are, the more flexible you will be during the shoot when unforeseen obstacles and ideas come up.

Preproduction starts as soon as you receive boards, as I mentioned in the previous chapters. For example, you and your production team will be looking for locations long before the award decision, because your producer needs to prepare a budget. Therefore, a few questions will already be answered to some degree at least.

While each project is different, there are certain things you will deal with in every prep. There are steps you can follow to stay efficient and organized and not get lost in the vast amount of work on your desk. It all starts with the concept and with the ideas you've had for it.

Although it's not necessary, it's great to be inspired by something when you prep a spot. For me, it's often a piece of music or sometimes an image. If I have the time to let things coalesce and develop at their own pace, I will let them. Of course, everyone works differently in this regard, and you should do whatever makes you tick. After all, this is your talent at work, your artistic viewpoint, your voice, and your vision.

The preproduction phase has something of a climax, which is called the preproduction meeting, or short prepro meeting, or even PPM. In this meeting, the director will present every major decision, and many minor ones, to the agency and the client for approval prior to the shoot. This includes shooting board, cast, crew, locations, wardrobe, art direction, music, and timing.

The PPM, which I will describe in detail, is probably the best expression of the hybrid nature of directing commercials. You will find yourself—and your production team—prepping the PPM as much as the commercial. In fact, a lot of the preproduction work is aimed at ensuring that the PPM is successful, because that is where the client has to sign off on most of your decisions prior to the shoot.

## Shot List

For me, the shot list is the basis of an organized prep. It determines the single most important decision a director makes: where to place the camera.

It is literally your angle on your object. It's your take, your viewpoint. As much as the action or dialogue in a scene, the point in space from which you choose to shoot is essential.

There are a lot of commercial directors who don't know much about the filmmaking side of their job. They came to directing from the agency or the graphics side. This is accepted in commercials, although it would be unthinkable in features. Some commercial DPs (directors of photography) come with the reputation of being able to "get it done." This means that they are capable of basically directing an entire commercial while the director sits around and chats with the agency.

One DP I know recently told me of a conference call with a director. He was amazed because the director asked *him* questions that *he* had expected to ask the director: What kinds of shots do we need to tell this story? How should we break it down?

The director pretty much expected the DP to come up with the shots. Don't get me wrong, I constantly ask my key crew members for advice and opinions. But you have to know what you want. You can't expect others to do your job.

## Beats

I usually work on story-oriented commercials, which is why I break each commercial down into beats: Husband enters kitchen, wife looks at him, husband takes mug, wife speaks, husband answers, and so on. If you are working on a more visual commercial that doesn't have a story, you will still have beats, such as: Car rockets down street, car brakes, car accelerates, bystanders are watching, and so on.

You must now decide how to cover each beat, or in other words, how to shoot it and from which angles. While this is somewhat similar to the movies, more coverage is usually shot in features, because the takes are longer and scenes tend to cut back and forth between the same shots.

In commercials, there used to be an ironclad rule: Never use the same shot twice. While this rule has become malleable, it's still a good guideline to remember.

## Editing in Advance

The next step is to create a list of the shots you'll need in order to cover the beats adequately. It's beneficial to have an editing scheme in mind when you do this, so that the shots cut well in the final assembly.

Let's use the preceding husband-and-wife story as an example. I decide to shoot the husband in a medium wide shot when he enters the kitchen. Then I would like to shoot the wife's look over his shoulder in a medium close-up. The next shot should be an insert of the coffee mug as he picks it up. One by one, my shot list is populated. Each shot is described briefly. Sometimes I do a simultaneous overhead scheme to plan out the shots.

This is quite similar to feature directing, where you break down each scene into coverage. However, in features you may do a master shot (usually the wide shot) and then pick up closer coverage. All those shots usually run the entire length of the scene. In commercials, shooting is more linear because of the "never use the same shot twice" rule. Shot 1 will take you through the first beat, shot 2 through the next two beats, shot 3 covers the fourth, and so on.

At the end of this process, I will have a list with all the shots I want, but not necessarily all the shots I need. In my case, the list usually contains a few more shots than I need. I may like a certain angle or want to flesh out a certain nuance—all of which may end up on the cutting room floor, but I still try to get it.

The shot list will give me a very good idea of how complicated and time-intensive the shoot will be. It will tell me about the order in which I should shoot, as well as what I need for each shot (cast, background, extras, equipment). This helps greatly when I sit down and schedule my shooting day.

I use a number system comparable to the old-style feature-film breakdown—long strips with numbers to schedule scenes. Only I do it on a shot-by-shot basis. Cast members will get their own numbers (and sometimes items like cars will also). On a simple chart, I can quickly see who is in which shot and then easily organize a schedule.

**CASE STUDY**

### Prep Time

I wake up to a phone call from John. We've been awarded the job. Great. Preproduction now starts in earnest. There will be a conference call with the agency planned, in order to answer a myriad of questions. My travel plans are being finalized. I'm returning to the States on the 28th, with a tech scout scheduled for the 29th.

Build day is January 2, and shoot day is January 3. It's tight, but doable.

I now have to prep this shoot. For me, this begins back at square one with the story. But before I can do that, the agency and I have to agree on the final direction. Thermos bottle, yes or no? Paige on foot, yes or no? One platform or two platforms? That's what the conference call is for.

In the call we agree that we should do the bottle drop, have Paige on foot, and put the car prominently in the background. Since I prefer the two climbers to be on one platform, Chris and Matt agree. We also talk about what else could be in the adventure backyard. As the

CASE STUDY *continued*

sweepstakes is apparently about winning the construction in general, and not about winning actual items, it seems we have all the freedom to put in what we like.

The agency mentions that a zip wire could be simple and cheap to do. My concern is that there has to be someone using it in order for the audience to understand what it is. Otherwise, all we would see is a thin black line. Since the backyard is still "under construction," it wouldn't make much sense to have someone zip through in the background.

A snowboarding simulator—although cool—is hard to find, complicated to build (even as a mockup), and even harder for the audience to recognize as such. Most people have never heard of such a thing. We agree that we should concentrate on the simple things like kayaks, a mountain bike trail (which is basically a heap of dirt with a few flags), and maybe a tent here or there.

All this is under the responsibility of the production designer. He has, in the meantime, created a production sketch for the wall (see Figure 5.1).

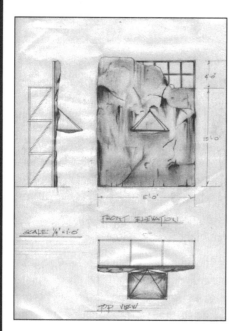

**Figure 5.1**
This is a production sketch of a 15 x 15 ft. wall with an extended 4-foot section on top where the scaffolding is half-exposed. Since we want the wall to still be "under construction," this is a good way to go. We could use one edge for the illusion shot without having to finish it full-size.

**CASE STUDY** *continued*

The wall he suggests has a 15 x 15 ft. base front and a 4 x 15 ft. section on top, which is half-finished. This design fulfills two important requirements: There is a 19 ft. edge of rock that I can use to frame the opening shot (in which I need a lot of height), and it shows exposed scaffolding, which tells us in later shots that the tower is still under construction.

There are also some photographs to look at for surface structures. In my opinion, the wall is "working," which means everything is on the right track. The production designer will complete a set sketch for the preproduction meeting, along with many, many photographs of gear and other props.

Now, we are entering the time when everything becomes about the shots. As a general rule, it's always good to spend your money in front of the camera. In other words, if you don't see something in the frame, why buy it, prep it, or rent it? The only person who knows what will be in the shot is me. On a very practical note, my job now is to define the shots in as much detail as possible to make everyone's jobs easier, and to free up all the money to be spent on things that are worth spending it on.

# The Art of the Shot

The shot list is an expression of your very own artistic viewpoint. Where you put the camera, which lens you choose—or in other words, what you choose to show—that is the truest and purest expression of your directorial art. Every shot is the culmination of so many different choices in so many different art forms. A true Gesamtkunstwerk.

Think about it: Cinematography originally stemmed from photography. Acting from the theater. Production design incorporates fine art, graphic design, product design, and architecture. Even makeup or camera moves with complicated blocking trigger associations with the performing arts and dance choreography.

In fact, only editing is original to film, but more about that later.

If you've gone through film school or are about to, chances are that you have studied the great masters of shots, like Hitchcock or Kubrick. To them, each time they started a camera it was like creating a painting. Each single frame was worth their diligence.

In the age of television, lots of this has gotten lost. Young artists have grown up watching sloppily shot TV shows in which the framing is unexpressive and dull. Unfortunately, many commercials look like that as well. Directors don't know (or don't care) about the power of framing or angles or lenses, and know even less about how to tell a story with these tools.

The art of creating shots is just that: an art. As such, it deserves its own book. But here are a few simple beginner's hints on the power of creating shots.

First, think about what you want to show—and what you don't want to show. Both are equally important. Think about what the beat is in each shot, and what the most important part is. Do you want to show that Jack is running? Or that Jack is running with a phone in his hand? Or that Jack is running away from Jane? And that Jane has a gun in her hand? All of this could be in the same story, and it is up to you to figure out what to show, in which order.

Consider your viewpoint—or rather, the viewpoint you would like the audience to take. You can steer the audience's sympathy or antipathy every which way. Do you show the preceding sequence from Jack's point of view? This would mean looking back with the camera at Jane running toward us with a gun in her hand. Or do you choose Jane's side and show Jack running away from us?

Also, think about the angle of the shot. If you leave the camera at Jack's eye height, you put the audience very much in his place. They can see what he can see, and they're in the midst of the action. Put the camera at a frog's perspective, and Jack is a running giant leaping over trash cans in very dynamic shots. If you put the camera on a crane with a wide lens, you could make Jack as tiny as an ant, a mere crawling insect in the giant anthill that is the city surrounding him. He could seem lost, desperate, and confused.

In each shot, you should also direct the audience's attention to what you want them to see. Kubrick was a master at setting up his shots so that the viewer's eye was automatically drawn to one point in the frame. You couldn't help but look there.

Kubrick used light and shadow, colors, movement, and the three-dimensional space's lines of perspective in a two-dimensional frame to direct your eye. For example, imagine a dark street at night, with a single lamp shining a cone of light onto the sidewalk. Your eye will naturally go to the light. Now add someone stepping into the cone of light. The human eye is always drawn to motion (a relic of more predatory times). This works even with products that are placed on a table or cars that shoot around a corner. The eye will *always* look there. If you now imagine that the person stepping into the light is a woman in a red coat, you can be sure that she will be seen. And even more, all the lines of perspective meet right at that lamp post.

You can also define relationships between characters by using certain angles. Looking down on someone puts him in a position of inferiority. If you have to look up to speak to someone, however, you define that person as the superior character. This is sometimes called the emotional close-up.

Obviously, once you move the camera, a whole other field of possibilities opens up. If you move in on an object, you underline its importance. If you move away from an object, you put it in the context of its surroundings. If you move alongside Jack in the previous example, you are saying that he can't get away. If Jane runs toward a stationary camera, on the other hand, it means that she is gaining ground.

The shots also work in sequence and are not stand-alone images. If you edit a series of shots in which Jack gets smaller and smaller, he is visually moving away from us and his escape is successful.

You can see that there are many, many techniques at your disposal, even with the simplest of technical tools. Study the masters and break down their shots and sequences.

CASE STUDY

## Break It Down into a Shot List

My own prep for the Ford spot starts with compiling a shot list. Once again, I go back to the story. Last we left off, there were these beats:

- ◆ Two climbers are hanging on a vertical wall, waking up.
- ◆ They're very cold. One hands the other a Thermos.
- ◆ When he tries to open the bottle, it slips from his hands and falls down the mountain.
- ◆ The bottle immediately lands in green grass.
- ◆ A woman appears from out of nowhere and speaks to the climbers.
- ◆ We reveal that it's an artificial climbing wall in a sunny backyard.

I will now break down these beats into actual coverage, or shots. For some beats, there is only one shot; for others, there may be several. Also, a single shot may have more than one beat. It's all about how you want to shoot it. I describe each shot with one or two lines, specifying who is in the shot, what happens, what size the shot is, and whether or not there are any camera moves. Let's start.

I want to open with a wide shot that communicates altitude, cold, exposure, and isolation. I need to set up the situation: climbers on a wall. If I use a low angle (the camera looks up), I can create the feeling of altitude fairly easily, particularly if I don't see anything but sky in the background. I also want to use a wide lens to create that sense of isolation. Thus, my first shot is this:

1. Low-angle wide shot of wall with climbers, sky in bg.

This short description contains a lot of important information, as I explained before. By the way, "bg" stands for background.

Next, I would like to show the climbers more clearly. In this shot, they will stir and wake up. We will see that they are packed tightly in high-altitude clothes, and that it is not the most comfortable place to be. To see the action, I need to be looking down on the platform. Also, for the shot to cut well, it's always better to have an aspect change if you remain with the same object. That is, unless you want to have the effect of a *jump cut*.

1. Low-angle wide shot of wall with climbers, sky in bg.

2. Medium-close climbers frontal on wall, stirring.

As you can see from the description, I also tightened up a bit, from a wide to a medium shot. I want to get closer to the guys visually and then be right there for the climax. Now it's time to introduce the *treasure* —that's story talk. In a melodramatic context, there is often a "treasure" of sorts, or the object of desire that the protagonist either is after or has to protect. Think of the Holy Grail in *Raiders of the Lost Ark*, the diamond in *Romancing the Stone*, and the ring in *Lord of the Rings*.

In this story, the treasure is the Thermos bottle. It's an important piece of gear, dispensing warm liquid in a hostile environment. The Thermos is very valuable to the two climbers, although it certainly doesn't appear obvious. Like so many things in life, they learn its true value only when they lose it.

In this shot, I'm going to jump to the reverse side of the platform to feature Paul as he digs for and finds the bottle. I will still be seeing Ed's presence in the shot. I like to keep the spatial relationship between them intact, and I increase the aesthetic quality of the shot by having something moving in-between my main object and the camera. You will see that I haven't specifically included Ed in the description. It's just something that I keep in mind for later.

1. Low-angle wide shot of wall with climbers, sky in bg.

2. Medium-close climbers frontal on wall, stirring.

3. Close-up of Paul, finding bottle.

If you compare this to the list of beats I compiled earlier, you can see that already we've covered two beats in three shots. Also, take a look again at the progression of shot sizes: wide, medium, close-up. Now that the treasure comes out, we're right there. No need to show the surroundings, the environment. That's already set up. I'm telling the story with the camera by guiding the audience's attention to the things that matter. This creates an unconscious expectation and dramatic tension. Unwillingly, we have the feeling that something is about to happen.

**CASE STUDY** *continued*

The following shot is going to enhance that even more. The bottle will now be handed over to Ed. By drawing the audience's attention to this, I increase the dramatic value of the Thermos, even if that is not obvious at all. The transfer to Ed is also important because it starts the fateful sequence of the losing of the bottle. This shot will be a reverse yet again.

Shots 1 and 2 are from the same side of the platform; then for shot 3, I jump to the other side. I do this so that in editing, it is easier to cut. The actors cannot possibly play each take exactly the same. In fact, most of these shots will roll longer than the "meat" of the beat. In performance-based stories, I always let the actors begin to play from a few moments before—if it's possible—and also a few moments after. The story flows better, and you get additional footage that you might be able to use in the edit.

1. Low-angle wide shot of wall with climbers, sky in bg.

2. Medium-close climbers frontal on wall, stirring.

3. Close-up of Paul, finding bottle.

4. Medium shot of Paul handing bottle to Ed.

The bottle is in Ed's hand. Now I have to fully trust the skill of the actors. Only they can make it funny. If we had a casting call for this job, I could make sure that the performer could do it. In this case—remember that we're dealing with celebrities from an existing TV show—I don't have much of a clue how good these guys are as comedic actors. They may play their respective parts on the *Extreme Makeover* show absolutely perfectly, but how they will perform here, I don't have a clue. I haven't met them, and I won't meet them until the morning of the shoot.

In this next shot, Ed has to fumble the bottle. There are a million different ways to act this out, from downplayed all the way to slapstick. I want to see a bit of physical comedy, stemming from that immature carelessness they've shown by camping on the wall in the first place. In short, I want them to behave like amateur climbers. As I said earlier, Ed is going to take the bottle in shot 4 and try to open it. Already at that point, he will be fumbling with the Thermos.

However, in the following shot, I want to push in a bit tighter on the bottle and change the aspect yet again. I want to have the freedom in editing not only to change the timing of the fumble, but also to tune the drama in it. I can make it more over-the-top or more subtle by choosing the intensity of the fumbling. It is very important to keep your options open and stay flexible. I can only reiterate that a commercial is made three times: it's written, it's shot, and it's edited. I prefer to have as much freedom as I can when I go into the third phase.

In shot 5, the bottle will be fumbled and will fall. I intend to have Ed go through different attempts to open it (almost as if the lid is too tight), as well as a version where he never really gets hold of it. On the set, we'll see how it plays during rehearsals. Then we'll go with the one we like the best—or shoot both.

1. Low-angle wide shot of wall with climbers, sky in bg.
2. Medium-close climbers frontal on wall, stirring.
3. Close-up of Paul finding bottle.
4. Medium shot of Paul handing bottle to Ed.
5. Close-up of bottle as it's being mishandled.

Okay, so the bottle is falling now. I'm thinking that before it goes off into complete oblivion, it would be a nice touch if it were to hit the metal edge of the bivi platform. It could serve as kind of an accent, both visually and audibly. Plus, it is another shot in the "action sequence," and every additional shot will make such a sequence easier to cut.

1. Low-angle wide shot of wall with climbers, sky in bg.
2. Medium-close climbers frontal on wall, stirring.
3. Close-up of Paul finding bottle.
4. Medium shot of Paul handing bottle to Ed.
5. Close-up of bottle as it's being mishandled.
6. Slow-motion close-up shot of bottle hitting edge of bivi.

**CASE STUDY** *continued*

I have noted shot 6 as slow motion simply because I want to have control over the speed in post production. By shooting 100 frames per second, for example, I'm getting four times as many images of the bottle's movement. In other words, I have more slices of the bottle's motion. This enables us in post to choose another speed without giving the motion a choppy, strobe-like effect. Think of it as resolution, although not in pixels like in a still photograph, but as steps in a sequence.

So, at this point, I'm not sure at all whether the shot will be in slow motion. But I may want to speed up or slow down the fall of the Thermos ever so slightly, and a higher frame rate allows me to do that.

Storytelling has two parts: action and reaction. Each on its own is fairly meaningless. Thus, whenever there is an action, there is usually a reaction, which tells the audience what the action really meant. Consider Jane saying, "I'm going to kill you." It wholly depends on Jack's reaction for the audience to figure out how this line is meant. If Jack runs away, it was meant seriously. If he laughs, it was meant as a joke. If Jane then says, "Don't laugh," yet another reaction is added to the meaning. You get the idea.

So now I need to see the reaction of the two guys as they are losing the bottle. This will again serve as a good cutaway to speed up the action. I will shoot this in slow motion as well, if only to be able to match exactly the frame rate of the shots before and after this.

1. Low-angle wide shot of wall with climbers, sky in bg.

2. Medium-close climbers frontal on wall, stirring.

3. Close-up of Paul finding bottle.

4. Medium shot of Paul handing bottle to Ed.

5. Close-up of bottle as it's being mishandled.

6. Slow-motion close-up shot of bottle hitting edge of bivi.

7. Slow-motion wide shot CU of Ed and Paul reacting.

The next shot I envision could be complicated. Incidentally, that's why it's good to think it through right now in greater detail. I would like a low-angle shot of Ed and Paul looking down after the bottle. The camera looks up at them almost vertically. The bottle falls past the camera lens (or even into the camera lens), and all of that is shot in slow motion.

I need to communicate this shot very clearly, because there are a number of technical aspects to be considered for the DP and his crew, such as the protection of the camera, the frame rate, and a possible low-angle prism—a device that lets you shoot extreme low-angle shots. If the lens is going to be down where the grass is, they will have to dig a hole for the camera body to fit in, or use a low-angle prism, which is basically a mirror.

1. Low-angle wide shot of wall with climbers, sky in bg.

2. Medium-close climbers frontal on wall, stirring.

3. Close-up of Paul finding bottle.

4. Medium shot of Paul handing bottle to Ed.

5. Close-up of bottle as it's being mishandled.

6. Slow-motion close-up shot of bottle hitting edge of bivi.

7. Slow-motion wide shot CU of Ed and Paul reacting.

8. Low-angle slow-motion shot of bottle tumbling toward camera.

The next shot is a possible "reveal" of the true situation. The bottle lands in green grass and Paige's feet step in. Sounds simple, but having a falling object hit a certain spot in a visually nice position can be tricky and time-consuming. Also, I need to carefully consider the angle of the camera and the direction from which the bottle and Paige enter the frame.

1. Low-angle wide shot of wall with climbers, sky in bg.

2. Medium-close climbers frontal on wall, stirring.

3. Close-up of Paul finding bottle.

4. Medium shot of Paul handing bottle to Ed.

**CASE STUDY** *continued*

5. Close-up of bottle as it's being mishandled.

6. Slow-motion shot of bottle hitting edge of bivi.

7. Slow-motion wide shot CU of Ed and Paul reacting.

8. Low-angle slow-motion shot of bottle tumbling toward camera.

9. Close-up of bottle landing in grass; feet step in.

Shot 9 poses the question of where these guys are and whose feet just appeared. So the next shot should be the answer: A close-up of Paige looking first at the bottle and then at the climbers. She also has a line of dialogue here, which I'm not specifically noting on the shot list. Behind Paige we will see the Ford Escape parked, as well as some background action from extras. Thus, the shot answers both questions.

1. Low-angle wide shot of wall with climbers, sky in bg.

2. Medium-close climbers frontal on wall, stirring.

3. Close-up of Paul finding bottle.

4. Medium shot of Paul handing bottle to Ed.

5. Close-up of bottle as it's being mishandled.

6. Slow-motion shot of bottle hitting edge of bivi.

7. Slow-motion wide shot CU of Ed and Paul reacting.

8. Low-angle slow-motion shot of bottle tumbling towards camera.

9. Close-up of bottle landing in grass; feet step in.

10. CU Paige as she looks at guys.

In this story, I now need to see the reaction of the climbers, because Paige just appeared from out of nowhere and said something along the lines of, "Are you ready to get back to work?" The audience thought we were dealing with two stranded climbers on a freezing, vertical wall at high altitude…but by their reaction, coupled with the newly revealed environment, we learn that they are only playing.

**CASE STUDY** *continued*

1. Low-angle wide shot of wall with climbers, sky in bg.

2. Medium-close climbers frontal on wall, stirring.

3. Close-up of Paul, finding bottle.

4. Medium shot of Paul handing bottle to Ed.

5. Close-up of bottle as it's being mishandled.

6. Slow-motion shot of bottle hitting edge of bivi.

7. Slow-motion wide shot CU of Ed and Paul reacting.

8. Low-angle slow-motion shot of bottle tumbling toward camera.

9. Close-up of bottle landing in grass; feet step in.

10. CU Paige as she looks at guys.

11. Medium shot of guys reacting to Paige, o/s Paige.

The o/s stands for *over the shoulder*, a common term in filmmaking that refers to someone's shoulder being in the foreground when filming another person. In essence, the camera is looking over someone's shoulder. This puts the two people who are part of the conversation into a spatial relationship. Are they close to each other, or is there distance between them?

This was the reason I wanted Paige out of the car. I like this moment better if she is right in their faces, confronting them with their own immaturity.

The following shot is the continued reveal. We haven't yet shown where these guys *really* are. We've established that they are not on a mountain. But what's really going on? There is not much of a choice but to go wide here. In order to reveal the wall, we have to show it in the environment of the backyard. Also, Paige needs to walk toward the Ford Escape and maybe even get inside.

1. Low-angle wide shot of wall with climbers, sky in bg.

2. Medium-close climbers frontal on wall, stirring.

3. Close-up of Paul finding bottle.

CASE STUDY *continued*

4. Medium shot of Paul handing bottle to Ed.

5. Close-up of bottle as it's being mishandled.

6. Slow-motion shot of bottle hitting edge of bivi.

7. Slow-motion wide shot CU Ed and Paul reacting.

8. Low-angle slow-motion shot of bottle tumbling toward camera.

9. Close-up of bottle landing in grass; feet step in.

10. CU Paige as she looks at guys.

11. Medium shot guys reacting to Paige, o/s Paige.

12. Medium side as guys begin to wriggle out of bivi; Paige climbs into car.

I think it can be a fun moment when the climbers try to free themselves from the ropes and sleeping bags. Again, I'm going to have to trust their physical comedy skills. This brings it to the final shot—the product shot. The car needs to be front and center with enough stuff going on around it. The wall needs to be in the shot, as well as other extreme sports equipment and workers carrying materials or tools. A wide shot, no doubt.

1. Low-angle wide shot of wall with climbers, sky in bg.

2. Medium-close climbers frontal on wall, stirring.

3. Close-up of Paul finding bottle.

4. Medium shot of Paul handing bottle to Ed.

5. Close-up of bottle as it's being mishandled.

6. Slow-motion shot of bottle hitting edge of bivi.

7. Slow-motion wide shot CU Ed and Paul reacting.

8. Low-angle slow-motion shot of bottle tumbling toward camera.

9. Close-up of bottle landing in grass; feet step in.

10. CU Paige as she looks at guys.

CASE STUDY *continued*

11. Medium shot of guys reacting to Paige, o/s Paige.

12. Medium side as guys begin to wriggle out of bivi; Paige climbs into car.

13. Wide shot of backyard, car in foreground.

There it is, my shot list. 13 shots in :30 seconds. It's a good idea to time the shots, but I will do that later.

| | FORD SHOTLIST | Ed | Paul | Paige | Extras | Car | Wall | Small Wall |
|---|---|---|---|---|---|---|---|---|
| 1 | Low angle wide shot of wall with climbers, sky in bg | 1 | 2 | | | | 6 | |
| 2 | Medium close climbers frontal on wall stiring | 1 | 2 | | | | 6 | |
| 3 | Close up Paul, finding bottle | 1 | 2 | | | | | 7 |
| 4 | Medium shot Paul handing bottle to Ed | 1 | 2 | | | | | 7 |
| 5 | Close up bottle as it's being mishandled | 1 | 2 | | | | | 7 |
| 6 | Slow motion close up shot of bottle hitting edge of bivi | 1 | 2 | | | | | 7 |
| 7 | Slow motion wide shot CU Ed and Paul reacting | 1 | 2 | | | | | 7 |
| 8 | Low angle slow motion of bottle tumbling towards camera | 1 | 2 | | | | 6 | |
| 9 | Close up of bottle landing in grass, feet step in | | | 3 | | | | |
| 10 | CU Paige as she looks at guys | | | 3 | 4 | 5 | | |
| 11 | Medium Shot guys reacting to Paige o/s Paige | 1 | 2 | 3 | | | | 7 |
| 12 | Medium Wide as guys begin to wriggle out of bivi, Paige climbs into car | 1 | 2 | 3 | 4 | 5 | 6 | |
| 13 | Wide shot of backyard, car in foreground | 1 | 2 | 3 | 4 | 5 | 6 | |

**Figure 5.2**
This is the finished shot list. Of course, it's never really finished and always changes. If it's close, though, things will run more smoothly. The numbers and colors on the right refer to who or what is in which shot. This makes for a quick and easy overview for everyone involved, and also helps tremendously with scheduling.

# Shooting Board

Using the shot list, I will begin to draw a shooting board. (Often, I draw shots beforehand and then compile them into a shooting list—whatever works best for you.) The shooting board is your version of the storyboard. In other words, you will have a number of frames depicting each shot that you are planning to shoot. A shooting board is mandatory so that the agency and the client can see and approve what you have in mind. It's one of the main courses in the PPM.

### Get Everyone on the Same Page

Tor Myhren, executive creative director at Leo Burnett Detroit, has this to say about shooting boards:

*Shooting boards are very common ,and it's always good to see them before a shoot. In fact, most clients won't buy off without seeing some kind of visual representation of the spot before shooting. I also think it's important to have shooting boards as a very loose guide, so the agency and the director know they're walking down the same path when they show up on shoot day. Sure, things will change. But the board helps get everybody on the same page.*

I make rough sketches and then sit down with an illustrator. Sometimes, I do a previsualization with simple 3D software to communicate even more clearly. The illustrator will do sketches (see Figures 5.3-5.5), which you can approve before he puts in detail and shading to make them presentable (see Figures 5.6-5.12)

The most important aspect of a shooting board should be the angle of the shot. While agency boards are more about *what's* seen, your shooting board should be all about *how* you see it. In other words, an agency board may have an image showing the characters, the car, and the background—the general information on what the shot contains. Your shooting board, on the other hand, will show exactly the angle from which you intend to shoot that moment, and quite likely you will have several shots for each of the agency's frames. Movement and action can be nicely integrated with arrows or dynamic drawings (see Figures 5.13-5.21).

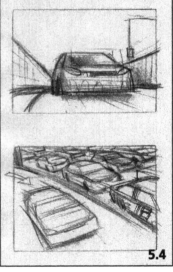

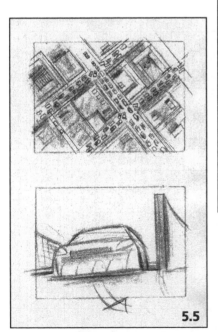

**Figures 5.3-5.5**
Here are some of the early drawings an illustrator
has done, before they get polished.

**Figures 5.6-5.12**
And here are some of the finished shooting board frames from the same project.

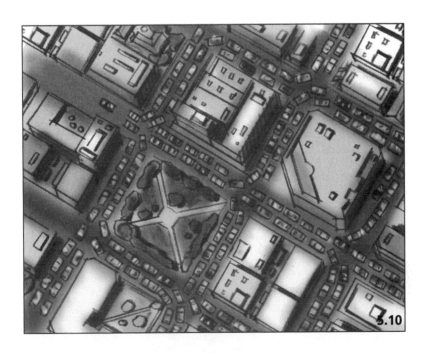

**Figures 5.13-5.21**
More examples of shooting board frames.
See how these frames are very specific in their angles and expression.

5.16

5.17

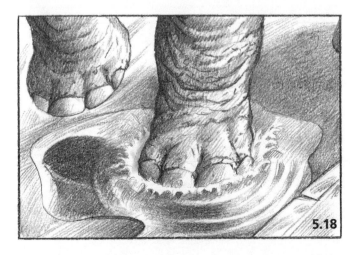

5.18

Both the shooting board and your shot list are also important tools for your crew. For example, an art director will see which part of the location he has to prepare, and a director of photography knows how wide the shot is and how much scenery he has to light. A lot of questions answer themselves, and you are free to think about more important things.

## CASE STUDY

### Previsualization

I mentioned earlier that I have concerns about the width of the wall. To make sure that I won't run out of background, I decide to do a simple previsualization (previz) for this one. In a 3D software program, I build the wall to the specifications of 15 x 19 ft., and I place the platform plus two cylinders as placeholders for the climbers (see Figures 5.22-5.26).

**Figure 5.22**
An overview of the relative sizes—the black cylinder represents Paige.

CASE STUDY *continued*

**Figure 5.23**
This is the opening shot of the spot. You can see that I need to
have lots of open sky and an extension on the height of the wall.

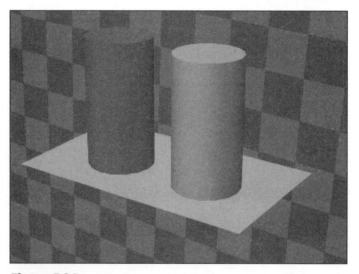

**Figure 5.24**
This corresponds to shot 2 on the shot list.

**Figure 5.25**
I'm testing out how far I can shoot from the side while still seeing all wall behind the guys.

**Figure 5.26**
Another test from a lower angle. The choice of lens influences the width dramatically.

CASE STUDY *continued*

Armed with the previz and my shot list, I meet the illustrator who is going to draw the shooting board. Again, the shooting board is mandatory and an important part of the preproduction meeting. Therefore, it should be as presentable as possible.

The illustrator and I talk through every shot, and I explain what I'm going for. For a few shots, he draws a quick sketch to see if we're on the same page. He then sits down and does a full board, which I have to look at for final approval and changes. Once it's okayed by me, he makes it pretty by filling in shading and the like.

Before it can be shown in the preproduction meeting, however, the assistant director takes all the drawings and creates a full shooting board with captions, descriptions, and shot numbers (see Figures 5.27-5.31). This board will be the basis for approval by the client and the subsequent shoot.

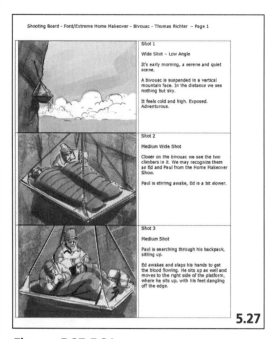

Shooting Board - Ford/Extreme Home Makeover - Bivouac - Thomas Richter  – Page 1

Shot 1

Wide Shot – Low Angle

It's early morning, a serene and quiet scene.

A bivouac is suspended in a vertical mountain face. In the distance we see nothing but sky.

It feels cold and high. Exposed. Adventurous.

Shot 2

Medium Wide Shot

Closer on the bivouac we see the two climbers in it. We may recognize them as Ed and Paul from the Home Makeover Show.

Paul is stirring awake, Ed is a bit slower.

Shot 3

Medium Shot

Paul is searching through his backpack, sitting up.

Ed awakes and slaps his hands to get the blood flowing. He sits up as well and moves to the right side of the platform, where he sits up, with his feet dangling off the edge.

**5.27**

**Figures 5.27-5.31**
This is the completed shooting board for the Ford job.
Compare it to the original boards, the shot list, and the previz shots.

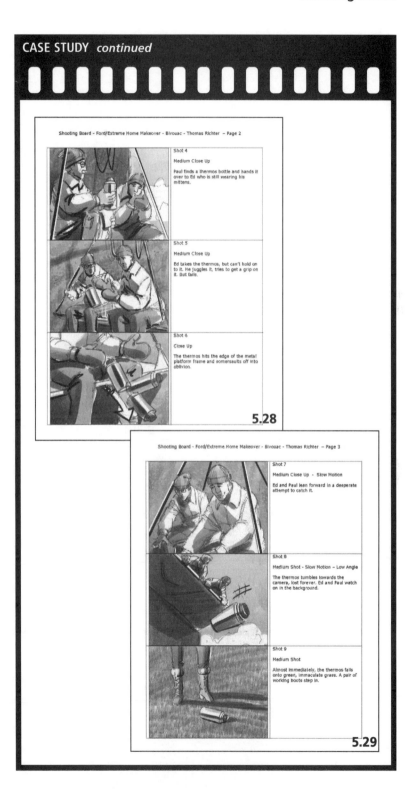

Shooting Board - Ford/Extreme Home Makeover - Bivouac - Thomas Richter – Page 2

**Shot 4**
Medium Close Up
Paul finds a thermos bottle and hands it over to Ed who is still wearing his mittens.

**Shot 5**
Medium Close Up
Ed takes the thermos, but can't hold on to it. He juggles it, tries to get a grip on it. But fails.

**Shot 6**
Close Up
The thermos hits the edge of the metal platform frame and somersaults off into oblivion.

5.28

Shooting Board - Ford/Extreme Home Makeover - Bivouac - Thomas Richter – Page 3

**Shot 7**
Medium Close Up  -  Slow Motion
Ed and Paul lean forward in a desperate attempt to catch it.

**Shot 8**
Medium Shot - Slow Motion – Low Angle
The thermos tumbles towards the camera, lost forever. Ed and Paul watch on in the background.

**Shot 9**
Medium Shot
Almost immediately, the thermos falls onto green, immaculate grass. A pair of working boots step in.

5.29

CASE STUDY *continued*

## CASE STUDY *continued*

Shooting Board - Ford/Extreme Home Makeover - Bivouac - Thomas Richter – Page 4

**Shot 10**

Medium Close Up

The boots belong to Paige. She looks up from the thermos at the guys: "You guys ready to work?"

Behind her the Ford Escape can be seen clearly. Also, workers are in the background carrying equipment and materials. Possibly we will see the house or other adventure improvements (dependent on location).

**Shot 11**

Medium Shot – O/S Paige

Ed and Paul react somewhat embarrassed or even disappointed.

The 'mountain' ends towards the edge of the frame and we can see green landscaping (or trees or structures).

**Shot 12**

Wide Shot – Dolly back

Ed and Paul wriggle out of the bivouac. Paige walks to and enters the car.

We can see that the 'mountain' is a climbing wall with a frame support in the back. Workers are in the background as well as in the foreground.

**5.30**

Shooting Board - Ford/Extreme Home Makeover - Bivouac - Thomas Richter – Page 5

**Shot 13 – Final Pack Shot**

Wide Shot - Dolly sideways

In the final shot we see the car, the adventure improvements (i.e. climbing wall, snowboarding simulator, BMX trail), and several workers.

The composition of this shot depends on the final location and setup in location. The angle in this drawing is not final.

There will also be room for the logo treatment.

**5.31**

# Chapter 6

# Preproduction

In preproduction you make the entire commercial. Yes, you still have to shoot it, but in essence you are laying the groundwork for what you will do on the set. After filming starts, you will add to what you've already done, work on the nuances, get the performances, and mix it all up in a great big pot.

Obviously, if you don't prep something, you can't shoot it. If you didn't rent that Ferrari to be there on the day of the shoot, you can't shoot it. Thus, in a sense, preproduction is about "enabling" your shooting day. You're making it possible to shoot what you want to shoot. That's why communication is so important. If your producer doesn't know what you want, he can't get it for you.

One of the main tasks in preproduction is casting. Joe Murray, who has been directing commercials for 20-plus years, says that "great directing is great casting."

## Casting

Anytime you use actors in a commercial, casting is a very important undertaking. That is because audiences react to humans in a very special way. Clients and agencies know very well the effect a performer may have on their customers and on their brand. Depending on the part, castings vary widely, but they are always a time-consuming process.

Let's assume that the commercial you are working on is using a spokesperson of some sort—not a celebrity, but a new character, like the Cranium Guy. In these situations, castings may take weeks or even months, and may be conducted all over the world to find the right fit. The same applies if you are dealing with models who don't even have to speak. It is not uncommon to cast in Paris, London, New York, Buenos Aires, and Milan. In such a case, hundreds of actors or models will be screened.

In a commercial where you have a couple in their kitchen talking about their day at work, you are looking to cast a husband and a wife. So, in this case, you would write a casting brief, which then goes to a casting director. The casting director will put out the call to agents and managers to submit head shots of actors they think are right for the part.

Depending on locality, the casting director may receive hundreds of head shots. Renita Whited, a commercial and music video casting director working on both the East and West Coasts, says for a regular part (male, Caucasian, 25-35), she receives as many as 2,000 submissions. Now, for two parts, that's 4,000 pictures to look at and 4,000 resumes to scan or read. In other cities or even countries, those numbers decrease dramatically, particularly when you are casting children or character actors, like seniors or odd characters.

The job of the casting director is to know what the director is looking for and to preselect. From the hundreds of submissions, a director may get to see 50 headshots, called *selects*. If there is nothing he likes, the casting director will have another batch to look at. The director and the casting director will then decide who to call in for an audition.

Auditions in commercials are usually extremely brief, as there are few lines or actions to perform. An actor will come in, do his thing, maybe do it one more time, and that's it. Besides the fact that this is an enormous challenge for an actor (to try to hit it just right at that one moment), it's an equally huge challenge for a director to gauge from those few seconds if the actor is right for the part or not. Most of the time, the director watches the casting on tape and can replay the performance. However, he is missing the vibe in the room when the actor was actually performing.

That's why there are callbacks. The director will select somewhere between a handful to a dozen actors to come in for a callback. Both the director and the casting director are present and spend some more time with each actor. The performance can be more nuanced, and there is more direction.

Finally, the director chooses his favorite person for each part, plus one or two alternatives, in case the client or the agency don't like what he's selected.

A lot of issues play into the decision to cast someone. The reason why so much time and effort is spent on it is because once you've miscast a role, there is little you can do to fix it—other than a recast. I've had to change actors on the set (on shoots where I had little input into casting due to time and place constraints), and it's not a pleasant experience. So you'd better cast right.

As a director, I look for a few things that are important to me. Obviously, I only select actors to audition whom I think will fit the part.

---

### Cast Away the Wrong Cast

I was once shooting a coach/team meeting scene with some famous real-life ball players. The coach, however, was an actor. He was supposed to inspire and motivate the players. I had only seen a videotape of the actor who was playing the coach, and the casting director on the job had not really asked for much acting during the casting session. The agency liked the guy's look, so we took the leap of faith.

Once on the set, however, the players would not "come down" from their celebrity pedestal and let a regular guy talk to them like that. They would just laugh and not really play along. We had to exchange the actor right there for a person who was familiar to the players and whom they trusted. The new coach wasn't an actor, so now the commercial had other problems.

However, there may be a certain openness in the interpretation of the role, in which case I will call in very different types and characters and see what they can deliver.

I look for an actor's energy, and I tend to prefer high-energy people. The reason is that it is simply much easier for an actor to take the performance down than to bring it up. I can't spend my time on the set coaxing an actor to show more zest and life. Time is too precious for that. If he is too big, however, all I have to tell him is to take it down a few notches.

If the energy is good, I throw out some challenges in the callback. I give the actor very specific directions, which may or may not be in line with the spot. What I'm looking for is whether the actor takes direction and adjusts. If someone repeats the same performance after being given three different directions, he is not an option. You will see quickly whether an actor knows his craft or not.

---

### Great Directing Is Great Casting

Again, Joe Murray's take on casting:

*Casting is a skill you have to learn. It's the most important part of the process. Don't spend time on things not onscreen. Casting is more than half the equation. The right person can be in front of everything. With the wrong person, [there is] nothing you can do to save it. I like to let people talk. You know, just hear what they have to say. That is, if I like their performance and if I think they can do it. I just give them some time to introduce themselves so I get a sense of their personality.*

*The worst is forced casting. When the client changes something, you run into trouble, so make sure you show them only talent that you can work with.*

*Also, I tend to look at a lot of people. I like to have choices. I think it's important not to waste their time—when someone comes in for casting, respect them. You give them everything you can to get the spot. You know, you help them be better.*

*Adjust them a little bit and see if they respond. Have a rapport with them. You can discover things in casting.*

I also tell actors to be open and bring their ideas. In fact, I learn a lot in each casting session about the project I'm working on. How do the lines sound? What is the timing like? Which are the funny lines? Where are good breaks and beats? Actors come up with suggestions that would never have occurred to me. I may steal them and use them in the spot.

Finally, I look for personality, and with it some sort of smartness or cleverness. I don't like to work with difficult people or divas. A high maintenance actor is of no use to me. I like actors who are polite and easy to work with, professional, and intelligent. It's good to be able to explain things only once.

Clients and agencies look for some other qualities, and the director has to take that into account in his selection. Companies are very careful, because actors will be associated with their brand or product. Therefore, they will usually go for more attractive-looking people, because they think that attractiveness rubs off on their product.

---

### Luck of the Draw

Sometimes, you get lucky. On a project in a foreign country, I had to cast two older men arguing about a famous cricket match. Now, it's hard enough to find good and trained older actors in Los Angeles. But this was in Jamaica! How on earth would we find someone who could do this?

On the casting tapes, we saw two gentlemen who seemed to have no fear of the camera and had the right look. We decided to hire them. On the set, I was pondering my options. How should I approach this? Should I talk to them in actor's language? Probably not. I was afraid they weren't going to be able to argue realistically without it seeming staged and contrived.

So, I walked up to them—they were already in their chairs on our set, a porch. I asked whether or not they knew about the famous cricket match in the sixties where there was a legendary play made by one of the out-fielders. Immediately, the two gentlemen started to argue about who the guy was. Was it Weeks? Or Worrell? They were at each other's throats in seconds, doing exactly what the commercial was all about. I turned to my DP and signaled him to let the camera roll.

Also, if you are dealing with food spots of any kind, clients are very careful about weight, health, and teeth issues. And clearly, if you show teeth or hands in a close-up, you usually want to make sure that all the teeth and all the fingers are still in place.

Commercial casting is very much typecasting, because the audience needs to be able to get a quick read on the characters. Clichés are unfortunate, but sometimes unavoidable. Doctors and bankers usually should look trustworthy, middle-aged mothers should be attractive but not sexy, and cowboys should be rough and weathered.

Finally, the casting director also makes sure that there are no conflicts with other commercials that the actor may have done.

## Crew

Part of your prep is the hiring of your crew. This is an important process because you want to work with people who not only understand your vision, but also add something to it. Your main team consists of the producer and the assistant director (on the production side), and the director of photography and the production designer (on the creative side). This is often described as the nucleus of the production team, because all the lines of communication flow from these five people.

On occasion, you have a stunt coordinator who has a special place on the set. Once a stunt scene is being shot, the stunt coordinator carries all the responsibility for the shot and the safety during that shot or scene, and thus has final say on a lot of issues regarding safety (which may impact your creative decisions).

The hiring of your crew is done by the producer, but you choose whom he ends up hiring. Look at reels and talk to candidates on the phone or in meetings to get a feel for who they are and whether you can work with them. It's a very personal working relationship with a lot of emotional capital at stake for everyone. The slightest remark of disapproval about your shot, the DP's light, the production designer's set, or the AD's schedule can create bad blood that carries through the day.

## Producer

The producer is in charge of running the production, including details such as where the trailers are parked, when lunch is served, and how to obtain insurance and permits. He, in turn, has his team, with a production coordinator and assistants. The job of a producer is extremely demanding, both in knowledge required and in the ability to be creative and endure long hours. During preproduction, he spends about 90 percent of his time on the phone.

His expertise has to encompass things like labor and tax law, as well as second-guessing the agency and clients on preferences and demands. While keeping an eye on the budget, the producer has to provide the director with the things he needs in order to shoot the commercial.

## Assistant Director

The assistant director, or AD, is in charge of the schedule and running the set. He will join the preproduction for a few days to look at your shot list and figure out the smartest way to shoot. His job is to have everyone coordinated when a shot comes up. He gets the talent into makeup, the stunt cars in place, and the extras in the background. While doing all that, he also keeps an eye on the clock.

In a way, he does all the technical and procedural directing the director does not do. Sometimes, however, the AD ends up directing talent, particularly when the director is not really good at that (think about a car director having to work with actors).

A good AD is necessary for a smooth and successful shoot. Too many people have to be coordinated for the director to do it all alone. At this point, the director should have a mind only for the creative part of the job, unless there are major obstacles to be faced.

## Director of Photography

The director of photography, or DP, is one of the two creative members of your team (the production designer being the other). The DP, obviously, is in charge of the image. Or, rather, he is in charge of making the image look the way you want it to look. Often, as I said earlier, the director relies heavily on his DP to take care of the scene breakdown and the composition of the shots.

The DP's main area is lighting. He looks at your shooting boards, and during the prep, he has extensive conversations with you about the look of the spot. Color, contrast, and brightness are the basic attributes of an image. However, there are a myriad of advanced techniques that he can use, from fairly simple slow motion to more complicated variable shutters or film flashing. For this reason, you need your DP to be experienced and reliable.

Because commercials are motion pictures, camera moves are also a big concern. There are endless possibilities for moving a camera, from dollies to cranes to wire rigs, helicopters, or steadicams. To achieve his job objectives, the DP has three key assistants: the assistant cameraman (AC), the gaffer (lighting and electricity), and the key grip (for dollies, cranes, and other equipment, such as flags and shiny boards).

If you do not have a DP in mind already, you should look at a lot of reels. I look at reels all the time, even if I'm not prepping a job. I tend to look for the visual impression of the image. To me, the DP is a painter with light, and I want to see his brush stroke.

There are a lot of DPs who would like to direct. A young, inexperienced director will run into old-timers who think they should be doing his job. The truth is that often these guys are hired for that very reason: The director is weak. The production company hires an experienced DP who can take over if things go haywire.

In general, the DP is your choice. Clients and agencies sometimes want to see the DP's reel (safety again!), but they should not have the final word on that. The DP is your closest creative ally on the set, and you need to have a good relationship with him.

## Stay True to Your Vision

Producers like to hire experienced DPs for younger or inexperienced directors. It provides them with a safety net, and sometimes the agency even asks for it. The result is often a DP who feels like he should be the director and a director who feels like no one trusts him. It's always difficult if a DP is forced on a director, and the best producers know that it's not a good thing to do.

I once had to work with a DP who had an existing relationship with the client. They liked him so much, they insisted that I use him. Although he was of the dominant kind of DPs, the ones who think they have to set up shots and change things to their liking, it took only a few hours of working together until he realized that I was not going to be deterred from my vision. I set up the shot, I chose the lens, and I placed the camera.

During preproduction, your DP has to decide on the equipment that the production needs to rent. Therefore, he will ask you many questions about your vision, some of which can become very technical. Moving shots in particular require great thought; for example, it is not feasible to rent four different platforms for the camera (such as a steadicam, crane, car mount, and process trailer) and then use only one.

You need to know what you want the shot to look like, and together with the DP you must decide which is the best equipment to achieve that look. Also, the appropriate types of film stock and lenses must be ordered.

Finally, the DP is usually a very creative person with a unique viewpoint. He will try to understand your concept and make suggestions. These suggestions may be specific shots, or even story ideas. You would be foolish not to listen.

**CASE STUDY**

## The DP Comes on Board

For this project, I have chosen Aaron Barnes as the DP. We've been in telephone contact ,and he is working on the camera and light lists. He and I went to Art Center together, and we each know how the other person works. For jobs like this one—where I'm prepping from Europe—it's good to have existing work relationships. If you know another person's style of approaching a project, you can concentrate on the important issues rather than having to get on the same page first. Aaron is writing meticulous lists of every piece of equipment we might need on the shoot day. He also attempts to hire his key people (gaffer and key grip) to complete his team.

## Production Designer

The other half of your creative team is the production designer. While the DP is responsible for how to shoot, the production designer is in charge of what to shoot. Anything and everything that appears in a commercial—except for the talent—should be within the realm of the production designer.

In your prep, you should compile lists of important props and set pieces so the production designer knows what to look for. However, he will also sit down and make lists that are even longer because they are extremely detailed. Again, everything you want to have in the shot has to be rented or bought, and must be brought to the set by someone.

The production designer has a number of buyers taking photographs and recording prices prior to the shoot. With the help of these photographs, you will narrow down the selection to a few favorites. If we're talking about cars or appliances (major art direction pieces), the budget might not accommodate more than one. In the case of hand props (bottles or umbrellas) or decorating props (flowers, chairs, tables, etc. ), the production designer will bring a variety of choices to the set.

The production designer's artistic vision comes into play when the commercial takes place in a fantasy world—for example, the center of the earth or a fairy-tale forest. A good production designer will create extensive production design drawings and sketches. The more input you can give him, the more his ideas will be in line with your vision.

Again, there are production designers who are talented at creating new worlds, and others who specialize in reality. Some may be more apt to build futuristic and modern sets, while others are particularly good at recreating medieval times.

## Location

The location is where you shoot the commercial. The entire spot could take place in the same location, or you could have several locations. There are commercials that are shot all over the country, even all over the world.

There are two ways to go: Shoot on a stage or on a real location. The stage is a bit easier to prep, because you don't actually have to search for it. Your producer will look for the best deal for the size of stage necessary, and the rest is up to the production designer.

The decision between stage and real location depends on a wide array of factors, including—but not limited to—weather, light, effects, feasibility, money, and even the existence of a specific real location in the first place. You will find that stage locations are much easier to control and coordinate. Stages often have everything you need right there (including overhead lighting rigs and high-voltage power). There are no major travel issues, street closures, permits, etc. However, you will lose realism. It is very difficult to create reality in a stage scenario, particularly when you're shooting exteriors. While digital post production has opened up new and amazing possibilities, there is a certain random reality in a live location.

I prefer a real location any day, because I like capturing the vibe of a place. Stage sets are often too perfect, even if depicting a trashy downtown alley. It's too trashy, too downtown, and too cliché.

The location is inextricably linked to your story or concept. Your final choice will depend upon your creative vision, as well as any production issues. However, in commercials, there is also the added layer of the client's and agency's vision of the spot. In choosing the location, you must keep in mind that you need to sell the client on it and convince everyone at the agency that it will work.

## CASE STUDY

### Location Choices

The location scout has sent dozens of photos from his scouts to me. For each location, he has every conceivable angle, plus shots of the skyline around the property, as I had specifically requested those. A few of the locations are already out, because I simply don't like the house in the background. Another two or three seem like their backyards are too small for our purposes.

I narrow it down to around five locations and choose one as a favorite location, based on photographs. Even though I'm still in Europe, I can actually do some more research on the different choices. Via Google Earth, I find the places and get a bird's-eye view of them. I'm able to see which direction the house is facing, and from which way the sunlight will shine and change over the course of the shooting day.

This is very helpful, because we have to place the tower in accordance with the sun's path, and we also have to plan our shooting schedule around that. The satellite imagery also allows me to gauge if there are mountains in the vicinity or very tall buildings that could inhibit the view.

My choices are preselected by the agency. It's good to have a close working relationship with the agency throughout the entire preproduction process. If decisions are made and approved by them, there will be fewer discussions later, and we can concentrate on the more important issues.

## Stage

Let's assume that for a commercial, you have to create an accidental water pipe disaster in an apartment. A woman is doing the
dishes when suddenly the wall bursts open and a swell of water
explodes out.

For obvious reasons, you cannot shoot this in a real location. The
cost is prohibitive, and it may be hard to shoot the exploding wall
more than once. On a stage, the wall is specifically built to explode
over and over again. There is a rigged water tank attached to a
pipe system that can deliver exactly the amount of water you
want. The drainage situation is taken care of, and there are no
downstairs neighbors to bribe when the water starts dripping into
their living room.

Your producer will look for a stage with a water tank and drainage
system already in place. All you are building is a kitchen that measures maybe 16 x 16 feet. So the stage can be comparatively small,
somewhere below 100 x 100 feet.

You and your production designer will decide on the design of the
kitchen, based on the types of shots you want to film. The production designer makes his construction drawings, and the set is
built—done! The advantages of shooting on a stage in this case are
obvious. You will have access to exactly the set you want. It can be
built to your specifications—with removable walls, ceiling or no
ceiling, moveable (i.e., an airplane fuselage on a giant gimbal to
simulate in-flight movement) or fixed. The huge advantage here is
that you can adjust the set to your blocking scheme, whereas in a
real location it's the other way around.

A lot of stage shooting these days is done on blue or green screen
for digital post production. You may not actually shoot full sets or
scenes, but rather elements that will be added into the footage later.
There are specialized green screen stages, often paired with expensive motion-control rigs. Again, the choice of which stage to use is
dependent primarily on technical, rather than creative, factors,
because you can usually build exactly what your vision calls for.

In either case, your set design prep is focused on working closely with the production designer. He'll make conceptual drawings for you to look at, and these drawings will also be subject to approval in the PPM.

## Real Locations

Besides the fact that some things simply cannot be built, shooting on location is good for realism, fun, and as one of the great perks of film production. The beaches of South Africa, the glaciers of Iceland, the mountains of Canada, or the deserts of California all offer beautiful, priceless backgrounds. Yet, the corner of Crenshaw and Jefferson in L.A. may be just what you're looking for. The realism in location shooting is hard to beat, and often you don't have a choice at all.

Once the director has taken a look at the boards, he or the producer will write a briefing or specs for location scouts—unless, that is, they already have a place in mind. Particularly in Southern California, there are certain places that are used a lot for shooting, such as movie ranches, roads, and buildings.

Where does the location scout look? That depends wholly on the concept. The spot takes place in the Midwestern plains. Do you have to go there? Or is there an area in Southern California that looks the same? (There is!) The commercial features European back alleys, a la Paris. Depending on the scope of the shots, you may be able to shoot this in L.A. If not, try Buenos Aires, which has doubled for Paris a hundred times—and it's much cheaper than France.

Whatever you are looking for, the location scout will go and shoot a huge quantity of pictures for you to look at. Also, the scout will make sure that it is possible to shoot what he's photographed in the first place. From any number of possible locations, you may decide to look at a few in person. I like to do my own recon of a location before I decide on it, because pictures can be deceiving.

The most important factor in selecting a location is whether it allows you to get the shots you want. For example:

- Does the composition work the way you envisioned?
- Is the look and feel right?
- Is there enough space for the camera to move?
- Are there trees in the way?
- Are the mountains in the distance a problem?
- What about that smoke stack or those power lines?
- What is the path of the sun?
- Is the location beautiful or trashy enough?
- How much art direction is necessary to make it work?

If you are looking for multiple locations, their proximity may be important. If you have to move locations during a shooting day, then you're losing valuable time. This is one of the major differences from feature production, where moves during a day are extremely rare. I've done commercials where we had to pack up twice during the day and move the entire show a couple of miles.

I often find that shooting interiors in a real location is an amusing undertaking. More often than not, a commercial crew will come in and change everything about the room, including the colors of the walls. Why not shoot it on stage, then? You may like the view out the window, or you may have another scene that takes place in the driveway.

Kitchens are a very popular location to search for. The reason is that building a fake kitchen on a stage with working appliances is often more expensive than renting an entire house.

For you, as a director, the most important thing is that the location gives you the necessary look, feel, space, backgrounds, and working area. Brief your scout well, and then look at the photographs and ask questions. I've used satellite shots to determine space and light issues, but I still prefer to have a walk around myself.

## Production Design

The production design of a commercial includes everything from hand props to major construction. Moreover, it is about the entire look and style of the spot, the color scheme, the textures, and so on. If your production designer is good (he'd better be, you hired him!), he will make certain that every aspect is covered and that all the different nuances make up a whole.

Some commercials are art-directed to the point that they are hyper-realistic. Others are designed to look like real life. Choose your production designer according to his strengths. Some production designers are very good at building extravagant sets, while others excel at creating just the right level of realism in any given location.

Your goal in designing the production is to make your creative vision become a reality. The preceding example of the kitchen with the exploding wall calls for a realistic set. A car spot in a beautiful location may have very few sets, but there is still production design to be considered: for example, the road or the desert floor or the tumbleweeds rolling across or the dust. A highly stylized perfume commercial may need to have all the trees in the vicinity painted gold (and thus must be carted in for that very purpose), or rose pedals strewn over an acre of perfectly green lawn.

In your prep, you need to think about every small detail. Someone has to go out and get every tiny element you want to shoot, prepare, or even create.

Also, in commercials you will often deal with certain color schemes. The company's logo or the brand's look may dictate or prohibit the use of certain colors. On occasion, clients demand a certain color to be used as a key color, which has to reappear in wardrobe, walls, and props. All of this has to be taken into account when your set is designed. You are half creative leader of a highly-skilled production crew and half artist-salesman, who must inspire and convince the client and agency.

### Production Design Preapproval

Our production designer prepared a set sketch to show the placement of the large items we plan to have in the backyard (see Figure 6.1). In this project, we need the agency and the client to approve some of the larger items before we head into the preproduction meeting, because of the tight schedule. There will not be enough time for all these props to be prepped or built before the shoot.

**Figure 6.1**
The texture and surface structure of the wall is also being decided at this stage. It will take at least two weeks to construct the wall, so time is of the essence.

# Wardrobe

Wardrobe is everything your actors wear. The client will have a close look at all the wardrobe items you propose, because the characters in the spot are greatly defined by what they wear. Their social status, their style, and their attitude are quickly communicated with just a few pieces.

**CASE STUDY**

### Wardrobe Briefing

I'm writing the wardrobe brief for the costume designer. This is a tricky case, because the climber's gear technically falls into the props depart- ment. The costume designer will be responsible for anoraks, climbing overalls, climbing boots, and mittens. The art department will be in charge of helmets, ropes, carabiners, backpacks, ice axes, and all the other climbing gear.

The only other person to dress is Paige. Word is that she likes pink. (She actually has a pink tool belt that she wears on the TV show.)

The brief will be appropriately short, because it is pretty self-explanatory. Mainly it will be about the colors. The wardrobe designer will then go out and take photographs of actual pieces or even rent or buy them. With every day that passes, the collection of pieces, grows in some corner of the production office. If I'm there, I'll look at things every once in a while and add my two cents.

In this case, I'm still in Europe, so clothes will pile up, and there'll be a lot to go through when I return.

Here, also, you will write a brief for the stylist. Some directors know every piece of clothing by its proper name. I don't, so I usually pull some pictures I like and include them in my brief.

Your wardrobe stylist will pull lots of pictures and make sugges- tions. Together, you decide on a general direction, and the pictures are prepared to be presented in the PPM.

## Car Prep

There are an enormous number of car ads, and there is a special process called *car prep*, which deserves a mention here. There are specialized companies for this prep, and I briefly mentioned what they do in the first chapter.

Anytime you see a car in a car ad, a lot of work has gone into it. The car has been prepped to look good and perform right. Days before the shoot, the car prep company usually picks up the car from wherever the advertiser or manufacturer has made it available. This means it could be at a dealership, a factory, or sometimes a car rental place.

The car prep company, by the way, is also in charge of the car's transportation. They will have a trailer on which the car rides to and from the set. Depending on the commercial, the prep company may do any of the following things.

Quite obviously, the car will be detailed to perfection. The car's paint will be polished to a perfect shine, without so much as a grain of dust on it. All the non-metal parts, like tires or bumpers, will be treated to make them as rich in color (mostly, they're black) as possible. Every inch of chrome will glisten like silver.

Very often the windows will be tinted. This can be done so that no driver is shown or to change the exposure inside the car. The grading of the tint goes from very slight percentages to almost complete black (called *limo tint*).

The car will be "blackened out," which means that any possible passageways for light through the chassis or the undercarriage will be blocked. For example, certain wheels and rims are see-through. For a commercial shoot, however, you want no light spots from these areas. The same goes for the grill, which often allows light to emanate from the engine compartment.

The electrical circuits, most specifically the lights, will be disengaged and run through a special switchboard so that they can be dimmed. A car's lights are very strong and would not look right on film at their standard setting. Once they are on a dimmer, the DP can set them at exactly the right strength. This includes all the interior and dashboard lights.

Also part of the electrical prep are things like alarms, automatic locks, or onboard plugs for small interior lights, which can be wired directly from the car.

For special effects, like an exploding airbag or smoke from the engine, even more prep is necessary. There are also special changes that a stunt or precision driver may ask for, such as disengaging certain safety features like the automatic brake systems, or increasing the tire pressure.

## Spin It!

If a precision driver is asked to perform a 180-degree turn, he will pump up the "load" tire to a very high pressure. The load tire is the tire over which the car slides. The high pressure is intended to prevent the tire from peeling off the rim during the maneuver. I had the pleasure of being in a car once during such a 180 turn, and it's great fun.

Finally, the car prep guys will take care of generic license or dealer plates, stickers, and all the other minute things on cars.

Camera rigs, however, are the job of a car grip. He is specialized in mounting camera platforms and heads onto the car. The most common mounts are the hood mount and the side mount. The rigs use both hard point tie-ins on the car's undercarriage and suction cups on the chassis. Their setup takes quite a while, and it needs to be planned accordingly in preproduction.

# CHAPTER 7

# PREPRODUCTION MEETING

The climax of your preproduction phase is the preproduction meeting (PPM). The purpose of this meeting is for the client to finally approve every aspect of the production. It's like looking at the architect's blueprint before the house is built.

A PPM can be daunting. You have to present the commercial you would like to shoot, and the client has to approve it. That is why a lot of the preproduction is geared not only toward producing a good commercial, but also toward satisfying the client's desires and making him feel safe. The agency's reputation with the client is on the line as well. After all, they chose you, and now their choice is being put to the test. It's really your meeting, your show.

In addition to the high stakes, there can be a lot of people at PPMs. Sometimes, the client arrives with a dozen top-level managers and a few gofers. The agency is out in full force as well, often with top management (people who haven't been involved in the project at all, but whom the client expects to be there).

## Marathon Meetings

I recently had a PPM with nine clients (from four different companies) and seven agency people. We had to talk about three spots, and the PPM lasted six hours. It's a physically and mentally tasking effort (even more so when you are jetlagged, as I was). There were many points of dispute between the agency and their client, as there often are.

Occasionally, agencies leave certain creative issues unannounced until the PPM, where the client then feels like he's been put on the spot. Usually, alliances are built in these meetings. For the director, it is important not to upset the agency or leave them hanging out to dry. At the same time, it makes no sense to take the bullets for them if they've screwed up.

In this meeting, the two sides of commercial directing truly collide. You had to sell yourself to get the job in the first place; now you have to justify your choices and sell your vision of the commercial on top of that.

Often, you will see the agency wanting to preapprove certain aspects, like locations or cast or major props, before the meeting. In fact, even a lot of clients like to see your choices in advance—the major ones at least. They want to feel safe going into the PPM, which then turns into a recap of the dozens of emails and telephone calls that were exchanged over the last few weeks. That's a good thing, in my opinion, because by the time of the meeting everyone is on the same page regarding the major decisions, and attention can be given to the details.

A word on length. I've had PPMs that lasted 30 minutes, and I've had those that lasted six hours. Depending on the scope of the project and the involvement of the client, there is simply no way to know how things will go. There are politics in the background and factors at play that you are not privy to, including a CEO's current mood or whether a client cares more about the shots of their product than the ideas you're presenting.

# Take Charge of the Presentation

Like in any meeting, it's good to have a certain amount of entertainment skills and showmanship. And once again, it is important that you are in charge—or at least appear to be. Talk directly to the client. When showing pictures or shooting boards, show them directly to the client. Despite the fact that they come in droves, usually there is one client decisionmaker. He is the one to talk to.

During preproduction, the producer will be putting together a PPM booklet, which serves both as agenda (see Figure 7.1) and presentation platform. The booklet contains names of all the responsible people on the client and agency side, as well as the production crew. And there are the original storyboards or scripts, and any other materials the agency wants to include.

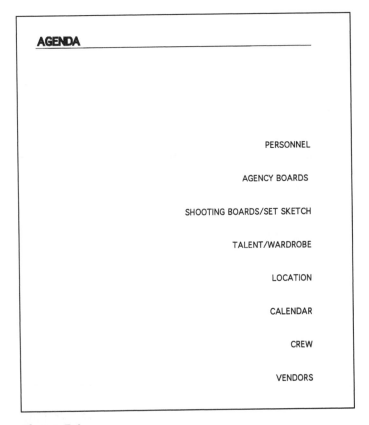

**AGENDA**

PERSONNEL

AGENCY BOARDS

SHOOTING BOARDS/SET SKETCH

TALENT/WARDROBE

LOCATION

CALENDAR

CREW

VENDORS

**Figure 7.1**
This is a typical agenda for a PPM booklet.

Usually, the shooting board is next, because it is the starting point of the director's presentation. Following that may be pictures of cast, locations, wardrobe, props, and any other visual reference material. Finally, there could be music descriptions or names of voiceover talent, and a schedule.

I often use my booklet to write down notes for my presentation, underlining nuances or explaining images or decisions. It is also a good idea to write down the names of the important people on the client and agency side, in case your memory fails you.

The PPM starts with appreciative niceties and introductions. As the client already knows the original boards (he approved them), the agency will usually hand the controls over to the director fairly quickly. However, there might be changes that haven't been approved by the client yet. The agency will then explain the changes and go through the new concept.

## Politics

Nothing could be more uncomfortable than a meeting in which the agency hasn't briefed their client (on purpose!). Sometimes, the agency will try to push through changes by simply having things prepped a certain way. By the time of the PPM, these things are then unchangeable. The client's options are either to accept the changes or to move the shoot, which often means more cost and delay in the media plan. This is a political gamble by the agency, because some clients will simply not concur and will cancel the entire production. The balance of power between agency and client is delicate and different with each project.

After the agency turns the meeting over to the director, it's your turn to step up to the plate. Each director has a different style in approaching PPMs. You can jump right into the story, have a few opening words, or go through a more conceptual speech. There is no set way for a director to hold the PPM. You are the artist, and this is your show.

I usually talk about the concept first: what I think the core idea is and why it appeals to me. Then I express my excitement to be working on the project and my belief that it will be the best commercial ever. Hopefully, there is no need for icebreakers, as no trouble has arisen thus far, and the premeeting chats with the client have gone over well. In general, clients are glad and happy to meet you, although there are those who see you as a mere service provider.

Obviously, there is a huge element of human interaction here. If you run into a difficult client, there are many ways to deal with it, depending on your own personality and style. Some directors cannot leave their own skin, and they behave whichever way they want to behave. This often creates problems when strong personalities collide.

I tend to be more on the diplomatic and psychological side. If I feel a client needs to pampered because they are full of themselves, then I use that to my advantage. Strong, dominant alpha male clients can easily be tamed by simply asking them too many specific questions for which they don't have an answer. The goal is to establish myself as the specialist.

Sometimes, a client needs a strong sparring partner. There are those who want confrontation and argument. I actually like that because it's quickly established that I know what I'm talking about when it comes to commercials and directing. In fact, I've told more than one client that they are the experts in making their product (be it cars, yogurt, or televisions), but I'm the expert at making my product.

The toughest clients are the quiet, sneaky ones, where you never know what's up. Or the ones who make decisions on a whim, simply because they enjoy the power of it.

Most clients I've worked with, however, have been extremely agreeable and wonderful to work with. Remember, though, that every client wants to feel safe about his investment. I said before that PPMs are a lot about making the client comfortable and reassuring him about the decisions he has already made. Always keep that in mind.

## Tell the Story

The shooting board frames are printed in the booklet, but you may want to use an extra presentation board with bigger images so that everyone is looking at you and not down at their paperwork. You obviously want everyone to pay attention to you and be on the same page. If the client or the agency start flipping pages in the booklet, they're not listening to what you have to say.

Try to capture their attention by describing the shots in a colorful, entertaining manner. Quite literally, tell the story. Don't use technical terms they may not understand. Use the beats of the story, short sentences, and active verbs.

I like to garnish the story with short, quick comments about how I intend to film certain shots or why a certain moment is special. Some directors act out the scenes, while others have a memorized speech they follow. It's a show, and you are the performer. The storyteller.

In a way, it's like the treatment you wrote, just as an oral presentation. Obviously, since you booked the job, there may have been changes or even new ideas. And the client or the agency will ask questions. If that happens, you should answer them and—before you go back to the story—recount the last few beats you've just explained.

Once you're done with the shooting boards, there may be a discussion or more questions from the client. Also, the client may express what is important to him:

*We really need to see the car clearly.*

*As long as people get that this is the best shampoo out there...*

*I don't want it to feel like these people are stupid. Just odd.*

*Is there any possibility of having an interior shot of the car?*

*It's important that the hand gesture is clear because it's our key visual.*

Obviously, these remarks are very important, even though they may come out of left field and have nothing to do with what you just presented. This is where a good agency will step in and help you out. They know their client, and they know how to handle these things.

## CASE STUDY

### The Performance

I do my presentations in the moment; in other words, I don't follow a manuscript. For the Ford spot, this is what my presentation could sound like:

*We open on two climbers in a bivouac hanging on the side of a mountain. A sheer cliff. It's cold. It's high altitude. Welcome to the North Face. I would like to compose this shot slightly off-center to create the feeling of a void around them.*

*We cut to a shot a bit closer, but still a wide shot. The angle is higher, so we can see the climbers more clearly. They're waking up. Stirring. Pulling themselves into a seated position.*

*We jump in for closer shots now, and we can see their faces really well here. They're slow and cold, slapping their hands together to get the blood moving.*

*I intend to shoot coverage here from reverse angles so that we have a lot of flexibility in the editing.*

*One of the climbers reaches for a Thermos bottle and hands it over with the words: "Here, drink this."*

*The other climber takes the bottle, but fumbles it. For a moment we think he may recover as he juggles the Thermos. But then it slips from his hands and falls. Into oblivion. Gone forever.*

*I'd like to shoot this really funny and interesting shot from below. The bottle falls toward us, and we see the climbers in the background. They simply stare after it.*

## Step by Step

The meeting moves on to the cast. In general, you will show a short casting tape with your choices on it. Be ready to explain why you chose these actors. If you are lucky, the client will simply nod it off, and you're good to go. However, often enough the client will take issue with a look, a hair color, an attitude, or anything else he may find wrong with another person.

## Guard Against the Bad Idea

I had a client once who suggested that the window curtains should be in the colors of his product. Only those colors were orange, yellow, and pink. Of course, you can't just say, "That's horrible!" Rather, you need to find a diplomatic way of making sure that orange curtains don't become a reality.

On another occasion, a client insisted that a girl's wardrobe had to be in the colors of the product. While the agency had described the girl as a shy, innocent Amelie-type elf, the client wanted a confident, sexy, kick-ass modern woman. Part of your job is to find a solution to these kinds of conflicts.

Don't budge. At least, not right away. Defend your choices and fight for them. Hopefully, the agency is on your side as well. If the client cannot be convinced, you should have backup talent on standby, ready to show. But remember, you are the one who has seen them in casting, and you are the one who has to work with them on the set.

After the cast is approved, you will cover locations, wardrobe, and props, usually by photograph, sometimes with video footage. The wardrobe may be present for inspection at the meeting. Again, it is important that you can justify your decisions, if need be.

One by one, all the important elements of the production are approved. Often, post production issues will be included as well, particularly if they have to do with computer graphics, which are being created simultaneously, or if they are an essential part of the commercial. Also, it's not often that you have the client, the agency, and the production team together at one table, so you may as well cover as much ground as you can.

At the end of the meeting, the producer will run through the production schedule (not the shooting schedule!), which is the day-by-day view of things to come: prep day, shoot day one, shoot day two, dailies transfer, editing day one, editing day two, first approval day, and so on. This is important because the client needs to commit his availability for certain dates so the production can move ahead on schedule. I will say more about that in the post production section.

---

### Allow For Input When It Matters Least

Clients need to feel as if they have input. After all, it's their commercial. There are some topics where I always feel it's good to let the client have a lot of input. Probably the best example is wardrobe and props. Unless there is a "hero" prop or piece of clothing, these items are not nearly as important as they're made out to be.

For example, during a recent PPM, there were a total of nine women from the client and the agency arguing over which handbag should be used for one of the women in the spot. Each of the women had her own taste and style. Who am I to interfere? Try to get a consensus on a handbag from nine women! Rather than jumping in, I let them continue their discussion, only to finally defer it to the shooting day where we would have a number of different handbags on standby. Of course, the discussion continued on the set, but I ultimately put my foot down and made the decision, citing time constraints. Everybody was happy, and the handbag ended up onscreen for a mere half a second.

---

# Play the Game

There are a few hints for sticky situations that might occur in meetings like this. All your choices were made for a reason—to support your vision. And the client hired you for your vision, after all. So stand firm on the decisions you made. Don't be impolite or arrogant. Just make sure you get your way. If necessary, consider letting him have his way on a less important issue (I mentioned wardrobe earlier).

The longer the meeting goes, the less focused and more tired everyone gets. At some point, everyone just wants the meeting to end. If you have an issue that you know is contentious or you suspect might be difficult to get approved, talk about it at the end. The chances that the agency and the client will be lenient are much greater at that time.

If you feel that the attention in the room is slipping, or that someone is trying to take over, a good tactic is to get up and walk around the table. You're taking a dominating position and forcing people to look at you. Also, if there is one person who is particularly contentious, you can stand right behind him just when the floor is open for discussion. He will be less likely to argue, because you have put him in an awkward position. However, never do this with the main client or the creatives. It is their project, their commercial, and they have every right to be heard. If, however, it is an annoying midlevel gofer who wants to shine, go ahead and set him up.

## CASE STUDY

### The PPM

In a very uncommon twist of events, it is decided that the PPM has to be done over the telephone. This is very uncommon indeed, and it's only possible if the client fully trusts his agency. In our case, Ford and JWT, and specifically the creative team and Senior Producer Kelly Trudell, have a longstanding relationship with each other, so this is possible.

The main reason for the teleconferenced PPM is the tight time schedule. There would be no time to prep if the meeting were to happen after Christmas, but there is no time to get everyone together before then. So the PPM happens over the phone on December 22.

The client fully trusts the agency and all the decisions we've made together, and only has a few remarks regarding the vehicle. In fact, it is one of the shortest and smoothest PPMs I've ever had.

After the PPM has concluded, the production team goes ahead and sets the wheels in motion. There are really only a few days left to prep, namely December 27, 28, 29, and January 2. I'm due to return to the States on the 26th (see Figures 7.2 and 7.3).

CASE STUDY *continued*

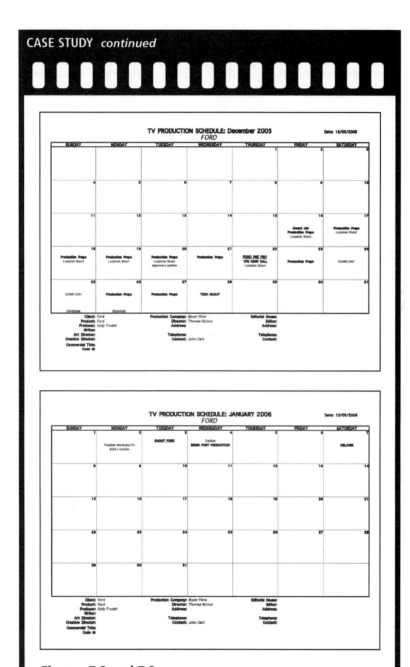

**Figures 7.2 and 7.3**
The production schedule for the Ford job is very tight.
Notice the delivery date.

After the PPM, a lot of decisions are final. The client has approved them and not much will change from this point on. The production team can now finalize all the bookings with crew, equipment, location, and cast. The wardrobe designer knows which pieces were selected. The casting director hears which cast was chosen. All the decisions once again trickle down the ladder into each department.

From the director's viewpoint, it is now time to think about the schedule (together with the AD) and to oversee the last few steps of preproduction.

## Tech Scout

A few days before the shoot (the sooner the better), there will be a tech scout—sometimes called *recce* (short for reconnaissance). You and certain crew members will visit all the locations and talk about the schedule, the direction of the light, the different setups, and all the equipment that is needed.

Participants in these scouts commonly are the following people:

- ◆ Director
- ◆ Producer
- ◆ DP
- ◆ Production Designer
- ◆ Assistant Director (AD)
- ◆ Gaffer
- ◆ Key Grip
- ◆ Location Manager

This will be the first time most of your crew will see the location or even hear about the concept. You need to communicate your needs and requirements clearly, because the gaffer and the key grip were not present for the hours of meetings and preparations you've had. Even the DP may have spent only a few hours looking over the boards and talking to you.

CASE STUDY

## Tech Scout

I landed yesterday, December 26. This morning my DP, Aaron Barnes, picks me up for the tech scout. We're meeting at the production company with the rest of the crew members. The location we've chosen is a good 40-minute drive out of Los Angles, in a place called Hidden Valley.

A small production bus takes all of us out to the location, and everyone gets to meet one another. Already the key crew members have questions based on the shooting boards.

Once at the location, the crew is completed by the production designer and his crew, as well as the location manager. I have my first real-life look at the place. Everything is pretty much as I anticipated. One of the most important and irreversible decisions we have to make today is where to put the climbing tower. Once placed, we won't be able to move it.

Together with the DP and the gaffer, we decide on the rotation of the front of the wall with regard to the sun, as well as its placement in relationship to the house and the car. We decide that it is better to have no direct sun on the wall's frontal rock part, in order to have complete control over the light. (Fighting the sun is one of the worst situations you can be in.)

The car will be parked in a nice spot on the grass, prominently placed in front of both wall and house. Since this is a residence, the location manager makes sure that we will have wooden boards to protect the lawn over the course of the day.

The key grip's main job is to make sure he can get the camera into all those places where I want it to be, and that he can move it the way I'd like it to move. We decide on the size of the crane and the length of the dolly track.

The AD figures out where to place the trailers, generator, craft services, and video tent, which is the place where the client and agency will spend most of their time.

**CASE STUDY** *continued*

With the production designer's input, we figure out the places for all the various items, like the mountain bike trail, the canoes, a work tent for the construction site, and building materials.

Then we have a dry runthrough of the entire shoot day and line up a schedule that we think works best, taking into consideration the sunlight and the amount of moving we have to do. For example, it's a bad idea to have to move trailers and trucks with each shot. Rather than jumping around with the camera, it's much more economical to finish all shots in the same direction in one block and then swing around.

There are many factors that go into the schedule, including talent availability, which in our case could be an issue because we're working with celebrities. We decide to start out with the very first shot of the commercial, the wide shot into the sky. Early morning light should lend itself to that shot, because it actually is supposed to be early morning. Should any of the talent be late, we can put anybody into the sleeping bag, since we're not really seeing them up close. The call time will be very early, as we're trying to get the first shot at 7 a.m.

The tech scout feels like the beginning of the real production phase because you're finally at the location and making nuts-and-bolts decisions: where to put the dolly, where to put the generator, where to stage the scene, etc.

As the name implies, the scout is mainly about technical aspects. The gaffer and key grip will look at their options for rigging lights and camera platforms, laying cable, and placing equipment trucks. They also figure out if they need extra gear or can leave certain things at home.

With your shot list in hand, go through each setup or shot. Explain what happens, how the camera moves, and what you see in the background. While the AD will consider how time can be saved by shooting out of order, the gaffer will decide where he can place major lights and cable runs. The key grip will figure out what he needs to build to enable the camera to move the way you want, and the DP will add his ideas to the discussion.

The more precise you can be about the shots you want, the better for your crew. If you can show them exactly how a shot is supposed to unfold, they can prepare exactly for that. Otherwise, if they're forced to improvise, you will end up losing time on the day of the shoot.

Personally, I take pride in being prepared and letting people know how things are going to happen. More than once I have wrapped sets early, to everyone's surprise. Crew members appreciate directors who know what they want and who can make decisions, because it makes their lives much easier. More importantly, it allows you as the director to get exactly the shots you want.

## Schedule

Each shooting day follows a (usually very) tightly set schedule. Your AD is in charge of that. However, as the director, you obviously carry the responsibility for anything and everything that happens. Together with the AD, you will figure out the order in which the shots are done. The tech scout is the first step in that process. After visiting the location with your key crew members, you will have a pretty good idea of the general shot order.

The AD will sit down and hammer out a timed schedule, allowing a certain amount of time for the setup and actual shooting of each shot. He uses this schedule not only to keep things on track, but also to cut down on certain costs or to call in people only when they are really needed (and send them home when they're done).

There are a few factors the AD takes into consideration:

**First, light.** If you are shooting an exterior, you may want to shoot certain angles at certain times of the day because of the sun. The larger the space, the less feasible it is to fight the sun. The DP and the gaffer know exactly where the sun will be at a given time, and they will tell you when to shoot a certain shot. Heed their advice.

Obviously, if you are shooting night or sunset/sunrise shots, the schedule completely shifts.

**Second, story.** For actors, it is much better to shoot the story in chronological order. They will have an easier time finding their characters and going through their beats. If you start shooting the story at the end, you also lock yourself into a destination without having scouted the route. In general, it is always better to shoot in chronological order, but it hardly ever happens that way. There are always a few shots that mess things up.

**Third, setups.** The things that take the most time in production are not the actual shots. Once the camera rolls, things usually go pretty fast. The time is spent setting up shots: placing lights, rigs, camera, background, and so on. It's not uncommon to spend two hours to set up a shot and 10 minutes to shoot it. Thus, logically, you will save time if you shoot all shots in the same setup, rather than changing setups. Often, you will have three or four shots looking in the same direction. Though not strictly the same setup, they still require much less moving. The background is already clear, the lights are on the correct side, the camera is almost in the right place, and so on.

**Fourth, shoot wide shots first.** In features, they're called *masters*. There are no real masters in commercials, but there are establishing wide shots (they sometimes cover the entire scene or run long, but are hardly ever used more than once). Since you see more in a wide shot, it is generally a good idea to shoot them first, because you set up the environment for all the other shots to come. Also, you may run into weather or lighting trouble later in the day, and then it is much easier to re-create fake conditions with tighter shots than wider ones.

**Fifth, fate.** I summarize "fate" as "everything that is out of your control." A celebrity only has two hours to spend with you. A location is only available during certain hours. A client wants to be present for a certain shot, but has to leave in the afternoon. There are a myriad of things that can influence your schedule, including so-called "acts of God," like heavy rain or extreme winds.

I have found that the more you work out your schedule, the more flexible you will be when things go haywire. An actor is late. There is equipment failure or a torrential downpour. An animal doesn't feel like acting. Whatever happens, you must be able to adapt to unforeseen events. The better your prep, the easier you will find it is to change your schedule and still get what you need. The fun of production is about to start.

# Chapter 8

# Getting the Shot

The shoot day is here. This is the moment that most people associate with filmmaking: The day you get to say "action" and "cut." Yet, as you've seen already, the actual shoot is the shortest of all the phases in the production of a commercial. After a week of bidding and a week or two of preproduction, you are on the set for only 10 or 20 hours. And post production will add another two weeks at the back end.

All the more reason to really enjoy this day. Hopefully, you've done your homework during the prep. You should be ready to put a lot of the elements together and create the footage that will be the basis of the final commercial.

There is not that much difference between regular film production and commercials, except for the fact that you have the agency and client on the set. I will deal with that issue in the next chapter. For now, let's concentrate on how to get the shots you need.

# Concentrate on Your Objective

Everything is laid out for you. The crew, actors, agency, and client —everyone is looking to you for direction. It can be a daunting moment. In fact, Steven Spielberg once said that the scariest moment for him is the moment before he gets out of the car in the morning.

Stick to your schedule. You and your AD have come up with an order of shots that makes sense. You should follow it unless unforeseen things happen. In which case, you can safely deviate because you made a plan. Some people think of a schedule as a limiter. I think of it as the tool which makes it possible to get everything I need in the short time available to me.

If the schedule is well prepared, I can concentrate fully on the objective at the moment. The shot at hand is what deserves all my attention. I can't be thinking about the next dolly move, when to break for lunch, what equipment has to prepped for the next few setups, or whether we are on schedule or not.

I need to think about what's in front of the lens right this moment. My objective is to make this shot the best shot I can. Right now.

# Discover Your Approach

Each director has a different approach for creating the shot. Some have a very clear vision in their minds, all the way down to lenses, lights, colors, etc. Others approach it much more free-form. It's up to you to figure out what works best for you. But I have some tips that have proven valuable in the past.

I always start with the camera. The technical setup is usually what takes the longest. If there are major props to be readied, crowds to be gathered, or streets to be emptied, it has usually been taken care of by your AD half an hour in advance. The camera, however, and the lights, and most importantly, the creative power of your team have been focused on the last shot.

The sooner you can give them "the shot," the sooner they will be able to work with it. Thus, I start with the camera. With the DP, the production designer, and the AD in tow, I stand where the camera will be, and I show them the angle and the lens. Within a few minutes, the camera is set up, and I can actually look through the lens and see if I was right or wrong.

I adjust the placements, angle, lens, or whatever else needs adjusting. In the meantime, the DP has already started to light the shot as I see it. See, he couldn't have done this before, because there was no way for him to know what exactly he would see or where he could place stands and lights. Everything flows from the camera's location.

### Establish Your Authority

It's possible that you may run into a DP who doesn't like the fact that you've set up the shots. Usually, this happens on projects where you were forced to use the client's or agency's choice of DP. Don't be afraid of the confrontation. It is your job as the director to set up the shot because that is the most direct expression of your vision. You must stand firm on that or else be labeled as a weak director.

I will then place any necessary art direction items, particularly if it is a new setup. Someone may stand in for the talent, in order to get a better idea about sizes or movements. Slowly but surely, everything comes together. The DP needs a short time to ready the lighting and other camera issues, and often the art department requires time to add or change things on their end.

Finally, everyone is ready for the talent to come and do some runthroughs or rehearsals. Sometimes, particularly when the talent is on top of their performance, we "shoot the rehearsal"—in other words, we shoot right away. But usually there is at least one quick rehearsal, to make sure that everyone in the crew knows what's happening and where they have to be.

It's helpful to record the rehearsal on videotape so that you can watch it a few times and see things that you weren't aware of when looking through the camera. It's also good to include the agency in this process and show them what you are doing. In fact, during the setup of the shot, it often becomes necessary to walk to the video tent and coach the agency and client as to what they're seeing on the monitor. More about that in the next chapter.

# Find the Moment

In the majority of shots, you will look for one specific moment. A shot can play out for two beats or more, but usually only one of those beats is the one you are going for. This is a necessity, because in the final edit assembly, there will rarely be a shot longer than two seconds.

You should concentrate on getting that one moment right, in the shot you need it in. In fact, it's not a bad idea to make notes on your personal shooting board during the prep. I write down all kinds of notes when I previsualize the shots in my head.

## The Meat

A simple note about the "meat" of the shot is extremely helpful when you're in the heat of production. Could be something like: *Turn! Realize! Reveal. Pain.* What is the essence of that shot? The chances of being sidetracked are too great. This will remind you why you created the shot in the first place.

## The Intensity of the Performance

I may need to make sure that there is an arc in the character's performance or a build in the intensity of reactions. Thus, I need to allow the right dose of intensity at the right time. Not too much, not too little. If you want a crescendo, then make sure you spread it out over a number of shots as the story goes along. Also, if you are looking for a sudden change in emotion—even a moment of shock—this is a good place to write it down.

## Movement

Right next to the shooting board image, I tend to draw a little overhead sketch of the move I want the camera to do. This is not necessarily to remember the move, but rather so I don't have to think it through once on the set. A small visual representation tells me all I need to know from having mulled it over during my prep. Overhead drawings will ensure that your blocking is correct, particularly when you shoot out of order or jump around in setups, because you need to stay on the right side of the line—unless you choose to cross it.

## Transitions

It may be helpful to have a character or an object move in a certain way at the beginning or the end of a shot, in order to be able to cut it well. For example, I could note to have a character start his action with the closing of a car door, even though that moment is part of the shot before. The editor will be grateful for every action that connects two shots. Cutting on motion will make the edit flow.

## Variations

Often, I'll have several versions of a performance or action that I want to get for both creative and time reasons. It's a good idea to get a range of reactions, rather than pretending you know how they're going to cut later. Do a few and have more freedom in the edit. Sometimes, it's a question of being safe and getting a certain action two different ways because the client may ask for it later. ("We don't have him entering the car?") It's also good to have a shorter version of a complicated action, in case the editor runs into trouble with length.

## Various Shot Sizes

Rather than amending the shot list, I might decide to get exactly the same shot in a different size. This means putting a different lens on the camera and getting new focus marks, but it's a lot faster than creating an entirely new shot. Various shot sizes are helpful if the order of your shots gets changed around in the edit, which almost always happens. Suddenly, the cuts fall differently than you antici-pated, and you want a wider shot where you had planned a closer one. That's where the various shot sizes come in.

Back to the moment. Each shot brings a lot of questions and confusion. The more you can concentrate on the moment, the better. The DP needs to know which part of a move is the most important part, and the actor needs to be aware that it's all about that specific beat. Once you have that moment on film, you can experiment and maybe find something else that is interesting in a different way. But rather than being sidetracked from the beginning, it's good to get the "must-haves" first.

## Go with the Flow

While storytelling is all about the moments, it, of course, isn't. It's about how those moments work with each other and how they flow. A beat by itself is useless. Much like the action-reaction relationship I talked about earlier, meaning is derived from the order of those moments. (This has been distilled down to both scientific and artistic perfection by Sergei Eisenstein—look him up if you don't know the name.)

For performers, it may be hard to "find the emotion" of a moment or beat from a cold start. Virtually every actor I've ever worked with prefers to get a running start. It's a good idea, therefore, to let shots begin a moment or two earlier whenever you can. This is referred to as the *full action*.

For example, let's say a man exits his house, can't see his car, realizes it's gone, and spots a tow truck down the road with his car on the hook. This brief action—four beats—could be broken down into eight shots, including the cutaways to the empty parking spot and tow truck.

I would have the actor do the entire action, from leaving the house, closing the door, turning, and realizing that his car is gone, plus his angry reaction in each shot. Each single moment will benefit from it. Yes, you'll be using more film, but the entire action is only 20 or 30 seconds long—so why not?

This also allows you to vary your shots a bit and get different moments in different shots that you hadn't necessarily planned.

For example, in the close-up, your main focus is his reaction when he can't see his car. But since you are shooting from the moment he comes from the house, you can do a pan up from the knob when the door opens.

It's always a good idea to shoot pickups of details and close-ups. Film some variations so that you can be flexible in the editing. Some directors are famous for shooting all the time. Literally. There is a camera running *all the time*. While lights are being set up, the director is off to the side, shooting little tidbits of interest to him.

They end up shooting 10 or 20 times the amount of footage that I would. Good for them, I say. If that's their style, more power to them. As footage is directly related to cost, my producer would probably kill me. But I also feel like shooting *everything* is not really making a choice.

On the opposite side of the scale are directors who shoot exactly what they think should be in the cut, and not a bit more. There is a story about a famous director who played basketball for six hours on the single shoot day of a commercial. With two hours left, he set up the shot, filmed it three times, and the spot was done. (It was a "one-shot" commercial, where there is no cut.)

## The Voyeur Cam

One great technique I often use is *not* to let the actors know I'm rolling film. This works very well for pickups or scenes where actors are not talking. Also, kids do really well with this style of shooting. Everyone acts natural and uninhibited when they think the camera is off.

Your DP should be aware of what you are doing, although sometimes I simply sit down at the camera and roll. The problem is that you need to have the right exposure and focus set—otherwise, it's a complete waste of film. I actually have a code word that I use with some DPs so that even if they are operating the camera, we can get footage secretly.

**Reality Bites**

While shooting overnight in a drugstore, we recently needed an actor to look tired. When we began setting up for his shot, we were in our 10th hour. Everyone was tired. We noticed that the actor was rehearsing his scene while standing in for the light setup. We rolled the camera without his knowledge and got a lot of good footage, including a great yawn, which ended up in the final commercial. Because he felt unobserved, the actor behaved completely naturally and yawned without inhibitions.

Also, you need to make sure that no one is running around in the shot who isn't supposed to be there. However, once you announce what you're going for, the moment is lost.

# Beware o' the Elements

With digital post production being as powerful as it is, you often need to get "elements" for later compositing. The live footage you shoot on the set is only part of the final image, sometimes only the smallest part. More often than not, several live-action elements are combined or composited. Some of those elements you may need to shoot include the following items.

## Background Plates

If you need to "paint out" or remove things like wires, stands, rigs, or even trees, it's a good idea to get the information of what's behind those objects on film. For example, if you have a person suspended on a wire (which is to be removed), you also need to get the same shot as a still, without any action and without any of the talent in it. This is often called "getting a clean shot." If the compositor has the background information, then he doesn't have to re-create it.

## Head Work

We were working on a scene once in which a group of five people were standing in an office kitchen. With his fingers, another worker was "squeezing" the head of one of his coworker's in his imagination. Finally, the coworker's head exploded spilling blood over everyone. This wide shot was actually composed of four layers: an empty background plate, the coworker falling on a stunt pillow after his head "exploded," the group of workers around him and a contraption that spurted blood from the falling coworker's position, and finally, the hand in the foreground, which was shot separately on green screen.

In post, the contraption was removed and replaced with the falling coworker. The head was "squeezed" and exploded (the background filled in from the empty plate), the stunt pillow was removed, and the hand was added in the foreground and with perfect timing. Finally, the entire composited shot was animated to look like it was shot handheld (see Figures 8.1-8.4).

8.1

**Figures 8.1-8.4**
These four frames are all from the same shot. The shot is composed of four separate layers. Where the hero stands, a special effects designer has been painted out (he was operating the blood-squirting machine), and where the hero falls, a stunt pillow has been removed.

8.2

8.3

8.4

## Moving Objects

It is always advisable to shoot small, fast-moving objects as separate elements. For example, if the camera follows a ball that is being thrown, you may want to suspend the ball from a wire, and rotate and shoot it in front of a green screen or a blue sky. This way the compositor can later use the ball and animate it exactly where and when you want it in the commercial.

### The Magic of Digital Post Production

On another occasion, we were filming a very complicated shot: A man was jumping out of a Cessna without a parachute. The shot I wanted was this: We see our hero crouched in the Cessna, then he steps forward and jumps out of the plane, while the camera looks after him as he plummets toward the ground. The hero was wearing a plain white shirt, so we could not hide any parachutes. Also, the actor was not going to jump himself. Instead, we would have to replace him with a stunt double. We rehearsed the jump on the ground so that the motions and body postures of the two men would match.

The first part of the shot we filmed while the plane was sitting on the tarmac. The actor crouched, stepped forward, and jumped out of the plane (see Figures 8.5 and 8.6).

**Figures 8.5 and 8.6**
These two frames were shot on the ground with the actor. A wind machine, hands on the fuselage, and appropriate camera movement sufficiently created the feeling and atmosphere of a plane in flight.

8.6

The second part we filmed with the stunt double in the air. The plane was too small to accommodate more than three passengers (and we would see the back of the plane, which would have to be empty), so I was operating the camera myself. Sitting on the threshold of the plane's open door, I filmed the stunt double, who was wearing a parachute over his white shirt and dark pants. I was also filming at 100 frames per second. On my hand signal (it was too loud to shout), the double did the action and jumped. I panned with him and managed to catch him falling off and away from the plane into the distance.

In post production, the compositor began the painstaking process of removing the parachute frame by frame. He created a new, clean background plate from the material on film, and used that to fill in the gaps where the parachute had been (see Figures 8.7-8.10). The result was an incredible shot and one of the most fun setups I've ever done.

8.7

8.8

**Figures 8.7-8.10**
This sequence was shot in the air. The stunt double was actually
wearing a parachute over his clothes, which was removed
frame-by-frame in post production.

**Figures 8.9-8.10**
Stunt double photos, continued.

## Different Exposures

In mixed-light situations or with car shoots, you may want to shoot a scene (or a background plate) at a different exposure to gain access to all the light sources. Imagine a sunset scene with a car in front of a motel. There are neon lights on the motel, there are some lights on the car, and the sunlight is quickly fading. It would be nearly impossible to balance all the light sources perfectly. Instead, shoot several exposures: Get the perfect exposure for the car, the perfect exposure for the sky, and the perfect exposure for the motel's neon lights. In post, you can composite them (if the shot is still, it's extremely simple) and create a perfectly exposed image. You may even want to shoot the car at several exposures (or frame rates if the light is too low) to bring out details like rims or black tires.

## Logo Backgrounds

Very often you will find yourself composing a shot that will be used later as a background or base layer for a logo shot. It's hard to imagine what the final image will look like with a graphic superimposed, so make sure you think about it beforehand. You may need to leave some empty space, be it through color or brightness. Here, as well, it is a good idea to shoot a variety of sizes and framings. Each of the plates should be about 10 seconds long, so that you're not wasting film by shooting more versions.

In general, it's a good rule not to limit yourself. The absolutely final image will be put together in post production, and you need to be flexible for all eventualities. You can always move the image slightly, or even zoom in later. Particularly for effects shots or for those compositions you know will be worked on later (sky replacement, removal of wires or rigs), it's mandatory to shoot a locked-off version so that the compositing artist has as much material as he needs.

## Listen to the Experts

As in all areas of filmmaking, you should be listening to the experts when it comes to such specialized areas as digital effects. Some of the preceding examples are part of a director's normal tool kit and will eventually come to be second nature as you grow and gain more experience. But as soon as effects enter a more complicated realm, you should have preproduction meetings with the effects house, and you should have a specialist on the set. Otherwise, all you'll be creating is trouble for later.

# The Atmosphere

A film set is a creative mill. Individual creative inputs are combined into one creative output. In general, people tend to be more creative when the mood and the atmosphere on the set are positive and open. This doesn't mean there should be anarchy. No one but the director has creative say. But the director constantly accepts creative input, whether he likes it or not, simply by virtue of having 100 people working for him.

Each individual crew member has a certain amount of influence on the project and the director, and, in essence, makes sure that the overall direction stays true to his vision.

A whole other story is the creative input from the agency and client. Again, more about this in the next chapter.

### Circuit of Communication

On a recent set in a foreign country, we had a sound system play music whenever work was going on. Apparently, that's the way they always do it. We also used the sound system to "direct" the set, rather than shouting. On most sets in the States, you will see several closed radio systems—one for each department. The key crew members are in constant contact with their crews, and everything happens in a very disciplined and organized manner.

Some directors rule by intimidation. Personally, I don't like screamers, and I can't imagine how anyone could enjoy working for or with them. Apparently, to some agencies and clients, a director needs to be a crazy, arrogant artist who is full of himself and untouchable. There is a difference between defending your vision and being impossible to work with, at least in my opinion.

I take pride in well-run, positive, friendly, and open sets where each crew member feels like they can talk to me. I try to shake everyone's hand, which is almost always impossible. I try to thank everyone for their hard work at the end of the day—equally impossible. But you get the idea.

## CASE STUDY

### Shoot Day

My alarm goes off at 4:30 a.m. I'm still jetlagged, so it's not too bad. My DP, Aaron Barnes, will pick me up at 5 a.m. for the 45-minute drive to the location. I take only a few items because I tend to lose things easily: cell phone, shooting board with notes, rain gear, sun gear (shades, hat, sunscreen), and that's it. We have to be prepared for all kinds of weather, even though the forecast says sun.

The last few days it has rained like crazy, though, which is a problem already. The lawn is drenched and soft, which presents a huge problem not only for equipment, but also may prevent us from being allowed to drive the car on the grass. At least the air will be clear.

On the drive out, we catch up on family and friends because we haven't really had any time to chat since I've been back.

We arrive in complete darkness. The parking and breakfast staging area is in a horse corral down the hill from the location. It's very dark, and people stagger around in the dirt to get some coffee. It's also freezing cold, being January. Everyone is wrapped up in down jackets.

I can't really eat this early anyway, so I grab a coffee, saying hello to a few people. Then I jump into the minibus that shuttles everyone up and down to the location. On the bus, I happen to sit down next to Paul DiMeo, one of our cast members.

I introduce myself, and we chat for a bit. We discover that we have some common friends. He seems like a great guy, and we hit it off well.

CASE STUDY *continued*

On the location, I climb into the production trailer, while Paul is off to the makeup trailer. John Quinn, the producer, is there and updates me on the status. So far, everything is good.

We want to be ready for a 7 a.m. sunrise shot—the first shot of the commercial. I walk across the set to look at the final rendition of the climbing wall. It looks ominous in the dark. I almost can't see the top of it. The surface looks great; so good, in fact, that I'm surprised it doesn't feel like cold rock at all.

Aaron and his core crew are already talking through the setup. My AD appears, and one by one the entire crew joins us. Everyone has had breakfast, and we get going. The camera is being built, the generator's fired up, and cables are laid out.

By 6.30 a.m., we are very close to being able to shoot, but Ed Sanders, the second climber, has not yet been sighted. He has called in by phone to report that his limo driver has no clue where he is going. The production crisis center shifts into high gear. The option is to use someone else in the rig, since we won't be able to see their faces here anyway.

Meanwhile, the wardrobe designer has clothed Paul, and I head over to the trailer to check it out. The agency is there already. We quickly agree on the outfit, and I explain the situation with Ed. No sweat. No panic. We're good.

Fortunately, the agency had arrived in Los Angeles two days earlier, and we'd already met over dinner.

6:50 a.m. Ed arrives. Quickly, we approve his wardrobe and get him and Paul into the rig on the wall. At 7:10 a.m., we shoot. Already 10 minutes behind schedule. The first shot is always the hardest to get because so many cogs in the machine have to get oiled. Once you're going, you're going.

We film shot-by-shot as the day grows warmer and warmer. Jackets come off, the mood rises, the schedule calms down. Ed and Paul, as well as Paige, who has a later call time, are fantastic to work with. No prima donnas.

CASE STUDY *continued*

As we had anticipated, we are no longer allowed to drive the car onto the grass because of the rain. I have to change the blocking of the shots at the end—effectively turning around the last shot by 180 degrees. Besides that, everything runs nice and smoothly.

The guys deliver a great, natural performance. Ed comes up with a line when Paul hands him the bottle: "You're a legend." We all love it, and it ends up in the cut.

The rig looks great and completely believable. The art crew has done an amazing job. We have two real-life climbers on the set who are in charge of hanging the platform and securing our talent. They're on top of it.

Ed does a great job fumbling the bottle. Paul's timing is impeccable.

The falling-bottle shot works great. In a few takes, the bottle hits the Plexiglas right at the center of the lens.

The agency and the client are happy. During the shoot, I'm in constant communication with them. We talk things through, approve shots, and decide which takes are our favorites.

Finally, at 4:30 p.m., we wrap half an hour early. We've got everything in the can. The weather was nice to us, and there were no major setbacks. It's a wrap.

# Chapter 9

# Working with the Agency—Dealing with the Client

The major difference between commercial productions and film projects is that the people who have the ultimate say are constantly on the set, watching every take you shoot or sipping cappuccinos. It's both a curse and a blessing. To be honest, the majority of agency producers, creatives, and clients I've worked with have been great people who gave me all the freedom and space I needed, while keeping an eye on what they wanted. In fact, a number of spots have greatly profited from their input on the set. And why not? The creatives came up with the original idea, and you should be on the same page anyway.

That said, I've also heard horrible suggestions from both clients and agencies. When that happens, you'd better have something diplomatic to say. Sometimes, you can defer the issue to a later time —by which time the person has hopefully forgotten about it. But I'm getting ahead of myself.

## Know Your Place

You have been dealing with the client and working with the agency since preproduction started. Hopefully, there is somewhat of a working relationship with the agency. The more back-and-forth conversation that takes place, usually the better the mood is. The client or clients you will have met at the PPM. That was your first and only impression of him or them, except for the stories the agency has told you.

It's important to remember that the client is the one who pays your fee. He is the one who pays for the production. The commercial is—if anyone's—his. You can hope that the client trusts his agency and—by extension—you. However, the client has a vested and completely justified interest in the commercial, which may or may not be aligned with your objectives 100 percent.

As much as you want to be an artist, free to pursue your vision, you are also a service provider, a craftsman, and a hired gun. You are not on the set for your own sake or to make the epic of the century (which you've been planning since age six).

Thus, you have a responsibility to the client and the agency and, in fact, everyone working with or for you on the entire production. You must always remember that in the grand scheme of things, the commercial director is replaceable. There are hundreds who could do the job just as well.

The reason you are on the set in the first place is because someone is trying to sell a product. It's not your self-realization project.

I've repeatedly said that you should see the agency as your partner in the creation of the spot. They are very creative people and have good ideas. Work with them, include them, and haul them into the boat, every step of the process.

The client, on the other hand, could be a creative person but may not be creative in the art of filmmaking. Or advertising. He could be incredibly innovative when it comes to leading a company. But most of the time, his ideas for the commercial are bad because they come from a different creative basis.

## Flexible Passion

Joe Murray, a veteran commercial director, says this about his relationship with the agency and client:

*It's about being honest. And there is that fine line...you have to be passionate about it, about your ideas. But not inflexible. Go in with a shared point of view. The art director and the copywriter and you are a team. If the client doesn't like an idea, it's incumbent on you to try to sell what you are doing, or you have to figure out if there is a shift going on. You've got to make it work; you can't let the agency fall on its face.*

*You see, we're dispensable. We're the ones who take the beach. You have to be a politician. You're not on the set for yourself. You're there to sell a product. A lot of what we do is craft, not art. What we do is a tool, it's utilitarian. The agency world is the exact opposite of our world; we live and die by our own sins. There is a lot of insecurity and fear on the agency side.*

*There is also an abundance of people who have an enormous appetite and a minimum of taste. Not many creative people. They have no passion for the medium or the art form.*

*But you have to cultivate relationships, learn stuff and cooperate, grow together, and then you will have a rewarding experience.*

A client usually knows nothing about filmmaking, just as you probably know nothing about manufacturing cars or writing insurance policies. Thus, it is part of your job to make the client feel safe about what is happening. See, companies invest lots of money in commercial campaigns. They're taking a risk, and the more you can comfort them on a very personal level, the better.

As I've said, you've already met the client at the PPM. It is possible that the client (or more likely the clients) will be on the set. The hierarchy on a film set, which flows from the director down to every single crew member, is there for a reason. It is to ensure that the director's vision is realized and that the production runs as smoothly as possible.

## Dealing with Ego

Once I had a very ugly situation happen. There were more clients than usual because it was a cross-promotion (several clients pitched in money). It was a sports celebrity shoot, and one of the clients considered himself a buddy of the players. Close to the end of the shooting day, we were rushing to get a shot before the sun disappeared. One of the players had to perform in front of the camera and, being "cool," he kept breaking into laughs and giggles.

Early on (this was the fourth shooting day), I'd figured out that I had to send everyone away from the set and out of this player's eye line if I wanted a usable performance. So before I even started, I told everyone to go get coffee, except those crew members who were absolutely necessary.

Simultaneously, the agency, with good intentions, had sent that client to support that player while he was on camera. That, however, put the player in a very bad spot. He now had to perform in front of someone he knew and had to impress him. Plus, the client had to be "cool" and was laughing along with the player. All of this was costing us serious time, because take after take, the celebrity broke into laughter.

Then I finally noticed that the client had come to the set, so I told him to go back to the tent, because I had just sent everyone else away. The client (I'll call him "D") and I had become friendly during the first few shooting days and had had pleasant conversations. In fact, he was trying to vie for my respect, just as much as for the players'.

So off he went. We shot the scene quickly and continued working, when suddenly my producer came up and said, "You have to talk to D. He is pissed." I didn't quite understand. Then the agency producer came and said, "You better talk to D., man, he is not happy." I was flabbergasted. What had I done? Well, it turned out that when D. got back to the tent, all the *other* players were mocking him because he had screwed up the takes. As soon as we wrapped, the client jumped into the shuttle and was gone.

The next shooting day, D. didn't show up for the longest time. Finally, after lunch, I saw him and walked up. "Hey D., sorry if I was a little hard on you yesterday, but he just couldn't get that shot right as long as anyone was there, and I had just sent everyone else down. It was a misunderstanding that the agency sent you up."

> I thought I'd done pretty well there. I'd taken the blame, although I didn't really think I was hard on him at all. I was just trying to get the shot done before the sun disappeared. Well, D. freaked and told me that he was "not amused," and that he was embarrassed in front of the players. After all, he was paying serious money for this spot, so he deserved respect.
>
> I apologized again and walked off. In fact, he had just lost all my respect by demanding it in exchange for money. This is a good example of how things can go when there are factors at play that you do not control. The agency realized its mistake and sort of apologized to me, but never made it an issue with the client.

The agency and client obviously take a special place on a set. They watch everything that happens and make comments. They have concerns, remarks, and ideas. They're not part of the crew, but they have an influence on the production.

For example, you don't want them to talk to the actors. You will not believe how often clients have expressed very specific wishes as to how an actor should say a certain line. It will happen to you, I promise.

*He says it like he doesn't like it.*

*Can he say it with more happiness?*

*His mouth looks strange when he says it.*

*I don't believe him at all.*

*Can he smile when he sees the car crash?*

That last line is a direct quote. A car insurance client wanted the actor to smile when he saw his daughter in a car crash, because in his mind, people should be happy that they have that specific car insurance—apparently, no matter what happens. It took a while to convince him that it would be a completely unrealistic reaction from a father seeing his child in a car accident.

**Misunderstanding Brand**

During a PPM, a brand manager once suggested that all colors on the set should be the colors of the product. After all, the colors of the product would then always be in the background and push the brand into people's minds. He completely neglected the fact that the colors of the product were pink, yellow, and red, and that they wouldn't work in the room, which was designed to be a calm, soothing, and tranquil environment.

Never let the client or even the agency talk directly to your cast. (In fact, no one on the set should talk to your cast except you, but your crew members already know this and need no reminding.) All they will do is confuse the actors and say things that are completely ridiculous and impossible. Any good creative will tell the director what he thinks and leave it to the director to translate it to the actor.

Hopefully, you have a producer worth his money. He will coach the agency and client and make sure that the information flows in the right direction. Or even better, you should act preemptively and constantly touch base with the agency yourself by walking over to wherever they are watching the shoot from. Remember that you and the agency are a team. Keep them in the loop so that misunderstandings won't occur. Once they come to you, they are in *your* working space. If you go to them, you can have conversations out of everybody else's—particularly the cast's—earshot.

## Video Village

Somewhere on the set there is an area which is sometimes referred to as the *video village* (or *video tent* if it's outside). There are a number of comfortable chairs aligned around a monitor, which alternately shows the camera video tap feed or the playback.

A quick discourse into video tap for those who are not familiar with it.

The camera has a built-in video tap, which records the image that is being filmed. To be technically correct, there is a rotating mirror —called the shutter—behind the lens, which alternately permits light to be exposed on film or the same light to be sent to the eyepiece. While the light is being sent to the eyepiece, the film is advanced so that the next frame can be exposed.

The same light that reaches the eyepiece also reaches the video tap. Thus, what your eye or the video tap sees does not actually end up on film. Usually, the time differences are so minimal that the images are pretty much the same. However, when you are shooting flashes or muzzle fire (things that possibly are shorter than one frame), you should know that what's on video is not on film.

The video tap, essentially, is like a live feed of what the camera sees. This is good while you are shooting. The agency and the client can see what is being shot live. Yet there are certain drawbacks. The image on the video tap is not "clean." It is a grainy, sometimes even black-and-white video picture taken through the ground glass. The ground glass is the framing device that is built into the camera (think of frame lines and crosshairs in the middle). Also, as soon as the camera runs, you can "feel" the shutter (mirror) rotating, and the brightness is decreased by half. Thus, the image is also darker.

Why is all that important? For three reasons.

## Never Light According to the Monitor

First, both the client and agency—particularly when they're not experienced in TV—will comment on the picture quality while looking at a horrible representation of the final image. They will remark that they can't see certain things because it's dark, or that the colors are too bright or too desaturated, or that things seem out of focus. From their viewpoint, that is perfectly justified. And you can easily explain it:

*You're not seeing the final image here.*

*I know it looks a bit dark, but this is just because of the video tap.*

*The colors here are not representative of the final look.*

*It's grainy here and soft. The final image will be crisp and beautiful.*

Quite honestly, it's sometimes good to use this argument, even if it is not the video tap. This is particularly true when you think an idea is bad, or if you know that you will adjust it later (in telecine). Just blame the bad video tap quality. Most of the time, you are right anyway. Yet it works even better if the image on the monitor looks good! Then you can point out that this is just the beginning. The final image will far surpass even the beautiful image on the monitor.

However, be prepared for unjustified comments—simply because clients don't know any better, and they are concerned. That is their right and duty.

## Less Is More

The second reason why video tap plays such an important role is that usually it's always "on." The clients and agency will see a live picture when the camera is being moved, the lighting is being set up, the actors are finding their marks, and so on. Often enough, a client or agency person will get a weird idea or a wrong impression from something he sees in a shot that is not completely composed or set up. This is particularly true when your camera moves. The client looks at position one—which may be completely different from the "meat" of the shot—and grows concerned.

Rather than having to explain away things that have lodged them-selves firmly in the client's head, I opt to prevent any opportunity for him to see something that is not finished. I shut it off. The video operator usually has a simple way—pulling the cable works well—to stop the signal from reaching the client's monitor. This way I can control at what point the video village sees an image.

## Roll Tape, Hal

Finally, video tap is used for playback. This is an important part of your job on the set. You are expected to watch replays with the agency and talk about the shots, critique them, and accept input.

## Pull the Plug

I once worked with a particularly inexperienced creative who had literally no clue when it came to film production. We were setting up a long dolly move when he came running to me, all in a panic. He wanted to know why I was showing what I was showing and why it was looking so boring. I looked at him in complete confusion because I couldn't even fathom what he was talking about.

We finally figured it out, and I told him to wait until we were done setting up, at which point I would sit down with him and explain the entire shot. He was finally consoled when he saw the finished product, but from then on, I had the monitors switched off as much as I could.

I tend to shoot a few takes and then walk over to the video village to look at those takes with the agency and the client. I may already be happy with what we've got, or I may just be trying to get a feel for what my clients think.

Often, the agency will ask you to shoot alternate versions of a shot. That's okay, as long as it doesn't develop into an "endless alternatives day." It also depends on whether you are going to be part of the editing process or not. If you have no input during editing, you may want to shoot in a way that limits versions you don't think will work.

During playback I also have a chance to look at every detail a few times. I decide for myself whether I'm satisfied with the take. There is usually no way to come back at a later time and shoot something again. So I'd better get it right the first time around.

On a lot of sets these days, the playback is no longer on videotape. The footage is digitized on the operator's laptop and can be replayed instantly. Also, you can actually edit certain shots and see how they fit. Once I actually edited almost the entire spot over the lunch break (of course, it's low image quality because of the video tap).

Particularly when you are working with effects, the digital playback comes in very handy. You can do simple chroma keys on it and overlay images quite easily. Additionally, the operator will often print out key frames, which are then taped next to the shot on the large board that carries your shooting board.

## The Attack of the Bad Idea

So what do you do if a client or agency person comes up with a bad idea? Well, don't tell him it's bad. In fact, you should probably tell him it's great, but not *right*. At least not at that very moment. Or not in the kind of spot you're doing. Not in that kind of story. Under different circumstances, it would be right. But not now.

This is a soft letdown. Whoever came up with the bad idea can save face, knowing that he had a "great" idea.

Or you can defer the idea. For example, "That's a good idea, but not right now." "This shot is about something else." "Keep it in mind for later; hold that thought for that shot we'll shoot in about five hours." Chances are that the idea has taken care of itself by then. This technique, by the way, also works very well for actors who, though well-meaning, sometimes come up with horrific ideas for their characters. Defer it for later.

By the way, when dealing with actors, it's not about upsetting the person who paid for the commercial. Rather, you need to make sure that they don't fall into that dark hole of insecurity that besets every actor once he emotionally opens himself up. It is very easy to have an actor lose confidence in himself, and that's why his ideas are always good. Just not right.

Another option is to shoot the idea—if only once and quickly—to satisfy the client's demands. This may be the path of least resistance, but it will also make the director look a little weak. Particularly if everyone realizes that the idea is bad.

For those few moments that get testy, you need to remember that the client pays for the spot and has the right to be treated nicely and with respect. It may feel like you have to explain things a dozen times—even the most basic cinematic concepts. I can't tell you how often I've had to explain that it's on purpose that we don't see an actor's face when we're shooting over his shoulder. He will get his close-up in a moment.

But as I said earlier, it's not their craft; they are not filmmakers. Yet, they have their own agenda, their own tastes, and their own way of looking at things.

You can see that the presence of the agency and client on the set can lead to tricky situations. You should work hard to prevent them because they will inhibit your ability to shoot. A good producer will do his part and play babysitter/buffer.

Luckily, most clients and agency folks are great people who are wonderful to work with. In fact, I rarely enjoy being anywhere else than a set. And, of course, there are a lot of agency creatives who you can tell that their idea isn't that good. It all depends on the relationship you've built with them.

## Juggling Egos

On another occasion, we had an agency creative who had just been promoted from art director to creative director. However, his forte was print, colors, and still photography, not film. He kept walking onto the set and rearranging props, in this case, vegetables. We were dealing with a close-up of the product—cheese—and had it laid out among a variety of greens, tomatoes, and fruits.

The creative kept moving veggies around, although we had a food stylist to do that. But the creative insisted that the tomato needed to be "in dialogue" with the lettuce and left us all shaking our heads. His ideas were pretty bad as well; the client finally came to me and said just to ignore the creative.

That put me in a very bad spot. On one hand, the client was the boss, and I would have loved to simply ignore the creative. On the other hand, the creative was part of the team, and ignoring him would lead to certain conflict. Luckily, my producer handled things really well and watched my back. It came down to a testy moment when the client and I talked about something, and the creative came running up, demanding to know what we were talking about. Again, I was the one who had to apologize for breaking the protocol.

# Be Part of the Solution

So how do you deal with a seemingly insurmountable conflict that has stopped all filming? These happen. I'm talking about the kind of conflict that is far more than a change to a line of dialogue or a piece of wardrobe. Sometimes, clients ask for changes that cannot be done.

A lot of it is about dealing with human emotions and egos. Very often when a problem arises, it doesn't really have all that much substance. Rather, you are suddenly at the center of a much larger conflict, one that started weeks or even months ago when completely unrelated issues in a company caused one person not to like another. Or back when the agency stood firm on something and upset some midlevel manager, who now has risen to a higher position and thinks it's payback time.

---

### Late Hit

I once had to deal with a newly hired marketing manager, who thought he had to change things to justify his position. I had done four prior spots for the same clients, all with great success. But in the PPM, the new guy chose to argue with me over a quite ridiculous point where everyone else agreed with me. He was alone in his stance and finally had to agree that I was right. However, this apparently upset him so much that during the bidding for the next job, we were told that the marketing manager no longer wanted me to be in the pitch. He said that I wasn't "able to listen."

---

Sometimes, these conflicts are fresh. They may even have started that very morning with the first shot when one of the clients didn't feel like he was being listened to. In any case, old wounds or new, you are in the middle. Your objective is to keep the commercial going, to continue shooting, to finish the project, and to deliver something that can go on air.

Very often you won't be able to do anything about the problem itself.

*Why is the car green? I thought we had a red car?*

*I don't like that actress. I just don't like her.*

*This location doesn't fit with our brand.*

*I don't think the concept works.*

There is little you can do to fix it without investing money and time—perhaps even moving the shoot. But these things happen, because in preproduction, people weren't listening, or they purposely wanted someone or something to run aground. It's very political.

---

### Agency Insecurity

On a commercial for a major retailer, I was working with an agency that had just won the account. The agency owner himself had written the commercial and was on set to oversee the production. His specialties, however, were hard-selling, shot-on-video testimonials of the worst kind. The kind of spot that has bad acting, bad lighting, and on-the-nose dialogue.

The commercial he had written for the retailer was a nice father-son story told in images—a complete departure from his usual work. Once we started shooting, however, the creative became uneasy. This kind of spot wasn't his territory. Finally, he decided that the actors should talk and praise the product and all its features. Exactly the opposite of what we wanted to do, but exactly what he had done all his advertising life. We hadn't even cast the actors for talking roles. I had no idea whether they could speak! I had to change my shots, and we had to hire a sound mixer. The agency creative changed the entire concept, and we ended up with a weaker spot.

---

As the director, it's probably better to stay out of the political stuff and be part of the solution instead.

*It's totally okay for the car to be green. It looks much better in front of the red brick buildings.*

*I think it's alright for the audience to feel a little antipathy for the actress because that's her role.*

*The spot really is about the people more than the location. I intend to shoot a lot of close-ups and concentrate on the faces, rather than the surroundings.*

You can see that it's a lot about talking. If the client doesn't like the concept, then what can you do about it? Unfortunately, in these situations, you are often reduced to offering alternatives.

# Extracurricular Activities

This may seem like a weird headline, but it's important. The commercial industry is an industry that runs on personal relationships. Thus, social events are very important. Every time you are working on a commercial, you will have dinner with the agency several times. You may have dinner with the client.

A lot depends on whether you are on location in a faraway country or shooting locally. If the agency and the client all live in Los Angeles, and you are shooting on a studio lot in Hollywood, everyone's lives will continue as normal.

But figure shooting on some island in the Caribbean, or in Capetown or Buenos Aires. You may all stay at the same hotel, and there is little escape. Even if the agency is in your town, they may expect to be taken out and shown around.

It's the production company's job to entertain clients and the agency to some degree. In fact, some creatives are known to enjoy that sort of treatment and choose their production partners accordingly. This reaches from outlet shopping malls to the best restaurants in town to the trendiest clubs. Nothing is out of bounds in these cases.

As the director, you are free to partake in these activities, whatever they may be. It is probably a good idea to participate in a few of them and stay clear of a lot of others. Dinners and drinks with the agency are almost mandatory, whereas late nightclub outings are purely on a volunteer basis.

Then again, it's a good thing to find common ground, particularly with agency folks. It could be a shared passion for a hobby or the same taste in restaurants or music that gets you to like each other.

## Check Out the Locations!

Once I was invited by a production company to visit their country in order to take a look at the locations available for shooting. A lot of service production companies do this sort of marketing, where they invite people in order to get their business. It was a great trip with a lot of wonderful experiences. For some reason, though, the producer thought he had to take me to a strip club—he said that directors usually enjoyed this place. It's not only the agency and clients who have special demands, apparently.

Once you've played videogames with a creative for four hours, your relationship has expanded beyond cooperation on a commercial.

These relationships should be built with an eye toward the future. Junior-level copywriters will climb the ladder. An art director may be promoted to creative director next year. You never know where people will go. One of my best contacts was a copywriter at a small agency when I met him. In the course of three years, he moved to a new agency as a creative director, and then to the next agency as the executive creative director.

This kind of networking doesn't only happen on jobs—it's a year-round thing at social events that are industry-related. Awards shows, festivals, and even specific networking events are all great places to meet people and make contacts. In Los Angeles and New York, the AICP has regular screenings and parties. Obviously, the Clio Awards show is always a good place to be, particularly if you are a winner.

Internationally, the single best place to make contacts is clearly the Cannes Lions Festival in the south of France. It's a week of partying, food, commercials, and extravaganzas. Even if you are merely short-listed there, everyone will want to talk to you.

CASE STUDY

## On-Set Etiquette

On the Ford project, the work process with the agency was very easy and productive. From the beginning, I liked their concept, and I also had the feeling that they liked my ideas. Throughout preproduction, Chris and Matt, the creatives, were very clear in their vision and open to mine.

During the shoot, it always takes a moment to get the flow of how the cooperation will actually unfold. In the beginning, John Quinn kept shuttling back and forth between the video village and my current position. As the day progressed, Chris and Matt felt more and more comfortable walking up to me and making comments. Being the professionals they are, they needed to figure out whether I was approachable or not.

We bounced ideas back and forth freely, which is always the best way to do it. Kelly, the agency producer, stayed mostly at the video village with the clients and voiced his demands when appropriate. His concerns were mainly forward-looking safety issues—the kind of foresight you acquire with experience. He would ask for one shot where Paige entered the car and one without. He would ask for an alternative lens when the car was being shot. He would ask for a pickup when he thought it would be helpful for post. In short, he made sure that his client was going to be happy, and that all possible elements that might be needed in post were shot.

The clients—and there were quite a few, both from Ford and ABC Television—were unanimously cooperative and almost inconspicuous. There were brief suggestions when I was at the village tent, but the trust in the agency and their choice of director was strong enough not to have major discussions break out.

By the way, if you are shooting with celebrities—as was the case in this project—it is a huge help if *they* are on your side. It's difficult for anyone to speak up against a celebrity. I've had this experience a few times, shooting with famous actors and sports celebrities. All it takes is for the star to slap my shoulder and say, "That's a great idea!", and the discussion is over. If you earn their trust, they will be your strongest allies possible.

# CHAPTER 10

# THE DIRECTOR'S CUT

The shoot is over. You're now officially in post production. Post production rivals preproduction in both length and intensity. It very much depends on the project, but a two-week post schedule for a two-day shoot is not unusual. However, the director may not even be involved in the post production at all. Post is very much agency territory. Very often, you will see that the agency itself takes care of the entire post process. It's not part of your budget, and you're not expected to participate in it.

---

**Follow-Through**

Here is what Tor Myhren has to say about directors in post production:

*I will only work with directors who want to stay involved in post production. For a director to shoot some film and then walk away, it shows me that that person really doesn't care. Would a feature film director shoot a movie and hand it over to the studio and post house and say, "All right guys, go make it great. I'll see you at the world premiere?" No. Would a great photographer allow a retoucher to manipulate his photo unassisted? Never. I think the director owes it to the job and to him/herself to follow the job through.*

---

However, because of the explosion of storytelling commercials and the simultaneous (though not necessarily combined) increase in visual effects, more and more directors are being invited, if not required, to take part in the post production. For storytelling and dialogue commercials, it makes a lot of sense to have the director there to see his vision through to the end. For effects-heavy spots, only the director can guide the effects artists through his vision (and this can take months). But when you're dealing with product shot-driven spots or action car commercials, the director's input is not as necessary.

It is pretty common, though, that the director does the director's cut, which is the best rendition of his vision and hopefully the commercial. This is not like the director's cut of a feature film, which is usually much longer than the original version. The commercial director's cut has to be in the right time frame and fulfill all the necessary requirements. There may be a version of the commercial that you cut for your reel. That is also referred to as the director's cut, and it can be, and usually is, longer than the on-air version.

---

## Strike the Balance

Here is agency producer John van Osdol's answer to the question of whether or not he wants the director involved in post:

*Absolutely. The director is part of the expanded creative team. The director should be involved with seeing his vision through to the end. This works best when the director truly understands the balance of art and commerce within advertising to ensure that the final ad communicates the message well and actually sells. Many directors can get frustrated during post because of the many compromises that can occur (longer product shot, anyone?), usually shorting the "art" portion of the balance. However, a director's passion can have wide influence, and can help continue the evolution of the creative through to the finish.*

In general, you can divide post production into the offline phase and the online phase. *Offline* simply means that you are not working with final-quality footage. Not only are you working with roughly transferred dailies, but also with footage that is often highly compressed from low-quality videotape. *Online* means that you are compiling the images for the final product—the master tape that will actually go on air.

---

### Project by Project

Agency producer Kelly Trudell has this to say about the director's involvement in post:

*It really depends on the project. Usually, I do want the director's input on the post. However, it sometimes depends on where we do the post work and the schedule. Occasionally, the timing of a project won't allow it. And, of course, a heavy effects project typically requires the director to see it through from start to finish.*

---

The differences are that in offline you work with a whole lot more footage, which translates into higher costs—meaning more film-to-tape transfer, more disk space for editing, and more hours to log. The machines used, however, are much cheaper than in online. The focus in offline is the *edit*.

In online, the focus is to finalize that edit in its highest image quality and with all the elements from different sources. More about that in the next chapter. In this chapter, I will describe the process through the director's cut, simply because that is where the director may check out and the agency takes over.

## The Lab

In post production, many processes run simultaneously. Post starts with the wrap of production. While everyone else is going home to catch some rest, the 2nd assistant cameraman, the loader, or some underpaid production assistant is off to the lab to drop off the film for processing.

## Captain EO

The loader, or whoever else is in charge of the film and magazines, carries a great responsibility. Any mistake in loading might not be visible, under some circumstances, until the film is developed and transferred. In other words, the shoot is long done, and the negative may be unusable.

During my time in film school, an AC once loaded an Eclaire magazine incorrectly—the film had the emulsion side out (which means the stock ran through the camera normally, except that the side exposed to the light was not light-sensitive, but rather opaque). He did that for the entire shoot, thinking that he was loading it correctly. After development, all they had was black film. Ever since, that AD's nickname has been Captain EO—for Emulsion Out.

If you are shooting on film (and most commercials are shot on 35mm), then your film negative has to be developed in a lab. This process runs automatically, and you usually don't have to think twice about it. However, there are certain techniques that you can use to change and enhance the look of your footage. Be careful, though, as these techniques may not be reversible. Once you have treated the negative, the process cannot be undone. A safer option is to re-create the same effect digitally, although any purist will tell you that it is simply not the same. If you are considering any of these techniques, it is advisable to shoot tests and work in close cooperation with the lab.

## Push Processing

In push processing, the film's development time is increased. The negative travels longer through the chemical bath, thus resulting in greater density. This is generally used to correct underexposed footage, but it also results in a grainier look, which may be a creative choice.

## Pull Processing

Pull processing is pretty much the opposite of push. If film is over-exposed, it can be developed for a shorter time than usual and thus reduce the overexposure. However, you also lose contrast.

## Skip Bleach/Bleach Bypass

The film stock contains silver, which is removed in the laboratory in a process called *bleach*. If this process is skipped or reduced, some of the silver is retained, resulting in a specific look called *skip bleach* or *bleach bypass*. The result is that the contrast is increased, and the colors are desaturated. While this process can be used in several stages of film production (negative, intermediate positive, duplicate negative, final print, or a combination of these stages), commercials tend not to go farther than the original negative, after which the footage is transferred to tape.

### Let's Get Dirty

I was supervising a telecine session in London once when a director/DP team next door took all their negatives out to the street and unrolled them. They literally stepped on them and pulled them under the soles of their shoes, foot by foot. Obviously, they wanted to scratch and deteriorate the film to give it a cool look. The director ran down the street with 400 feet of film trailing behind him. After they had rolled it all back up, they demanded that now it must be transferred with "organic and realistic" scratches.

The only problem was that the telecine operator certainly wasn't going to let dirty and dusty film run through his expensive machine. So the director and DP had to go to a lab and get it re-cleaned. But the lab said they would only clean it as the last footage on the last day before the chemical change (labs change their development chemicals once a week, and the cleaning baths are part of that), because they didn't want the dirt to compromise anyone else's footage.

Depending on the stage of the film, the effects are different. Applied to the original camera negative, the process will result in blown-out highlights, higher contrast, and more grain. If you want to achieve results associated with the other stages, you have to cut the negative after you finish the offline edit and go through the process of film printing.

## Dailies

Most of the time, your negative will be processed and readied for dailies transfer. This means each lab roll is specially cleaned to achieve the best results in telecine. The dailies are, of course, what you edit with. While the transfer of the negative to videotape is usually a routine process, nevertheless, it can have huge consequences for you.

Again, the dailies are the footage you will be editing with. That means the agency and the client will get to see many of these dailies. Unfortunately, they may fall in love with the look that's set during the dailies transfer. And then you're stuck with it, and all the "great look" ideas you had are no longer an option.

---

### Back to the Backup

On a recent project, we had done a "normal" one-light for the offline cut and much more intense select takes with fairly wild colors. The agency simply didn't want it to look like anything else at first, and it certainly didn't. I was very happy with the look, but the agency grew more and more uncomfortable, feeling they had stuck their necks out too far. We finally ended up going with the one-light footage that we had luckily transferred onto DigiBeta as well. We were able to color-correct in online without having to do another third telecine session.

---

There are a few different options for the dailies process, which I will describe later. But if you are doing a one-light transfer, it is advisable to give the dailies transfer operator very clear directions. I can't tell you how often I have had to fight for my visual intentions because someone had color-corrected my footage with a completely different sense of style and taste. As for dailies and the final setting of the look, there are a few different possibilities.

## One-Light

In a one-light, there are actually two telecine sessions. The first telecine is called a *one-light*, which is an old term from movie times when negative film was printed to positive film for editing. Since there is usually a lot more footage than what actually ends up in the film, it makes no sense to color-correct every foot of it to perfection.

Rather, in the one-light process, the operator sets the exposure, contrast, and color balance to a medium setting, and pretty much lets everything run through at the same values. The DP or the director may actually have given the colorist more specific notes, like "Make it cooler" or "Make it contrasty."

In any case, a one-light is not the final look. It's working footage, which is usually transferred to low-grade videotape with a window in the image that shows the time code and key frame information.

After the editing, there are only 30 seconds of footage that are actually in the commercial (depending on the length, obviously). A second telecine session, called *select takes*, is then booked in which *only those 30 seconds* are transferred again. This time everything is scrutinized to the tiniest detail. A lot more work is being put into each shot in this very expensive process. More about that in the next chapter.

## Safety One-Light

This is a fairly recent addition to this process. Everything is the same as the one-light process mentioned previously, except that parallel to the low-grade video, a high-grade digital videotape runs at the same time and records the entire footage, but without a time code window (also called "clean").

Thus, on the morning of the edit, the editor has both low-grade video to edit with and a high-grade digital tape for safety, and possibly to *skip* the select-takes telecine. If time is of the essence and the commercial needs only moderate color correction (like many storytelling commercials do), then the grading can actually be done in the online process on a digital editing machine.

The reason this process is so new is that color correction on online machines has gotten a lot better over the past few years. However, there are obvious drawbacks: The sharpest, highest-resolution image with the most color and contrast information is the film negative. In a telecine bay, that is your basis.

If you do color correction on the online machine, the basis is the digital videotape from the one-light telecine, and thus it is vastly inferior. Again, because of the quality of film stock and digital transfer, as well as online machines, this has nevertheless become a viable option for many projects. Don't forget that telecine with a good operator is very, very expensive, so the budgetary savings could be substantial.

---

**CASE STUDY**

### High-Quality Dailies

On the Ford project, we decide to do a safety one-light, hoping that the quality of the one-light is sufficient to do only one pass. The reason for this is primarily the extremely short post schedule.

When the dailies come back, the word is that they are very warm in color with lots of red and yellow chroma in the image. This is, however, fairly easy to correct. The footage is being loaded into the Avid at Boxer Films where the editor Rob Groenwald will start working ASAP.

## Transfer All

This option is often used if there is not that much footage to transfer. Basically, the one-light is skipped, and the entire footage is transferred in a supervised telecine session. The final look is set here—before editing.

The advantage is that the offline edit, or rough cut, already looks pretty close to the final image, albeit at a lower resolution. Often, there will be a tape-to-tape color correction after the online, in which the final touch is added. A tape-to-tape, however, is not as powerful as a film-to-tape telecine.

# Let the Editor Have a Look

Once the dailies are transferred, they are delivered to the editing house for cutting. Generally, there are a number of different paths your editing process can take, depending as much on the routine of a production company, agency, or post production house as on the project's parameters. Avid is the standard platform in commercial editing. However, there are other platforms that work just as well and may have slightly different features. These range from Final Cut Pro to Lightworks.

Whichever system you use, you will probably be working with a low-quality image on a digital editing system. But it's not about the system, it's about the editor—he is the one who will make the cut work, sometimes create a little magic, or even save a project when things go wrong.

Usually, the editor has not been part of the production. He has not seen any of the footage, and he has not been present at conversations with the agency. This is actually a very good thing. The editor is in the unique position to look at the footage with a completely fresh eye. The images speak to him without the baggage of knowing what it took to get them. He is unconditioned to the problems, troubles, changes, ideas, or chance attached to each shot. To the editor, it is only an image.

As the director, you often have a certain order of shots in mind to tell the story. But the editor may see two shots and edit them together in a way you have not anticipated. The editor may think a shot that you didn't like works as a reaction shot. In his initial look at the footage, the editor creates entirely new relationships between shots in his head, because he is not locked in to your order. No shot lives on its own. It is usually dependent on the context of the other shots. Thus, if your sequence of shots was 1-2-3-4-5-6, the editor may cut it 5-4-2-3-1-6, thereby creating new relationships, connections, associations, and meaning between the individual frames.

For this reason, you might want to let the editor work initially without your input. This is sometimes a luxury, particularly on tight schedules. But it's a huge advantage to see someone's neutral reaction to the images you have created.

The editor takes the footage, the script, and the board. In a day or so, he assembles a rough cut, or even several versions, and then you join him to take a look. As I said, editors often come up with amazing new ideas, which may or may not be right for the spot. But in any case, an editor's input can help you think in new ways about your own shooting board.

The editor, by the way, is one of your most important crew members, for all these reasons—and for a lot of other reasons. Too many people see editors as operators who press buttons. You need to work with an editor you like, one you can talk freely with, and one who feels he can tell you what he thinks. The editor is the most important bounce board for you at this point. He'll ask you questions, such as: "How about this?" "What about this shot?" "What about this reaction?"

Remember that a film or a commercial is made three times. First, it's written, then shot, and finally edited. You can forget all the work you've done before, because now all you've got is the footage at hand. It's a limited supply of images, but they are your raw material.

# It's Your Vision

The director's cut should be the expression of your fullest and best vision. Use the best takes and work on nuances that are important to you. Create your story. You will now find out if your initial beat breakdown works as well as you thought it would.

Moment by moment, you can chisel out the timing, the joke, the drama. You may have had a very clear previsualized idea of the cut. But things may have changed during the shoot. Now is the time to go through the variations. Which reaction is the best? Too much, too little? Is this shot needed? What does it say? Does it take too long to get to the main turning point?

I usually have a pretty good idea of where I want to go with the edit. But I'm frequently surprised by editors. If I come in and see something really great, I would be foolish not to consider it for the edit.

Nevertheless, I always try out "my version," which is the version I shot—if only to see whether what I had previsualized works in the way I intended it to work. It's sort of a self-check. It's a learning experience. It's always a lesson.

Did I get this or that moment right? Did I need it to tell the story in the first place? How was that camera move? Too long? Note to self: No more 10-second camera moves in 20-second commercials. All that stuff is invaluable. I'd like to think that I'm my own harshest critic, although not necessarily in public and with the agency. But I certainly work through things with the editor if I know him well.

So, together with the editor, we do a first cut, which is always too long. Sometimes by a whole lot. Then we chop it down to the required time. Obviously, you must fulfill the parameters of the commercial in terms of pack shots, logos, brand communication, and time frame. Later, you may get a chance to work on your "perfect" director's cut. It can be longer than the on-air version, and you can use it on your reel to feature your directorial talents.

At this early stage of the process, though, your cut is the one you want to see on-air.

The chopping down is where you have to "kill your babies." Your babies are the shots that you have in the commercial simply because you like them, not because they absolutely need to be there. That line of dialogue which sounds so cool. The shot that looks so dramatic. The 10-second camera move. Time to chop.

**CASE STUDY**

### The Edit

Wednesday, January 4, the day after the shoot. Rob, the editor, has done his first pass, and I come in to take a look. The falling-bottle section is bumpy, and he didn't use some of the shots that I liked. But, in general, the cut works pretty well. We're discussing several options for the reveal—the moment when we show that the climbers are not actually at high altitude.

It could be the bottle hitting the grass, or Paige stepping in, or a wide shot. We're still way long, but right now we're not concerned with that. There is always "air" that can be taken out.

For some reason, the bottle hitting the platform, tumbling, and hitting the grass is all very complicated and takes a while to develop. Time that we don't have. We opt for a shorter, clearer version where the bottle drops out of sight, but we stay on the climbers to see their reaction. The shot where they look down (which is the shot where the bottle hits the camera lens, but we cut in later) is hilarious.

We let all of the shots run in real time rather than slow motion. It just takes too long. A good lesson to learn: There is just not enough time in 30 seconds to have four slow motion shots in a story of 13 or 14 shots.

Our padding is the performance of the two guys as they wake up and pull out the bottle. We have a lot of great footage there, but we can pretty much cut it to any length we want. We reserve a good 10 seconds for the two ending shots, which have logos, legal text, and voiceover on top.

# Enter: The Agency

Once you achieve a version you like, it's time for the agency to have a look. By the way, if the director is not part of the editing process, the agency still goes through much of the same steps with the editor.

The agency will have yet another viewpoint. Again, the collision between art and commerce takes place right here. Although the agency is generally on the creative side of things, they know that their client has parameters that need to be met. They will make sure that the cut is "showable" to the client.

Here, as well, you and the agency are a team. You will come up with one edit. Hopefully, your vision is already fairly close to what the agency wants the cut to look like, and the discussions are merely about details.

*I don't like his reaction here.*

*The car doesn't look good enough in this shot, let's use another one.*

*I feel like the wide shot is unnecessary there.*

*I'm put off by the way the line is delivered.*

If you've stuck close to the shooting board, things should go smoothly. If you've found a new idea—or your editor came up with one—then you will need to be able to justify it in case the agency doesn't agree. Often, the agency will want to look through various takes and see if they find alternatives. They may even remember a specific take from the shoot.

A lot of time is spent trying out alternate versions, exchanging takes, flipping the order of shots, and cutting this or that moment. It's also a very good idea to sleep things over. The next morning—with some distance—you may have a better and clearer look at the cut.

If there are major problems in the cut, this can be an intense process where you should try to position yourself as a problem solver rather than a roadblock. You should fight for your vision, though, but you have to be able to justify it. As in every step along the way, diplomacy is a good skill to own.

## Over-Editing

On some commercials, the agency and client go through hundreds of edits. This may sound crazy, but it comes from a place of insecurity. There are too many people involved at that point, and too many comments and remarks need to be taken into account. The result is a "safe" cut or a mixture of compromises, neither of which is really pretty. In some cases, an entire commercial is finished online and ready to go on the air when the top managers finally take a look and decide they don't like it. Everything has to be stopped and redone.

In usually two or three days, there will be a tight cut that the client can look at. These days, much of the approval process happens over the Internet. Clients, wherever they are, have almost immediate access to what you have just edited. The client may have changes or remarks, which are then addressed.

Step by step, the cut is polished and fine-tuned until you have a version that is approved. The approved version is called a *locked picture*, because the cut will not change any more.

During the offline editing, you will be working with a rough soundtrack. In fact, the soundtrack is very important in "selling" the cut and getting it approved. With sound, each cut will flow better and be more presentable. Good music will actually improve the image in the viewer's imagination. Additionally, some effects or music may even have to be timed to the cut, or vice versa. But all these elements are temporary, mere placeholders. For now, the online process begins when all the elements are put together.

## The Agency Edit

Still Wednesday, January 4. Due to the extremely short schedule, the agency comes in the same evening we begin cutting to have a first look. The response is positive, and together we work on the reveal. We all agree on a specific choice for that moment—Paige (over her shoulder) steps into a shot of the climbers, and their heads snap up to look at her. This shot wasn't intended to be used at that moment, but we like the reaction of the guys, and it makes everyone laugh.

Again, I had let the shot run from a few beats before and had Paige step in, to be able to cut it. A shooting technique I use as second nature—start the shot a few beats earlier—gave us the moment we liked the best. Had Paige already been standing in place, it wouldn't have worked.

We add some sound effects, such as wind and a screaming eagle, plus game-show music for the retail section, and the cut is ready to be shown to the client. We will get feedback tomorrow, and will have almost all of Thursday to do changes and finalize the cut.

# Chapter 11

# Director's Prep

The online process, from beginning to end, involves a great number of specialists. Each one has a specific expertise to bring to the commercial. Your post producer, the agency producer, and often the editor are the supervisors of this process. Depending on the project, you may be involved heavily or not at all.

I said earlier that *online* simply means that you are now in the final compilation process of the master. The edit has been decided on, and there is an edit decision list (EDL). Basically a collection of time codes, the EDL is used to re-create the edit you did in the offline editing system, frame by frame, on an online machine. But before I get into the onlining of a commercial, let's take a closer look at telecine.

## Telecine

The telecine or film transfer process is basically the same as the dailies transfer, but now it's the real thing. Most of the time, you will only be transferring the takes that are actually in the final cut. This process that I already mentioned is called *select takes*.

The original, developed negative is loaded into a film scanner, called a *rank* or *datacine*. It is much like a projector, except that it projects the negative image onto a chip, similar to those in high-end video cameras. The ranks can vary greatly in resolution and capabilities. Common rank names are Spirit, URSA, and Quadra Vision.

The color correction software and hardware attached to a rank is as important as the rank itself. You may hear names like DaVinci or Pogle, as well as a variety of plug-ins, such as Power Windows. These systems are complete, which means that, for example, a DaVinci has both proprietary software and hardware.

The telecine systems are highly advanced digital machines that are kept in climatized, dust-protected rooms and are calibrated on a regular basis. Each system has different strengths and weaknesses, but they are all high-tech toys.

The most important factor in color correction, however, is the colorist. He is the operator who adjusts the track ball controls like a virtuoso. If you have a good colorist, then things will go fast and easily. He will not only save you time, but will also offer you great looks and interesting ideas. In fact, some of the colorists are minor celebrities in the industry because they have such a great influence on the final spot.

That is because the film transfer defines the look of the commercial. You are working from the highest-quality material—the original negative—and you are setting the colors, contrasts, hues, and saturation. Once you have the footage on digital videotape, you are limited when it comes to adjusting all these values.

## Who Needs an Adjustment?

The possible adjustments are vast. There is primary color correction and secondary color correction. There are curves, gradients, crushed blacks, and blown-out highlights. Experience is the best way to learn about all these possibilities—by sitting in as many telecine sessions as you can and asking questions. The colorists are highly specialized professionals who will gladly answer anything you throw at them. You are well advised to listen to what they have to say.

## See What's Possible

Whenever there is some leisure time in a telecine session (which isn't very often), I ask the colorist to experiment a bit with the extreme limits just to see what's possible. We once managed to bring out a face that was five stops underexposed. In other words, on normal settings there was nothing but black. With the system all the way cranked up, though, we could recognize the actor even if the quality was extremely grainy. As a possible "look," it certainly was interesting.

The SPIRIT rank is known for being able to zoom in on the negative without losing much resolution. While transferring footage from a job shot on stage, we tried something else. The footage was very high-resolution because we had lots of lights, ultra-prime lenses, and very dense film stock (low ISO). When we began to zoom in on the negative, we could go up to 80 percent without noticing a difference between the original size and the zoomed-in version. We transferred a close-up shot of a person and then zoomed in on his eye for an extreme close-up. The quality was impressive.

For example, by drawing masks or windows over certain areas, the colorist can correct the entire image or only parts of it. If the wheels of a car come out too dark, the colorist simply puts a circle mask over it and raises the brightness locally. This can become complicated if things are moving, which they usually do in a commercial. However, the masks can be animated and to some degree even tracked directly onto the image. Tracking is an automated process where the computer tracks the motion of a specific pixel and applies it to another layer like a mask.

The colorist can pull in colored gradients to make the sky bluer or the beach whiter. He can pick one specific color and only correct that. It's beyond the scope of this text to go into all the possibilities of transferring your footage to high-end videotape. And in fact, it's not the director's job to be the specialist.

You, the director, must tell the colorist what you want in layman's terms.

*Can you make it darker?*

*I would like it a bit warmer.*

*How about a bluish feel?*

*I think the contrast can be increased.*

*I like it when the highlights blow out.*

*Can we make the edges darker?*

*I'd like to have this area be the lightest area in the frame.*

Or, even better, show him color references. Because, despite the technical aspects of telecine, deciding on the look is ultimately an emotional, gut decision. You are creating a painting, a piece of art—and that's how you should look at it.

While the operator has to ensure that the images are within the technically possible limits for broadcast, and that all the shots match, you should concentrate on the creative visual experience you want your audience to have.

- ♦ Does it serve your story?
- ♦ Does it set the right mood?
- ♦ Does the eye go where you want it to in the frame ?

Telecine is an incredibly powerful tool to determine, stylize, push, create, and shape your vision. Never again will you see the images you've shot in such perfect and pristine quality. Enjoy it, because from that point on, your commercial will be shown on television sets nationwide, where you have no control over the settings.

Also, one thing to keep in mind is that moment when you see the footage for the first time. I try to let it impress me as "cleanly" as possible. I try to forget all the work that had led up to it and put myself in the position of the audience. This very first moment I need to remember for the rest of the process. My initial reaction to a shot or a performance will be valuable later when I've seen everything a couple of dozen times. By that time, I may have lost objective judgment and need to think back to that moment when I first saw the shot.

### Hello, Operator?

I've walked into telecine sessions and known as soon as the colorist had put up the image and adjusted a few things that we would be fine. In fact, more than once I've been blown away by the images I've shot myself, because the colorist had made them incredibly beautiful and taken them to the next level.

Unfortunately, the opposite can happen as well. Some colorists are too technical and not artistic at all. They look at curves and videoscopes, rather than the image. If you are unhappy with a colorist, do not hesitate to replace him. Ask for someone else. This is such an important moment in the production of the commercial that you should not accept any shortcuts or compromise.

## Nitty-Gritty Telecine

Here are some practical hints to enrich your experience in telecine. Your eyes get used to colors very quickly, and when you stare at a set of chromas for a long time, your visual nerves lose sensitivity to them. In fact, you may experience visual distortions or small optical illusions, like traveling colors or focus shifts.

Immediately behind the main monitor, there is usually a lighted gray wall area. It is there for you to stare at in order to reset your optical cells. Close your eyes and open them, looking at the gray for five or six seconds. You can actually feel your eyes relax because there is nothing to focus on, no contrasts to adjust, and no colors to read. It's completely neutral. In fact, you should look at the monitor as little as possible and even leave the room occasionally to see some daylight, get some air, and refresh your retinas as well as your pupils.

If you are working on a project with effects, specifically with green screen shots, you may want to do several "passes" of particular shots—in other words, transfer them several times. One pass is for the look, the next one is for the green screen. In the second pass, the colorist will ensure that all the green screen is technically perfect for the later stages of compositing, although the look is off. Because of the time code associated with each shot, footage will later line up perfectly, and the compositing artist can use the green-graded version for his mask (more about that later).

You may also want to do several passes for specific elements in the frame, like the product. Sometimes, it is easier to grade the entire frame first so the product looks perfect, then grade the image so the environment looks perfect, and finally, composite the two at a later stage.

With car shoots, you will often have to do several passes for the car's lights. It's very difficult to get the sheet metal to look good without having the headlights blow out completely. So simply do several passes, which you can overlay later.

## Digital Elements

You may have noticed that commercial filmmaking is at the forefront of new technologies. Most of the digital wizardry now common in features was tried and tested in product spots long before it ever ended up on the big screen.

Most commercials today are digitally post produced, if only for a logo, a sky replacement, or a small touch-up. Somewhere, inevitably, the image has been adjusted. However, it is important to distinguish between the different stages of the spot's digital enhancements.

The online edit, which I will explain in detail later, can include small enhancements, sizeable adjustments, or even huge compositing tasks. But you may be dealing with much more involved computer graphics (CG). Computer graphics provide everything you can't shoot on actual film, including aliens, dinosaurs, explosions, flowing lava, flying elephants, and submerged cars. It's limited only by your imagination.

More and more, we rely on computer graphics to perform various wonders: fill in gaps, draw backgrounds, create winter effects in summer, or change blue skies into a snowstorm. These elements must obviously be an integral part of your preproduction. You must direct them just as thoroughly as you do any actor on camera. You have to set up the shots, pick your lens, and choose your moves.

Yet the process of creating these digital elements takes far longer than shooting. Compared to only two shooting days, for example, computer graphics may take six weeks. The CG artists will build wireframe models, animate them, skin them, shade them, light them, put them in the scene, and sometimes even composite them into your footage.

Even with mere 2D graphics and not full-scale 3D models, the production may take weeks. Depending on your project, it is more effective to shoot liveaction footage first and then go into computer graphics production. Often, particularly with green screen shots that include a moving camera, the CG artists will ask to be on the set. Without impeding your creative vision, they need to watch for technical issues—like tracking marks—that will make their work easier.

Computer graphics are a vast field in today's commercial production. Like cameras, lenses, lights, and cranes, the computer is simply a tool to accomplish your vision.

## 3D Graphics

Three-dimensional graphics are used to create a greater sense of realism over 2D. However, the final image is not true 3D (for example, IMAX 3D, in which each eye sees a different image than the brain and then merges into a spatial illusion). The final image is only a 2D image (like your television screen). The 3D refers to the fact that the models are built in 3D and can be animated in a 3D world.

If 3D graphics involve more dimensions, they also require more time and money. Three-dimensional models must be seamlessly integrated into live-action footage, and therefore need to be photorealistic. This requires perfect lighting and a model with flawless attributes, including shading, color, material, and texture.

The 3D engines used in the industry are Maya, Softimage, 3D Studio MAX, Amorphium, Poser, Ray Dream Studio, Bryce, Blender, and Truespace. Many computer graphics houses have their own proprietary software. And there are various plug-ins available for specialties such as water, fire, or grass.

Yet, as always, it is not about the software, but about the artists who are using it. Some are better at animation, while others excel in modeling. Some are great for realistic landscapes, others for cars or futuristic buildings. Usually, you are dealing with a computer graphics house with in-house or freelance artists.

However, there are certain specializations among companies, which you should research by looking at reels and talking to them about your project. In fact, if it's a big CG job, you will probably take bids from more than one post house, carefully considering the ideas and the technical solutions each one has to offer your project.

In 3D graphics, even more than in live-action shooting, it is essential that you know what you want and that you communicate it exactly. The 3D artists create a world from scratch, according to what you tell them, and once they've started their creation, it is not easy to change it. Use picture references, photographs, drawings, or whatever it takes to make clear how you want it to look and which elements you need.

There will be a constant conflict between your creative vision and the feasibility of accomplishing that vision. Is a certain thing doable in the amount of time and for the amount of money available? How can you simplify your shot to save both time and money? Your vision, for example, involves a moving camera shot—this will require the move to be re-created in the computer, a process for which there are two options: motion control or tracking.

Motion control systems record the camera's moves and can execute them time and time again with perfection. The spatial data can be downloaded into 3D software, and the camera's moves can be re-created exactly. (This process also works the other way—importing a digital move into the motion control system.)

Tracking is the more common (and cheaper) way to do it. The computer uses points in space to deduce the camera's moves. These points can be random spots or specifically placed marks. Tracking complicated moves is harder. Obviously, if your shot moves only slightly from left to right, the tracking will be easier and will require less time.

Another issue is aspect change. The more aspect change a model undergoes (the more sides you see of it), the more complicated the CG gets. For this reason, it is important to sit down with the specialists and talk through every detail of the shot.

Three-dimensional graphics are tools to serve your vision and nothing more. Get the most out of 3D graphics, but don't compromise. This is particularly true with photorealistic models: It is very, very hard to make a CG object seem real. And only half of that realism is achieved in the model building. The other half is done in the integration, called *compositing*, which I will talk about later.

Generally, CG artists will want the object to look as perfect as possible. But if you are not happy with any element—texture, reflectivity, patina, or "feel"—you need to be adamant about what you want, because your requirements and standards are different from those of the CG artists.

### And Then There Was Life

On a spot for tea, we once built an entire 3D world. The camera was flying through a cherry-blossom tree, across a plain of flowers and grass with a creek-bed, toward an antique mill, and up into the sky. Additionally, before the move started, the world changed from a dark, depressed state to a colorful, uplifting mood. The tree appeared dead at first, and then it began to blossom.

The 3D artists built a single blossom, which was animated so it opened up in a beautiful little sequence. It was copied 250,000 times, placed along the branches of the tree, and then time-delayed so that the blossoms opened at slightly different moments. The effect was incredibly wonderful. A dark, dead, black tree transformed into a pink, blooming, living thing. For the grass, a plug-in was used: Like a spilling paint bucket, the artist filled the landscape with the plug-in color. When rendered, blades of grass were created all over the place, 50 million in total.

## 2D Graphics

Most of the 2D graphics you will be dealing with are logos and type. If your niche is graphics, you probably know more about 2D graphics than I do. However, in virtually every commercial, there are logos or type somewhere. The 2D work that is being done on the image is almost always done during the online process. Only if it is a heavily graphics-laden spot will there be any preproduction for it.

In most cases, the agency will provide the post production house with logos and sometimes even fonts. The work is done in programs such as Adobe Photoshop or Adobe After Effects (for animated 2D graphics), or on online machines such as the Flame or the Henry.

## Online Edit

The online edit is the final image assembly. All the elements—live-action footage, computer graphics, logos, and fonts—are brought together and composited. There are two major lines of online machines, with different levels of processing power and capabilities.

There is Discreet's line of Flint, Flame, and Inferno. And there is Quantel's Q series. Finally, there are a number of specialized software solutions, including Adobe After Effects, Apple's Shake, and Eyeon's Digital Fusion, all of which have their niches and applications. Some are geared toward compositing, others toward graphics, commercials, or feature films.

In general, the final image assembly involves loading all the elements into the online machine and combining them into a final image. In commercials, the online machine will lay back the final version of the spot to digital videotape. That videotape is the master source for all the tapes that go out to be aired by broadcasters.

There are various stages between loading in the elements and laying back the final version: removal of unwanted parts of the image (i.e., wire or rig removal), replacement of backgrounds or skies, compositing of separate elements, addition of effects (smoke, sparks, lens flares), color correction (to match elements and blend the image together), speed changes, animation of logos, and type.

The live-action footage is loaded from the digital tapes made in the telecine session. An edit decision list (EDL) is loaded from the offline editing system to re-create the cut exactly, down to the frame. Then layer upon layer is added to achieve the final image. The layers are composited with masks, and this is where green screen shooting finally comes into play. The computer easily recognizes the extremely green color and creates a mask from it. Another layer can now be used in its place.

Sometimes, an object needs to be separated from the background or touched up in footage that was shot without green screen. Then the operator has to work on each frame and separate the object by hand in a process called *rotoscoping*. Obviously, this is more time-consuming than the virtually automatic use of a green screen.

Again, the operator is crucial. Some operators are fantastic with masks and compositing, while others are experts in effects creation. A good post production house will have several people working on a project if necessary.

For the director, this is the final chance to enhance or adjust image values, gradients, dissolves, and shot sizes. If you have done your job well, all the elements will be great, and you need be concerned only with compositing and adding new elements, plus small adjustments here and there. Compositors are perfectionists, and there won't be many decisions to be made. Your main job is to make calls on new effects, final color, and a myriad of other details.

No doubt the agency will be present, and time will be spent placing logos and type, as well as color correcting and touching up product shots. The entire online process usually takes between a few hours and a few days, although when there is a lot of compositing to be done, it can take more than a week. In the end, you'll walk out with a digital master of your commercial, the finished image. All you have to do now is add sound.

CASE STUDY

## Online Session

It's Friday, January 6. The client has approved the edit, and we're going into online. The agency, my post producer, and the editor are all there. The footage is already loaded into the Inferno, and the computer has automatically re-created the commercial. For comparison, the Avid output is loaded in from U-matic videotape.

In the first shot, we have to paint out a branch. When I was setting up the shot on the set, I knew that I could easily get rid of the branch, so I concentrated on the composition rather than getting a "clean" sky. In fact, during online we not only delete the branch, but end up replacing the entire sky with a bluer, high-altitude version.

During the Avid edit, we changed the timing of Paige stepping into a shot by just a few frames. The EDL does not reflect that, and the effect is re-created manually. There are a few other shots, notably the frog's perspective shot looking up at the climbers, where the sky has to be replaced. In this case, we actually animate clouds in the background to give it just the slightest bit of motion.

The last two frames are a bit more work because we layer logos and type on top of the image. The next-to-the-last shot is blurred when the logo comes in, so as not to take away attention from it. In the final shot, the shot of the car, we've decided to go with a still shot rather than the slight move we shot on the set.

We're adding a vignette here, a slight darkening of the edges, which acts like a visual upgrade, bringing out the colors and the contrast even more. The car needs just a little bit of work on the license plate (which we took off, but the empty screw holes look weird). The animated Ford logo is placed, and there is some discussion about size and position.

Finally, we decide to go into a tape-to-tape session in a telecine bay to adjust the colors. Remember that we didn't do select takes on this one because of the tight time schedule. So rather than going back to the negative, we will correct the digital footage from the online bay.

CASE STUDY *continued*

In the telecine session, we work with a great colorist, who quickly and without any of our input, nails the look. We actually have a change in mood in this spot: While the beginning is cold and bluish, everything changes to a warm and sunny feel when Paige steps in.

The colorist adjusts the contrasts to bring out the texture of the rock even more, and the spot looks fantastic.

# Audio

Audio is an often-underestimated part of filmmaking. In commercials, music plays an important part because it quickly sets the tone and mood of a piece. The audience is taken in by the communicative power of music—an important asset in a 30-second spot.

Much like the picture, the final audio track is a combination of several elements from several sources. There is the sound originally recorded on location, aptly named *location sound*. Then there is the music, which may be composed or purchased. Additionally, you will have effects, which are either recorded separately or taken from sound effects libraries. Finally, you may have a voiceover, which is recorded in the studio.

Your editor is already working with a few tracks, most notably the location sound and temporary music tracks, called *temp tracks* or *temp music*. For important effects, those which are part of the story, sounds may be added as well. With the advanced digital post production available, the quality of the offline edit sound is often very good. The editor will export his soundtracks and make them available to the mixer, who may or may not use them in the final mix. However, he will certainly use them as reference tracks to locate certain cues.

## Location Sound

One of the decisions you face on the set is whether or not to record synchronous sound. Some cameras are too noisy for recording sound; on the other hand, some cameras specifically made for sync sound may not be able to shoot at the frame rate you desire.

The process of shooting sync sound is more complicated because another, separate tape has to be included in the process; this issue is negligible, however, when using a professional crew. The major advantage of shooting sync sound is that it provides the true sound of the location. When shooting actors in a storytelling situation, real sound is a priceless asset because it becomes as much a part of the performance as the picture. It includes not only dialogue, but also the noises involved in moving and breathing, which add a layer of realism that's very difficult to achieve in post production.

The sound mixer and his boom operator will try to record the best possible sound. Often, they will ask if you have a preference for a particular kind of microphone. Each recording device has a different sound quality. Wireless mikes attach to the actor and deliver a very close sound, but it can be slightly muffled or dull. Boom microphones are brighter and crisper, but they present the complication of needing an operator who must put them in exactly the right place. Boom mikes come in different sensitivities (zoom factors) and record more of the surroundings than wireless mikes.

The sound mixer may offer to record both—a wireless mike on the actor on channel one and a boom mike on channel two. Often, however, you won't have a choice because the scene you are shooting is not recordable. For example, on a process trailer (where a picture car sits with camera, lights, and crew), there is too much engine and wind noise for a boom mike. The only choice, if you have actors who are talking, is an interior microphone. The car's noises have to be recorded separately.

Be sure to record *fill*, or the ambient noise of the location—this is something that any good filmmaker knows! Record fill for about 20 or 30 seconds while everyone on set stops and stays completely quiet. This short moment can have huge payoffs in post when you're filling in gaps.

## CASE STUDY

### Location Sound

On the Ford shoot, we recorded location sound because we had lines of dialogue and lots of natural sounds, like rustling clothes and clinking gear. We had both a wireless and a boom working, and were able to choose the cleaner track in editing. The slow-motion shots we couldn't record in sync because of the different frame rate, but we let sound run anyway as wild track. *Wild track* is everything you record that is not in sync with a specific picture. It's always advisable to grab as much extra sound as you can.

## Music Composing

As I said earlier, music plays a huge part in commercials. Whether it's a famous song that is being (ab)used or an original piece, nothing sets the tone and mood of a scene as quickly and unobtrusively as music. In fact, images seem to change when you watch them with different music tracks. Music is so emotional that actors' performances can be shaped by scoring them wisely.

The choice of music is not something to be underestimated. When you are not using canned music, you will be working with one or more composers at a music house. Depending on the budget, the score will be recorded with real instruments or created from samples. Or sometimes it will be a mix of both. It's rare—although fascinating—to get to work with a full orchestra.

The huge advantage of composing the commercial's music, rather than using preexisting tracks, is that the timing can be perfect. The beats, crescendos, climaxes, and counterpoints can be placed exactly in order to tell the story. It is also much easier to make "comments" with the music when creating it from scratch.

The process of working with a composer varies greatly. Some composers hide away in dark rooms and emerge with a track they like. Others value cooperation, want to hear your references (temp tracks), and try to fulfill your vision as well as their own. Both approaches can work.

Because of my own musical background, I tend to talk in detail with the composer. I bring in references, and sometimes I even create a visual representation of my take on the music. Be aware that there are styles of music that are too commercial. Also be aware that some composers have been doing commercial work for so long, they can hardly come up with anything noncommercial.

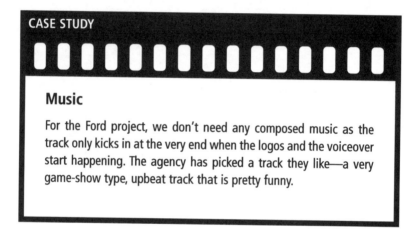

**CASE STUDY**

### Music

For the Ford project, we don't need any composed music as the track only kicks in at the very end when the logos and the voiceover start happening. The agency has picked a track they like—a very game-show type, upbeat track that is pretty funny.

## Sound Design

A commercial's sound design is a kind of music. Instead of instruments, however, it consists of sounds, like those made by cars, birds, creaking doors, or footsteps in the sand. These effects enhance the realism and the substance of the commercial, and they complement the story told by the images. Try listening to a commercial without looking at it. Can you follow the story? Can you hear what's going on?

From the recorded sound on the set, you probably have many sounds available in the edit. Also, you may add an occasional effect from a sound archive. And, to make something sound like it never would in reality, you might want to create a completely new or different sample.

The sound design process begins with a list of sounds, compiled by you or your editor, which is sent to a post house. Their archives will yield numerous existing effects, ready to be cut in. Sometimes, there is time to create a separate sound design before going into the mix. In most cases, however, the sound design editing and the mix happen together over the course of a day.

Your focus should be on effects that tell the story or help to communicate your vision. Background tracks provide a base layer, while certain beats may need enhancement by specific sounds, like the slamming of a door or a swoosh of air.

Make sure that you have all the pieces of sound you need before going into the mix, particularly if you want to record something that's not in the archives. You absolutely cannot send someone out during the mix to get a recording done. You must have specifically engineered sounds prepared in advance.

## CASE STUDY

### Sound Design

In our sound design, we're trying to create the atmosphere of high altitude in the beginning. Howling wind and a screaming eagle in the far distance create that setting perfectly. We also add some creaking noises for the platform, as well as the occasional clothes rustle to make the cut feel more realistic in its texture. Later, when music and voiceover begin, there is not really any room for additional effects.

## Dialogue and Voiceover Recording and Re-Recording

Dialogue recorded on the set is not always usable because of background noise, like airplanes or generators. In that case, the actors are brought into a studio to re-record their lines. This process is called ADR (additional dialogue recording). The actors, while trying to stay in sync, attempt to hit exactly the tone and mood of their original performance.

Additionally, you will often have to record a voiceover for the product shot, or even for conceptual text. The voiceover talent is cast and approved by the client. In fact, it's not uncommon for companies to use the same voiceover talent for several years, in an attempt to create a "voice" for a product or a brand.

In most cases, the agency will be in charge of booking, selecting, and even working with the voiceover talent.

## Audio Mix

Much like the online edit for the picture, the audio mix is where all the elements are brought together and molded into a complete piece. The music, the effects, the dialogue, and the voiceover are laid out on separate tracks, and their values and balances are adjusted.

As I said, in most cases, the sound effects editing is accomplished while doing the mix. This is possible due to the relative brevity of commercials—in features it would be unthinkable.

The audio mixer will adjust volume and equalization, add filters, and fade tracks in and out. His job is also to make sure that the track stays within legal broadcast limitations and is audible on all speakers, whether of high or low quality. You may listen to state-of-the-art speaker systems during most of the mix, but you should also check the soundtrack on $10 computer speakers. On inexpensive equipment, the lower frequencies will drop away, and the volume will sound much different. Unfortunately, you have to aim for the lowest common denominator—at least a medium-grade consumer speaker.

**CASE STUDY**

## Sound Mix

In our mix for Ford, everything falls into place nicely. It's Friday afternoon, and online and telecine were completed this morning. By tonight we have to be finished, because the spot will air on Sunday. Our mixer does a great job, and there are not really many remarks or comments from the agency or me.

We watch the commercial on the big screen in the studio and over the nice speakers. We take it in. This is probably the last time we will see and hear the spot at this quality. In fact, right after this, we will watch it on a consumer-grade TV set with tiny speakers to make sure that everything is audible there as well. It's a very good idea to check your audio on $10 speakers before it goes out. As a film-maker, you are the victim of people's TV sets. Your project is subjected to literally millions of different audio and video setups.

Anyway, the spot is mixed down (the voiceover had been recorded while we were onlining in the morning), and we're done. The master tape is being recorded, and copies will be made and sent out.

A fun project has been finished in an incredibly short amount of time. It was a real stretch, but we did it.

Make sure that everything important on the sound track is "in the clear" and not obscured by other sounds. It's better to cut some effects in the interest of clarity. Sound mixing is often intuitive, and if you feel there is a gap, or if you are confused at certain points, you need to fix those problems.

## Putting It All Together

Eventually, you will reach the point where nothing needs to be added or subtracted. The mix is done. The balances and volumes are right. It feels rich and complete. All that remains is the layback, the final technical step in the production of your commercial. The sound is added to the final picture, and your spot is finished.

Now it's really time to breathe and give yourself a pat on the back. The spot is done, and hopefully you'll get to see it on the air soon.

Remember to stay in touch with the agency on a private basis, if you were able to strike up that kind of a relationship with them. It's a business run on personal contacts, and if everything went well during your project, you should harvest those contacts.

# Chapter 12

# The Next Step

It is actually very hard to make a long career out of commercial directing. While it may take you a while to get to a place where you feel like an established director, you may only spend a few years at that peak. It is rare that directors continuously work on the same level for more than 10 years.

The ones who have managed to do so were able to reinvent themselves and change their style along with the times. Some people have that capacity, others don't. The vast majority of commercial directors have a peak period of two or three years after which work begins to slowly fade out.

Make no mistake, in those two or three years, you stand to make as much money as regular folks make in 20 years. If you are among the A-list talent, you can rake in a couple of million in those two years, and that ain't bad.

But you have to bake bread when the oven is hot. Or better—when you are hot. Remember that you are a product, a commodity, a brand. Once you reach a certain level, your value is obviously higher, and you should rightfully gain as much as possible from that.

I want to touch on two opportunities that are obvious. For one, there is international representation. Working abroad is a rewarding experience for a director of any level.

But first, there is the inevitable desire for a movie career. A lot of commercial directors' ultimate goal is the big screen. Commercial directing is merely a stepping stone on the way to the acceptance speech. I've had the chance to sit down with Sony/Columbia Pictures Entertainment's President of Production, Matt Tolmach, and chat about the studios' take on commercial directors.

## The View from Hollywood

Matt Tolmach has been working in the film industry ever since he started in the mailroom at William Morris. His focus has been the development of scripts, and he has climbed the executive ladder with blazing speed. He is now in the top echelons of Hollywood as President of Production at Sony/Columbia Pictures. His credits include the *Spider-Man* franchise, *The Da Vinci Code*, *Ali*, *Panic Room*, *Lords of Dogtown*, and many other major studio productions.

> *Q: What is the attitude of the film industry towards commercial directors, and how has it evolved?*
>
> *A:* I think it's a very healthy attitude. People in the movie business are constantly on the lookout for talented directors, those who can tell a story combined with powerful imagery. It's been cyclical, though. A few years ago there were an enormous number of commercial directors who made the transition, like David Fincher, Michael Bay, Mark Romanek, and Gore Verbinski. Studios were always on the search for the next guy—who will be the next hot guy?
>
> You have to be careful as a studio, though, because movies are all about creating great characters, and it's hard to show that in a :30 spot. How much of a character can you create in that time? How much dimension can you convey? If a guy can blow you away with his images, great—but does that mean he can tell a layered story with great characters, one that has to hold your attention for two hours? Not necessarily.

So if he's got the imagery and he can tell a story, then that's an option. Commercials are definitely a great training ground for filmmakers, because spot directors usually are very aware of schedules and budgets, and they are very advanced technically. But it's still a huge leap of faith for a studio to hire a commercial director who has never done a feature.

**Q: What's your best advice for those commercial directors who want to make the transition? How should they go about it?**

*A:* I think directing an indie film may be the best way to go. It's very unlikely that a studio will just give you $50 million to do a film. But you can get $10 million for an indie feature, and prove that you can tell stories and create characters. Then you become more viable.

**Q: How do you get reels from commercial directors in the first place?**

*A:* Their agents send them in and introduce people, and our younger executives are always looking for new talent. If we like someone, it doesn't mean we're going to work with him—say, this year. We may track someone's career and see how they develop.

And we actually watch commercials on television. I know it's kind of a cliché, but we watch the Super Bowl ads, and that's kind of the Super Bowl of ads, too. The next morning we talk about them, which spots did you like, which one was your favorite, who did this, who did that one?

*Q: In commercials, the director bids against other directors with treatments and phone calls. How does it work in the movie industry? Is there an equivalent?*

*A:* We take lots of meetings and hear how directors would make that film. We're interested in that director's vision. They come in with images sometimes, but mostly it's story talk. If we're interested, we'll go into development, which means we give the director some time to work on the script, budget, and cast. Usually, when a director comes aboard, the script is not done, so he is expected to work with it and improve it.

We really put them through the paces. What's their vision for the movie? What does it look like? How does it make the audience feel? What's the movie *really* about? In the executive job, you learn (through failure) that these are the most critical and telling conversations. Directors almost always direct the movie they talk about in the first meeting. So we really listen. In other words, come prepared to be fully interrogated!

Again, it's a huge leap of faith, and so there are many meetings and many questions, and we listen very carefully.

But a director may be attached to a project and develop the script, and the movie never gets made. The green light comes at the very end—we must like the script, the casting, and the vision.

As a commercial director, you are between a rock and a hard place when it comes to breaking into features. You know you have the skills, but how do you prove it? Making a 30-second commercial for $2 million is as high-stakes as it gets. That's $4 million per minute and would translate into a $480 million feature. Of course, it doesn't quite work that way.

There is no question that your chances are much better than most other wannabe Spielbergs. If your commercial reel is strong, and if you can find a way to market yourself as a writer/director or short film director, you will get the opportunity to jump into the fray that is Hollywood.

No question, from there it's still a long way to the red carpet. But if you can tell stories in 30 seconds, work with actors, shoot beautiful images, and run successful productions, you are light years ahead of everyone else. And the main lessons from this book certainly apply in the film industry: Stay true to your artistic vision, because people want a strong director; market yourself; and continue to build your network, since talent is only half the equation.

Know what you want. That's usually the best way to get it.

# International Representation

Most of this book has been written from the U.S. perspective, because much more production happens in New York and Los Angeles than almost anywhere else in the world. As a result, most directors will ultimately strive to be represented in the States.

The problem is that in the U.S., it is very hard just to get a foot in the door. The competition is fierce and unrelenting. If you want to work continuously, gain experience, and further your education as a director, look for jobs abroad.

The major markets outside the U.S. are Canada, Europe, Asia, South America, Japan, and Australia. Each region has its own idiosyncrasies, but many of the issues and processes explained in this book are applicable to most countries and markets. (The client-agency relationship and the director as artist-salesman, for example, are similar almost everywhere.)

## How to Make International Friends

There are a few ways to get representation abroad. You can either travel there in person and take meetings, or you can send your reel after contacting producers by phone or email. No question, traveling is the more expensive option. But meeting someone in person certainly creates a stronger first impression, and your reel won't be lost in that big stack.

The resources listed in the appendix of this book have directories with addresses, names, and phone numbers. Before you travel to a certain production hub, make sure you call around.

*I'm in town and I'm meeting with some companies. I love your work and would like to come in for a meeting.*

Set up appointments, if possible, and try to get recommendations. It's always better to have someone else call for you.

Next, know what you want from the meetings. In many countries, companies have lists of directors whom they can offer on a project-by-project basis. In other words, if a board comes up that calls for a tabletop/food director, they look in their stack of reels. But they don't actively market that reel.

You definitely want someone to actively market you. Particularly in the major markets, you hardly stand a chance if you are just an "Oh-wait-I-think-I-have-someone" guy. It's better if you can get a company to push you, get behind you, and use their contacts to place you.

Also, standards of production are very different, depending on the country. You should be clear on your demands and requirements, and see how the company reacts.

Often, you will find that production companies trade directors. Sometimes, your U.S. company has contacts in Canada, who have contacts in the UK, who have contacts in Sweden, and so on. They will offer to represent each other's directors in their respective portfolios, essentially enlarging their product palette.

However, this can also create problems. Some of the directors from another company may be your niche competition.

### Six Degrees of Representation

My German production company represented a Canadian director who subsequently started his own company in Toronto, and I got signed there. The Canadians then showed my work to a company in London, and they signed me for UK representation. Next, the UK folks had ties to a Spanish production house, and I had representation there as well.

## Cannes You Look at My Reel?

Another great way to meet people is by going to festivals, especially Cannes—the number one international venue. Cannes is a week-long party, and you will run into any number of folks from all over the world who will gladly look at your reel. Because of the vacation-esque quality of Cannes, people are very open to meeting and exchanging information.

It's good to have reels and business cards to hand out. Obviously, if you are somehow "in" the festival—say, short-listed, your chances to have people look at your stuff are even better.

But even if you are simply a visitor, you will make friends quickly, and you can get access to some of the parties quite easily. There are coveted shindigs that are almost impossible to get into without serious contacts, but for a lot of the production companies, it is advantageous to have as many people show up as possible.

In Cannes, there is also a Young Directors showcase run by advertising agency Saatchi & Saatchi. It is meant for fresh talent, although frequently, powerful production companies push their established directors into it.

Cannes is definitely worth the trip, even if you have to spend $40 on a drink. If you are lucky, you'll be treated to a lot of them.

## Work the Web

And, of course, there is your work. Once you do a commercial that gets some decent air time or hits the trades, you will get calls from people wanting to rep you. I had a spot on a "What's Hot" list for a few weeks, and I couldn't answer my phone fast enough.

The promotion of your work can be tricky because clients don't want their commercials "out there" before they actually hit the airwaves. But hopefully, once the spots can be seen on TV, the agency will also have an interest in promoting it in trade magazines and on Web sites.

The Internet is a great place for sharing and trading . There are newsgroups, as well as professional Web sites where companies will research both directors and spots. You will find some of those Web sites in the appendix. Try to get on them. Advertise yourself!

And obviously, this is where your own Web site comes in. It's very easy for people all around the world to look at your site and see your reel. Send out newsletters every time you update the site. Have links to other Web sites, and try to be linked by other sites. The more traffic, the better.

### Link Up

I started my Web site right out of film school, and it has helped me numerous times to get jobs or representation. It's also linked to some of the subscription research Web sites out there, which increases traffic even more. The site is a great way for people to get a quick look at my work before there is a reel. I also use my site to post treatments, artwork, and presentations for agencies and clients.

## Canada

The most obvious and common choice for U.S. directors looking to work outside the country is Canada. It is close geographically, the system is much the same, agency folks float back and forth, and there is a lot of cross-shooting. (Americans shoot in Canada for budgetary reasons; Canadians sometimes shoot in the U.S. for the locations.)

However, the main reason that it is so easy for U.S. directors to work in Canada is the shared language. As a communicator, language is an important tool in achieving your creative vision. Naturally, you will have an easier time working in largely English-speaking Canada; even in the French-speaking regions, people speak English well.

The geographical proximity is yet another reason, as well as the fact that many agency folks go back and forth.

Many Canadian production companies are interested in representing U.S.-based directors. You approach them in much the same way you would a production company in Los Angeles or New York, although their production hub is Toronto. (Vancouver has a lot of shooting, but not many agencies.)

I have found that the bidding and shooting process in Canada is virtually indistinguishable from the U.S. (if a bit more relaxed). One difference is that you may have to shoot two language versions of a spot (English/French) or direct actors in French dialogue.

Post production facilities and shooting equipment are top-notch.

## United Kingdom

The United Kingdom has the same language advantage, and there is a lot of sharing of directors going on. However, it's considerably harder to get representation because the creatives in the UK are on a different level altogether and being U.S.-based is not necessarily seen as an advantage. Obviously, the top dogs will be repped in London, but for mid- and low-tier directors, it can be problematic if you don't live in the UK.

London is a hotbed of creativity. Many internationally successful campaigns originate there. Most directors will want to have representation there, if only for reasons of prestige. It's a metropolis with style, and a hip culture with many ethnic influences. The winners of international awards are frequently British campaigns and spots.

The competition in London is as fierce as in Los Angeles. However, I've found that it is much easier to get meetings and find open doors. You can call executive producers, and they will actually pick up the phone themselves. People's offices will be open for walk-ins, and, in general, the atmosphere is less pretentious.

Production and post production are on the highest level. In fact, some of the CG facilities in London are the best in the world. Some of the most expensive commercials ever made have originated in the UK, but lower-budget productions are common as well.

The best way to find representation is, without a doubt, to travel there for a week and take meetings, which are much easier to get than in the States. Like the U.S., the UK has exclusive representation; you will end up signing with one company only.

## Italy

Italy has a very active commercial industry, centered in Milano. Most of the agencies are there, with a few in Torino. It is quite common to be repped by more than one company. In fact, my production company in Germany gets frequent calls from Italy for my reel.

Italy is one of those countries where production companies have a long list of directors, and they see who can fit each project. You may get a call out of the blue, perhaps from people you've never even talked to.

Shooting in Italy was one of the best experiences I've ever had. The director is king, and the crews are great. I was working in Rome with a film crew from cine citta and had a blast. However, there is a somewhat unfortunate practice in Italy: Often you will get bid on a project as the international choice director, while the project ends up being awarded to a local guy. Some directors have told me that whenever they get a board from Italy, they quote an insanely high fee and pretty much forget about it.

The *creative*, in other words, the work that comes out of agencies, can sometimes be odd and is often driven by visuals. Storytelling commercials exist as well, but the dramatic structures are not as pure as in the States or the UK. The Mediterranean taste is a bit more on the melodramatic and colorful side.

## Spain

In Spain, most production takes place in Barcelona, one of the creative centers on the Iberian Peninsula. Barcelona happens to be one of the greatest cities on the planet, and I could think of a lot worse places to work.

Besides the local productions, there are a whole lot of service productions going on in Spain. Therefore, the crews are well experienced and speak English. Getting repped in Spain is somewhat like Italy: You don't necessarily have to sign with a company. They'll have your reel, and if they have something for you, they may give you a call.

The locations in Spain (and Portugal, which is, of course, a different country) are beautiful and can be quite exotic. The deserts and coastlines in the south have been used as sets for many a feature film.

## Germany

In Germany, you can be repped by more than one company. There is not enough turnaround per production company to keep a director busy. For local directors, it's therefore common to have representation in different cities. The agency and film centers are Hamburg, Berlin, Munich, Frankfurt, and Düsseldorf. It's not uncommon to be with a company that has branches in more than one city, or to be repped by separate boutiques.

International directors tend to stick with one company, simply because they don't rely on work from that country only. The creative is not as good as the UK, but most of it is solid. Car advertising, in particular, is a top-notch, high-stakes business. Some of the comedy work has gotten international attention as well, and a few German agencies are even lead shops for global campaigns.

As an international director, you will be considered for the higher-budget stuff unless you make a real effort to get smaller jobs. Of course, it takes a lot longer to get to the higher-budget stuff.

Agencies tend to be weaker in their relationship with the clients. The economic upheaval over the last few years has caused a lot of changing accounts and fear in the agencies, and at times it seems like everyone is complaining.

Germany is on a very high technical level. Munich-based ARRI provides world-class German engineering in cameras, lighting, and post production equipment, and there are many top-notch post production houses.

Like many other Northern and Central European countries, German production often takes you around the world into warmer climates in South Africa, New Zealand, or South America.

I've had plenty of experience shooting in Germany. As long as you get good creative, it can be an all-around rewarding experience. The crews are excellent, and the work atmosphere is generally pleasant. I've found that the agency-client relationship is more complicated than in most other countries, for whatever reason. That can make things a little more difficult to get done.

## Scandinavia

I haven't worked in Scandinavia myself, but over the past 10 years, it has become a spearhead in creative advertising. Its conceptual thinking and style have transferred somewhat to the rest of the world, along with directors such as Traktor.

The humor is odd, and the look is drab and almost unappealing. The cold, underplayed style of acting, which emphasizes a sort of uncomfortable realism, can now be found in ads all over the world.

Denmark and Sweden are the two countries with most of the production companies, but I've found that being repped in England or Germany might also open you up to Scandinavian business. In other words, it's not necessary to be represented by a company in Scandinavia, and their work very often is done by locals anyway.

## Eastern Europe

The political changes in Eastern Europe have resulted in a surge of agency and commercial work, albeit on the low-budget end of things. Some of the creative can be interesting, if weird at times, and the director's fees are not what they are in the rest of Europe— although it's not unheard of to get a regular rate.

Nevertheless, it's work. You can earn money, and young directors, especially, can gain valuable experience. The main centers are Moscow, Prague, and Warsaw. It's likely that you will eventually be approached by companies from Eastern Europe; they are constantly looking for international talent.

There are also independent agents who connect production companies with directors, in effect, acting as your sales rep.

You will be working on a job-by-job, rather than an exclusive, basis. While English is fairly common in Western Europe, you may run into some substantial language barriers here. Sometimes the translations of boards are broad or confusing. Just ask questions to find out what people really are looking for. And it's great fun to have conference calls in Russian or Polish. You feel like a politician at the U.N. being translated simultaneously.

Also, many clients produce spots for several Eastern countries at once, which can lead to a variety of versions being shot. I once did a chocolate commercial that was post produced in Russian, Polish, Ukrainian, Rumanian, Bulgarian, and Czech. The model in it, famous in all those countries from having appeared on their billboards, was, however, from Argentina.

The craft of filmmaking is very established in Eastern Europe, and most of the time you will find good, professional crews. In post production, although there is a fairly high standard of equipment, there are few high-quality operators. When I did telecine in Moscow, the operator had come straight from Bollywood (which was, I guess, a good thing).

Budgets are definitely small and in currencies that don't hold up on the international stage. Only in Russia is the money available to shoot large-scale productions abroad, not in the least because Western companies are moving in with major investments.

## Asia

I've never shot in Asia, but according to those who have, there are significant cultural differences when dealing with clients and agencies. Preproduction is taken extremely seriously—to the point of verbatim realization of reference images and storyboards.

One director told me that he *had* to shoot each shot *exactly* the way it was drawn on the shooting boards. If the actor depicted on the boards was using his right hand to do something, for example, it *had* to be the right hand in the actual shoot. If he was shown cocking his head to the left, he *had* to do that.

The agency wanted to make sure that everything approved by the client was in the can, down to the most minute detail. Once you had shot it, then—and only then—could you shoot something else.

Needless to say, Japan is the major market in Asia for commercial directing, although good work also comes out of South Korea, Taiwan, Singapore, Malaysia, and India. Finding representation is usually a networking task, since any interest in you derives from your reputation or from direct connections between producers. Japanese clients occasionally shoot in Los Angeles, and production companies do look around for U.S.-based talent.

Some countries, particularly Japan, are famous for shelling out huge amounts of money to hire superstar celebrities and the top directors that come with them. In general, though, budgets are modest unless you are dealing with major car or electronics manufacturers.

## Middle East

There are three centers of production in the Middle East, with a fourth one rising. Clearly, Israel has the most depth in terms of filmmaking, mainly because there is a strong local market. Although Israeli agencies like to shoot abroad, there is plenty of production in-country. The equipment is top-notch, and the crews are well-trained.

Dubai is the other major center, but not so much as a vertically integrated industry. Rather, Dubai is a service production hub for a great variety of locations and equipment services. There are agencies and production companies that work for the local markets, but they alone could probably not sustain the production infrastructure. On the technical level, the production here leaves no wishes unheard. The influx of car-shoot service production money has undoubtedly contributed to that.

Finally, there is Beirut. Interestingly, there is a proud tradition of filmmaking in Lebanon, and Beirut can be used as a production base camp when you shoot in the Middle East. While the equipment is inferior to that in Israel and Dubai (both in quality and quantity), there is much less red tape and cost involved if you are shooting in, say, Jordan. To get a camera from Israel into Jordan and back out is quite a nightmare, even though the distance between the countries' two capitals is a mere 200 km.

However, if you get your camera from Beirut, some guy in a beat-up van will drive it through Syria in a day, no questions asked, for a fraction of the cost. If you have the luxury of time to address possible snafus, this can be the best way to handle it.

In a lot of other countries, there are local crews and equipment, particularly TV crossover stuff like lights and grip. Jordan and Egypt have some infrastructure, but it is impossible to get a 35mm package. Production there is possible, however, as proven by *Lawrence of Arabia* and *Indiana Jones and the Last Crusade*, both of which were shot in Jordan).

## South and Central America

The major markets in South America are Mexico, Brazil, and Argentina. Buenos Aires, which has a European look, is a big film town because it attracts service production from Europe. Language is an important factor, and any native will tell you that Argentinean Spanish is not like Spanish spoken elsewhere.

There are many native Spanish speakers in Los Angeles who work frequently for the Mexican market. In fact, many commercials run south of the border, as well as in the Latino markets in the U.S.

The creative in Brazil has been making waves over the last few years with its international awards. However, in general, the creative is not considered extraordinary in South America. Production is solid in the main markets, while the quality drops severely elsewhere. Budgets are much smaller than in most places, although large companies spend top dollar on their advertising.

I have never had a chance to shoot here myself, so I can't attest to the quality of production services, but the work done certainly speaks for itself.

## Australia/New Zealand

Australia and New Zealand are very active markets that often use local talent. Rarely have I heard of directors shooting for the Australian market. A great deal of service production takes place Down Under due to its financial benefits and beautiful locations. This could be as odd a constellation as a U.S. director shooting a Polish beer commercial in Auckland with a Russian agency.

The local budgets are on the small side, but the quality of production and post production is very high. Sydney is the business center of the region, whereas Auckland is the major destination in New Zealand. The production of the *Lord of the Rings* series has certainly established the area as a post production possibility, particularly with the flexibility of online cooperation.

The creative from Ozland has been great—at least judging by the campaigns that have been seen and recognized internationally.

# Appendix

## The Interviewees

I've had the great pleasure of interviewing some very smart and helpful people for this book. I cannot possibly do them justice with the following few paragraphs, but I will try.

In alphabetical order:

### Joe Murray

Joe Murray has enjoyed a highly successful career directing and photographing television commercials and music videos for the better part of 20 years. He has worked with celebrities such as Cindy Crawford, Celine Dion, Aretha Franklin, Randy Travis, Graham Nash, Johnny Miller, Dale Earnhardt, and Richard Petty.

His clients include General Motors, Ford, Lincoln Mercury, Peugeot, Honda, U.S. Army, U.S. Air Force, Budweiser, Coors, Miller, Dr. Pepper/Seven Up, and Dreamworks (for which he won the Country Video of the Year award in 1999 for Randy Travis's "Spirit of a Boy"). He has also worked as a second unit and additional scenes director/director of photography on feature films for Warner Bros. and Lucasfilm Ltd., most notably *Star Wars Episode IV: A New Hope* (1977) and *The Adventures of Young Indiana Jones: Masks of Evil* (1999).

## Tor Myhren

Tor is executive creative director, EVP, at Leo Burnett Detroit, and he oversees all creative development for the agency and its clients. The agency's main client is GM, with accounts such as Pontiac, Cadillac, and GM Service Parts Operations (SPO).

If you've noticed a change in GM's advertising after 2005, it's because Tor is now in charge of it. His work for the Solstice and the Cadillac Super Bowl '06 ads speak for themselves. He is a superstar creative who went to Leo Burnett from TBWA/Chiat/Day Los Angeles, where he was the lead creative on Infiniti.

## Matt Tolmach

Matt started his career as a trainee at the William Morris Agency and quickly moved into producing where he got his start in TV movies of the week. Soon he was tapped by Michael J. Fox to run his production outfit, Snowback Productions.

His move into the studio world came when he hired on with Turner Pictures as a junior executive, focusing on the development of scripts. When Turner closed, Matt went to Sony/Columbia Pictures where he had an incredibly successful run developing and overseeing major studio productions, such as *Panic Room*, *Ali*, *The Da Vinci Code*, and of course, the mega-franchise *Spider-Man*.

## Kelly Trudell

Kelly is senior producer/partner at J. Walter Thompson Detroit, the world's oldest advertising agency with a 140-year history. JWT has 300 offices in 87 countries.

Kelly was hired at JWT in 1984 to manage the audio/video department. Subsequently, he moved on to produce his first TV commercial in 1988; ever since, he's produced primarily Ford Division spots. His most notable work over the last few years has been a series of Ford F-150 spots and a Mustang spot featuring the ghost of Steve McQueen.

## John van Osdol

John is executive vice president and director of broadcast at Leo Burnett Detroit, a unit of Leo Burnett Worldwide, the world's eighth largest agency network (*Advertising Age* 2005), which in turn is a wholly owned subsidiary of Publicis Groupe.

John started his career at Ross Roy Advertising, working on Kmart, Blue Cross, Michigan Travel Bureau, NBD Bank, and other clients. He subsequently moved to Campbell Mithun Esty/Bozell/FCB, working on Jeep, Eagle, and Chrysler. His latest stop is D'Arcy/Chemistri/Leo Burnett, which became Leo Burnett Detroit in 2005. At his current agency, he is responsible for work on Cadillac, Pontiac, and Goodwrench.

In 1994, John and his team received one of the world's most prestigious commercial awards, the Grand Prix Cannes, for the Jeep commercial "Snow Covered."

## Jim Zoolalian

Jim grew up admiring Steven Spielberg, George Lucas, Francis Ford Coppola, and Martin Scorsese, and began pursuing a career in film in high school by taking cinema classes at the Art Center College of Design and Pasadena City College. After graduating high school, he enrolled in UCLA's film program.

His diligent work moved him up the ladder of film production, eventually landing him his first directing jobs for local TV commercials and industrials. He briefly ventured to the other side as an agency producer, but returned to directing TV spots with even more experience.

His credits include commercials for Sprint, Lexus, NASCAR, McDonald's, Suzuki, Cingular, and dozens of other big name brands.

# Resources

## DGA

The Directors Guild of America is the most powerful guild in the entertainment industry and represents directors for TV, features, commercials, music videos, and documentaries. The yearly DGA awards for commercial directors are coveted and recognized worldwide. As soon as you are shooting a union spot—which pretty much is any major commercial—you will have to be pay guild fees and maybe even become a member. As a member of the DGA, you enjoy a myriad of benefits and protections, but it also can hinder young directors in their flexibility. Nevertheless, the DGA is an organization any director will want to be associated with.

Directors Guild of America
Los Angeles Headquarters
7920 Sunset Boulevard
Los Angeles, California 90046
(310) 289-2000
**www.dga.org**

## AICP

The Association of Independent Commercial Producers is the representational organization for production companies. When unions like the DGA or SAG negotiate, they do it with the AICP. If a production company is an AICP member, you know that they generally abide by a certain code of conduct and accept the common industry rules. Membership information can be found on its Web site, and it is a good tool for finding addresses and names.

**www.aicp.com**

AICP/National HQ
3 West 18th Street
5th Floor
New York, NY 10011
(212) 929-3000

AICP/National LA
650 North Bronson Avenue
Suite 223B
Los Angeles, CA 90004
(323) 960-4763

## WheresSpot

WheresSpot is a Yahoo newsgroup that was started by sales reps Perry Schaffer and Michael Porte. It's an incredibly useful tool for getting answers to all kinds of commercial production-related questions. Someone posts a question, and usually within a few minutes someone else has an answer. Additionally, producers put out calls for directors' reels, ask for recommendations for crew members, and search for locations or contacts. You can meet people from all over the world, although the focus is clearly on the U.S. market (there is a WheresSpot Europe, but it's slow). This is a free community, which makes it even more worthwhile to check out. I actually booked a job off WheresSpot once.

**www.wheresspot.com**

## *Shots Magazine*

London-based *shots magazine* is probably the most respected publication in terms of the creative edge. You can subscribe to its monthly print edition, complete with a DVD that's filled with the best work out there, both commercials and music videos. *shots* also offers a directory service, as well as an online portal, www.shots.net. Some of the news is free, but the more in-depth information is subscription-only. If you watch the monthly DVD, you can pretty much stay on top of the best work in the industry. *shots* also has a "New Directors" section in which this author has been privileged to be featured.

**www.shots.net**

## *Shoot Magazine*

The biweekly trade publication *SHOOT Magazine* and its Web-offering, www.shootonline.com, are almost mandatory reading in Los Angeles and New York. It's a press release platform, as well as a site for features about directors, locations, and technologies.

**www.shootonline.com**

## 'boards Magazine

The Toronto-based monthly *'boards Magazine* and its online version, www.boardsmag.com, are more feature- and article-oriented, and the magazine even has its own awards festival. You can find a board-flow meter describing the current state of business/busyness in Los Angeles, New York, Toronto, and London.

**www.boardsmag.com**

## Adweek

*Adweek* is a print and online magazine (www.adweek.com) focused on the advertising side of the industry. This magazine not only covers TV commercials, but all aspects of advertising, as well as insider news that is of little interest to directors. It is helpful, though, to track creatives when they move from agency to agency or to see what work gets featured in this magazine.

www.adweek.com

## Advertising Age

This is another advertising-oriented print and online magazine (www.adage.com) with a lot of inside industry information. Some of the articles about market research and target groups are interesting, if only marginally useful to directors.

www.adage.com

## Post Magazine

This print and online magazine (www.postmagazine.com) is the leading resource for all things technical in the post production world. New telecine ranks, 3D software, compositing machines, and editing systems are reviewed and introduced. Lots of good information here when you are looking for technical solutions.

www.postmagazine.com

## Group101Spots

Group101Spots is a collective of filmmakers that shoots one spec commercial per month for its directors. The scripts are real agency scripts, and the group gets a lot of resources from production companies and ad agencies. Although it's meant for aspiring directors, a lot of the folks that have come out of it already have spec reels and have revived their careers here. Incidentally, the group's founder turned it into a production gig for herself quite successfully. And why not?

www.group101spots.com

## FastChannel

FastChannel is a subscription-only online research tool. There are some public pages on the Web site, but the main information features complete reels of directors and DPs. Production companies sign up their entire roster, and it's a great way to showcase talent, as well as to research spots, directors, and even styles or looks. The articles are mediocre, but the newsletter at least lets you know who's moved where. It's also a good resource to get up-to-date information on phone numbers and addresses.

Creative.fastchannel.com

## AdCritic

AdCritic is a site much like creative.fastchannel.com where you can see the latest work and find out who has done what. The site is run by the magazine *Creativity*, and offers search tools, as well as articles. The site also sends out a regular newsletter.

AdCritic.com

## Source TV

Source TV is another research site that offers targeted research for subscribers. They will actually put together reels and host them as well. Furthermore, they offer clearance services and several up-to-date databases on companies, spots, and even creatives.

www.sourcetv.com

### LA 411 and NY 411

The 411s are essentially Yellow Pages for the film and commercial industries. The listings include ad agencies, production companies, directors, crew, sets, stages, post production, equipment rentals, location resources, and even additional information such as city guides and festival data. The 411s are definitely great resources for finding addresses, phone numbers, and names.

www.la411.com, www.newyork411.com

# Technology Glossary

Just a few technological terms:

### Avid

The Avid is one of the digital editing systems in use today at a great number of editing houses. There are different variations of the hardware and software, allowing for a different level of resolution and image quality to work with. You can actually online on an Avid, although the capabilities are inferior to a bona fide online machine.

### Frozen Moment

This effect, sometimes referred to as Frozen Moment (incidentally, that is also the name of the Nike spot that made the effect famous), shows an object that is seemingly frozen in time while the camera continues to move around it. *The Matrix* made this hugely famous, but it was used in commercials years before that.

The effect can be achieved in a number of different ways. Either there are hundreds of still cameras arranged along the path of the camera move, or there are a smaller number of film cameras at certain places on that same move. In the case of the still cameras, they all shoot a frame at the same time. All the frames are then scanned in and assembled to make one piece of film footage.

In the case of the film cameras, computers are used to fill in the gaps with the help of morphing software.

## Green Screen

The color called "chroma green" is a color that rarely exists in nature, and it is used as a background whenever a chroma key needs to be done. A chroma key lets you replace the color of your choosing (in this case chroma green) with another source. This is probably best known from the weather guy on TV. In commercials, the effect is much more subtle and used in a multitude of instances that most people won't be able to notice.

The green screen needs to be lit evenly, if possible, and you may need tracking marks on it for post production. Often, smaller mobile screens are used as well to separate a specific object from the background, and sometimes humans, human heads, dummies, cars, or the like are wrapped up in green screen to "make a hole" in the image, which is filled later.

## Helium Balloons

Pretty new toys, helium balloons are large spherical balloons in different sizes with light sources inside. As helium is lighter than air, they float and provide a very soft, wide light source for night scenes.

## High Definition (HD)

HD is a term used to describe any number of high-resolution digital video formats. Some U.S. channels already broadcast in this format. In commercial production, HD means that a project is being shot in high-definition video rather than on film. There are a number of camera manufacturers with different approaches to this, but the quality is getting better and better, and the number of spots done in HD will certainly rise. You can also post produce a commercial shot on film in HD, so that it can be broadcast in that format. Generally, most commercials are post produced at DigiBeta quality anyway.

## Motion Capture

Motion capture is a technique in which motion is recorded as digital data rather than visual data on film. A person may have hundreds of little white dots on his body, and their spatial movement is recorded by a number of computers' cameras. The motion data can then be transferred to a digital model, such as King Kong or Gollum.

Motion capture helps make these movements seem more natural, rather than pure animation by hand. It's an expensive and long process because the data has to be cleaned up and tweaked a lot. But it's very effective.

## Motion Control

Motion control refers to a camera rig that is automated and computer-controlled. Basically, it's like a robotic arm that can move the camera around in the same path over and over. This may be needed for effects work. Motion control rigs are usually installed on a motion control stage, complete with green screen. The data can be transferred into compositing machines in lieu of tracking. There are a few portable motion control rigs, and even those that mount on a simple tripod, but their range of motion is obviously much smaller.

## Photosonics

This line of cameras is high-speed specialty gear, which means that it shoots very high frame rates. Whenever you see a drop of water falling in extreme slow motion, it was shot with a photosonic camera. These cameras can shoot up to 3,250 frames per second. The company also produces a number of other technical toys, but in the filmmaking world, this is what they're known for.

## Previz

Previz is short for previsualization, a technique used to create shots in a rough 3D environment before the shoot for planning purposes.

In a complicated effects situation, this puts everyone on the same page, and elements can be worked on before the actual shoot. There are companies that specialize in previzing, but it's an expensive process.

## R1 Rig

The R1 rig is a camera rig primarily used for cars. It attaches to the underside of the car and extends an arm out from it, enabling the camera to be mounted in a fixed position in relationship to the car. When the car drives, the effect is that everything in the frame moves except the car.

Often, though, the extension arm has to be removed in post because you want to see the car in its entirety, in order to have the full effect of it.

## Remote (Stabilized) Head

Remote heads are camera mounts that can be controlled by wires. The camera can be tilted and panned, and sometimes rotated, depending on the model. The huge distinction is whether they are stabilized or not. Stabilization means that the image will be smooth and not shaky, whereas a nonstabilized head will transfer all the vibration onto the camera directly. For example, if you see a driving car shot where the camera travels with the car, it's most likely a stabilized head. Most helicopter shots are stabilized heads.

The head uses gyroscopes to keep the shot smooth. There are several models, all of which have their own weaknesses and strengths. The operator of the remote control head, as well as the operator of the platform—be it a car or a helicopter or a crane—needs to cooperate with you closely to get the shot you want.

## Repeatable Heads

The term *repeatable heads* refers to any camera head that can repeat a certain movement exactly. Motion control rigs have repeatable heads, but there are smaller, cheaper versions that mount on a tripod, with which you can repeat a tilt or pan endlessly. For effects shots, this is very helpful because several passes of the same shot need to line up perfectly and repeatable heads make sure that they do.

## Russian Arm

The Russian Arm is a cool tool that mounts on the roof of a car. Basically a remote-controlled crane, the camera can move around the side of the car that it is mounted on, or it can be used to shoot another car driving next to it. Since the crane is mounted on relatively small vehicles, it is a very flexible system.

## Snorkel Lenses

Snorkel lenses are a range of lenses, such as the Frazier and T-Rex lenses, that look like snorkels. They have a moveable front end that allows you to pan the lens without moving the camera. This is great for tight spaces (such as a move through the wine glasses on a dinner table) or for macro and no depth-of-field shots. Due to the large number of glass elements in these lens, they require more light and have very little depth of field.

## Swing and Tilt Lenses

Borrowed from still photography, swing and tilt lenses feature a moveable front element that changes the focus plane in the image. Such a lens can be used to put things in focus that otherwise couldn't be, but more often it is used to place a traveling focus on a single object. These lenses create very beautiful images, but are somewhat inflexible and tricky to use.

## Techno Crane

The techno crane is an expensive piece of equipment that has an automated telescope arm, which can cover a lot of ground very fast. There is usually a gyrostabilized head at the end of it. The crane can be controlled directly by hand or can be run through a preprogrammed path. It's definitely one of those items that you want to make sure you actually need before booking it.

## Wire Cam

Any camera suspended from a wire qualifies as a wire cam. There are a number of systems available. Imagine a shot following a downhill skier, which would be impossible to achieve without a wire cam. Another huge advantage is that wire cams can move over crowds or uneven terrain. For example, wire cams have recently been introduced to football games, where they show a unique perspective from behind the quarterback without inhibiting game play.

# Commercial Director's Sample Contract

Here is a sample contract. There are many versions around, because there is no official DGA version of this. Contracts of this sort are not bound by any industry standards (for example, TV directors). Each production company may have its own version. It is certainly a good idea to consult an attorney.

---

### DIRECTOR'S AGREEMENT

This Director's Agreement ("Agreement") is made effective as of the date it is signed by both parties between (Production Company), a California Corporation with offices (address) Los Angeles, California, and (Director Co)., a Corporation ("Lender") for the services of ("Director").

A. (Production Company) is engaged in the business of Commercial Film Production and Post Editorial Services and will be primarily conducting business at Los Angeles, California.

B. (Production Company) desires to have the services of Director.

C. Lender is entitled to the exclusive services of Director and is willing to sign an agreement with (Production Company) for Director's services.

---

## 1. ENGAGEMENT

Lender will provide to (Production Company) the exclusive services of Director as a director of television commercials, and agrees to be represented exclusively by (Production Company), for all projects originating in the United States (the "Territory").

Director has the right to approve or disapprove all jobs.

Any projects originating outside the Territory by Director can be run through (Production Company), but will be negotiated on a job by job basis.

All services anywhere in the Territory by Director must be performed for (Production Company). Director shall not perform services or become interested in any business competitive with (Production Company) in the Territory.

## 2. TERM

2.1 The term of this contract shall be for two years, beginning on the last date that Director, Lender, and (Production Company) sign it (the "Term").

2.2 Should Director be engaged in any feature film or other project outside the scope of this agreement, Lender will provide written notice of unavailability within 10 business days prior to the proposed engagement, describing briefly the nature of the engagement and the length of the engagement.

2.3 (Production Company) will have the option of suspending and extending the term of the contract, by written notice, for the length of time that Director's services are unavailable to (Production Company), due to projects outside this contract, and for an additional period up to 30 days.

## 3. COMPENSATION

Lender's total compensation will be composed of the following:

3.1 Director's Fees: (Production Company) will use its best efforts to obtain a day rate of not less than $xx,xxx per shoot day, unless Lender agrees to a different rate.

3.2  When bidding, (Production Company) may, where possible, include an additional $775.00 (or whatever the required DGA amount) to pay Company's share of DGA pension and welfare contributions.

3.3  (Production Company) will pay directly to the DGA the employer's share of Director's DGA pension and welfare contributions. Director shall remain a member in good standing of the DGA during the term of this agreement.

3.4  If a job actually comes in where the production company makes a net profit of less than that of the director's total day rate (as bid on the AICP bid form), then both parties agree to negotiate in good faith regarding a reduced director's fee.

3.5  Profit participation: In addition to Director's Fees, Lender will earn profit participation of 20% on the jobs that Director directs ("Profit Participation"). "Actual profit per job" will be defined as the total amounts received from the client in connection with each job that Director directs, less all of direct cost of productions, including but not limited to:

a) All costs listed as items A to K on the standard A.I.C.P. bid form.

b) Director's fees.

c) (Production Company) overhead of 8% of the bid A to K. (Which includes sales commissions and sales cost.)

d) Insurance.

e) Talent.

f) Sub-contracts.

g) The cost of Director's Cuts.


## 4. SPEC FUND

4.1  A spec fund of $20,000 will be provided to lender for the purpose of creating additional commercials for his reel. Lender will repay monies spent on spec commercials from first monies accumulated in Director's Profit Participation (see 3.5).

## 5. INPECTION OF RECORDS

5.1  Lender or its appointed agent will have access to a copy of the A.I.C.P. bid form that was submitted to the agency for each job awarded to Director.

5.2  Lender's representative shall have the right to inspect (Production Company)'s books and records (as they relate to this agreement) once during the Term, and once during a period of 12 months after the termination of this contract. Any such inspection shall be made at (Production Company)'s offices during regular business hours, upon reasonable notice.

## 6. ARBITRATION

6.1  Any controversy arising out of or relating to this agreement, or performance or breach thereof by either party, shall be settled by binding expedited arbitration in Los Angeles, California, before a single mutually approved arbitrator, who is experienced in the commercial production business, under the auspices of the American Arbitration Association. The rules then in effect of the American Arbitration Association shall govern any arbitration or litigation hereunder. The prevailing party therein shall be entitled to recover the unsuccessful party such reasonable attorney's fees and costs as the court or arbitrator may determine.

## 7. SCHEDULE OF PAYMENT

7.1  Lender will be paid Director's Fees within 10 business days of the end of the shoot on which the Director's Fees were earned.

## 8. SALES

8.1  Director shall have the right to approve the reel that is used to represent him.

## 9. EXPENSES

9.1  (Production Company) agrees to reimburse Lender for reasonable and approved business expenses, including first class travel incurred by Lender in connection with the performance of his duties.

## 10.  NOTICE OF BREACH

10.1  (Production Company) shall have the right to terminate this agreement:

a)  If Lender or Director are in material breach of any provision of this agreement and, if the breach involves failure to perform services, such breach continues for a period of 5 days after written notice thereof. In the event the material breach or failure involves other curable breaches, Lender shall receive 30 days notice. In the event the material breach or failure is not curable, (Production Company) shall have the right to terminate this agreement immediately upon written notice;

b)  Upon Director's death;

c)  If Director is physically or mentally disabled and unable to perform his services, or if any event of Force Majeure exists for a period of 6 consecutive weeks or for 8 weeks in the aggregate during the term.

10.2  Lender may terminate this agreement in the event of any material failure or breach that continues for a period of 30 days after written notice thereof, unless such material breach or failure is not curable, in which event Lender shall have the right to terminate this agreement immediately upon written notice.

10.3  In the event that this agreement is terminated by (Production Company) as provided for above, Lender shall not be entitled to receive any further compensation, except for Director's Fees and Profit Participation earned and payable pursuant to this agreement prior to the effective date of the termination.

10.4  Written notification of the breach can be delivered to the parties at respective addresses as set forth on the first page of this contract, in a manner as follows:

a)  Federal Express. UPS. Any licensed courier company.
(Signed for by an agent of either party.)

b)  Hand delivered.

c)  Fax or email.

10.5 Copies of notification will be given to:
Director
Lawyer

## 11. AMENDMENT

This agreement contains the entire agreement between the parties. There are no other agreements, representations, covenants, or warranties. This agreement may be modified or amended only if the amendment is made in writing and is mutually agreed upon and signed by both parties.

## 12. INDEPENDENT CONTRACTORS

Lender and Director acknowledge that they are independent contractors and that neither is an employee of (Production Company). All payments made to Lender by (Production Company) shall be in gross, without deduction. Lender shall be responsible for the withholding and payment of all Federal and state taxes on amounts paid to it by (Production Company). Lender and Director agree to indemnify and hold (Production Company) harmless from any obligations with respect to the same. Nothing in this agreement shall create or constitute a joint venture or partnership between Lender or Director and (Production Company).

## 13. INDEMNIFICATION

Each party hereto agrees to indemnify and hold harmless the other party for any costs (including reasonable attorney's fees, if any) incurred arising from the breach of any of the indemnifying party's obligations hereunder.

## 14. CONFIDENTIALITY

Lender and Director recognize that (Production Company) has and will have information regarding the following: Client/Agency lists, operation of business affairs, agreements, contracts, bids, corporate obligations, and vital information items (collectively, "Information"), including but not limited to the terms of this Agreement, which are valuable, special and unique assets of (Production Company). Lender agrees that Lender, and his assigns or agents, will not at any time or in any manner, either directly or indirectly, divulge, disclose, or communicate any Information to any third party without our consent. Lender and Director will protect the Information and treat it as strictly confidential.

## 15.  APPLICABLE LAW

This Agreement shall be governed by the laws of the State of California.

AGREED TO AND ACCEPTED

(PRODUCTION COMPANY) FILMS, INC.

By_____

Date: _____

Production Company

By_____

Date: _____

By_____

Date: _____

I agree to be bound by the foregoing agreement insofar as it pertains to my services, duties, responsibilities, and obligations.

By_____

Date: _____ Director

# Index